NINE GATES
TO THE
CHASSIDIC
MYSTERIES

A Jewish Legacy Book

JIRI LANGER
NINE GATES TO THE CHASSIDIC MYSTERIES

Translated by Stephen Jolly

Published by
BEHRMAN HOUSE, INC., NEW YORK

A Jewish Legacy Book
Series Editor: Seymour Rossel

Published by arrangement with David McKay Company, Inc., New York

Library of Congress Cataloging in Publication Data

Langer, Mordecai Georgo, 1894-1943.
    Nine gates to the Chassidic mysteries.

    (A Jewish legacy book)
    Translation of Devět bran.
    1. Tales, Hasidic. I. Title.
[BM532.L313   1976]   296.8'33   76-5859
ISBN 0-87441-241-2

Manufactured in the United States of America.

10 9 8 7 6 5 4 3 2   82 81 80 79 78 77

Written with the help of God in the town of Prague which between two castles lies at the confluence of the waters of the Veltava and Botitch in the country called Bohemia: In the six hundred and ninety-seventh year of the sixth millenium since the creation of the world: Enter his gates with song and his courts with praise as is written by the hand of King David, Amen.

A WORD BEFORE THE FOREWORD

I t is several hours after midnight when, say the teachers of our mysteries, the hidden may become clear, and I've just finished another reading of *Nine Gates to the Chassidic Mysteries*. Why, I ask myself, does the prospect of seeing this book reprinted give me a sense of urgent need fulfilled—a need not only personal but what kabbalists call *Tzorech G'voah*—a "Higher Need."

Surface reasons come easily. This book belongs to that intriguing category of reportage which can be reproduced only by an inside-outsider—a person who, while deeply and personally involved with the milieu he is describing, is still able to look at it from the outside with a smile, maybe even with a smidgen of skepticism. Such a position is costly. He who occupies it may begin to look like those Picasso faces which have one eye staring forward and another eye looking sideways. His inner being may take on the characteristics of what the Kabbalah calls a *neshama Artla'it*—a naked soul which flies from world to world seeking its clothing, seeking in vain. Such people don't usually have it "together." Harmony, fulfillment, happiness is not likely to be a major mood of their lives; it doesn't seem to have been Jiri Langer's life portion, as his brother's intelligent introduction makes clear. But it is precisely problems and ambivalences which can—when combined with genuine writing talent, a delicious sense of humor, non-ponderous scholarship and a *heiche neshama*—a "high soul"—produce a very good book.

And this is an excellent book. For this judgment I cite no less an authority than Gershom Scholem, Professor Emeritus of Jewish Mysticism at the Hebrew University in Jerusalem. My own opinion, offered not without a bit of envy, since I've written in the same field, is that Langer's "Nine Gates" offers just about the most authentic and delightful entry into the world of chassidic mysteries available in our day to a serious seeker.

As for the deeper reasons which move me—well, Chassidism divides everything into *pnimiut*—"innerness," and *chitzoniut*—"outerness." Sometimes it calls the outer coverings *klipot* or "shells." That's not necessarily a pejorative term for there can be no inside without an outside, no soul without a body, no content without shells. *(Klipot* become negative when they become too thick, too obscuring of the inner light.) But it seems to me that much contemporary writing about mysticism, though it may use terms like soul, light and love, is really *klipot* literature—concerned with external matters: scholarly information, techniques for breathing, sitting, thinking or not thinking. It hardly affects the soul of the reader. Or, to become a bit more technical, it impinges on the lower levels of the soul for the Kabbalah sees the soul as an entity with potential for several levels of existence. Its higher levels, being close to the source, can involve a phenomenon which Judaism calls *Tshuvah*—meaning "return" or "turning." A person meeting this level of soul may feel a call to change his own life. There is an urgent need, a "Higher Need" in our day for this "inner" word, especially in the Jewish world.

I believe that Langer's book, though offering simple delight and entertainment, fits this category of mystical literature. And it may be especially effective precisely because it is so light of touch. In any case, I urge the reader to savor it in small sips, with long pauses for inner-directed reflection. Its bouquet improves with age.

I want to add a final word about the exotic aspects of the world to which Jiri Langer introduces us. Certainly it is a strange, foreign, almost paranoically, Jewish scene. Most seekers in our day are attracted by the non-parochial, the universal, but somehow eastern robes, mantras, and rituals do not put off seekers for universal truths. Yiddish, chassidic garb, and rebbes are a different matter. Well the fact is that Judaism does try to set itself apart and Chassidism is an extreme expression of Judaism. But in the world of religion as in the world of physics, the deeper our exploration of the concrete, the more we encounter universal laws and truths. Depth calleth to depth and the exotic and exceedingly particularistic world of Chassidism, as many non-Jews have discovered, can offer universal soul food.

But it's nearly dawn and I must take myself out of the way so that you can enter the gates—so unsophisticated, even primitive when compared to the gates offered by other worlds. But, reader, enter them with respect. The ground upon which you are about to tread is holy.

HERBERT WEINER
South Orange, New Jersey
December 18, 1975
14 Tevet 5736

FOREWORD BY FRANTISEK LANGER

My Brother Jiří

To write this book my brother Jiří Langer had to transport himself from the living reality of the twentieth century into the mystical and ecstatic atmosphere of the Middle Ages. Nor could this be effected merely in a metaphorical way, on the wings of fantasy. It had to begin with the reality of purchasing a railway ticket at a station in Prague to a little place in Eastern Galicia. This was very easy to do, for at the beginning of this century the Austrian Monarchy was still in existence, linking together a variety of distances and nations. Thus it was that after twenty-four hours of travel, or a little longer, in a dirty train, Jiří found himself five hundred kilometres away to the east, and simultaneously two, or even five centuries back in time. A lad from the beautiful city of Prague, a lad from a Jewish family accustomed to a twentieth century environment with all the advantages of modern town life, had taken up his abode among fellow-believers living as a little nation entirely on their own, beyond some inner frontier, and hence all the more inaccessible to time and space. They were a people who had their own religion and languages, their own traditions and history, their own education, a people who had retained ancient customs, disputes and quarrels, who cherished superstitions and backward ideas, some of which belonged to earliest times, often as far back as four thousand years ago. They were a people who had rejected everything spiritual and material which the contemporary present or their surroundings, whether near or distant, could give them—all those practical advantages which the new age had brought. The inventions of this new age, as far as they were concerned, ended presumably with the printing of books and the pleasures of tobacco. The most devout communities in these Chassidic colonies lived their lives in an un-

vii

broken mystical trance, a state of unending ecstasy entirely beyond time, space and matter. A traveller who wished to visit these strange people would not find the journey in any way difficult, but should he desire to meet them face to face, to lose himself amongst them, to live their life and acquire within himself the spirit of the most uplifted of them—an essential prerequisite for the writing of so truthful a book as the present one —his task was indeed both hard and long.

At the turn of the twentieth century Jewish families in Central Europe were for the most part lukewarm in the practice of their religion. In fact the way of life in which religion played an important role had ended with our grandfathers. My grandfather on my father's side lived in a mountain village called Ransko which had been established a long time ago in the vicinity of an ironworks; the latter was already a mere ruin when I was a child. This ironworks had been built by Cardinal Dietrichstein in the middle of the seventeenth century. From Holland the Cardinal had brought with him his "Hofjude" who came to live at the village. The Hofjude was our most notable forbear. For more than two hundred and fifty years our family lived in the same cottage in this village. I can recall my grandfather vividly, since I often went to visit him and once spent the entire school holidays with him. He was tall and thin, and like all the villagers he was clean-shaven on his cheeks and chin. His shaving however was not performed with a razor, which no honest Jew should allow to touch the skin of his face, but with a lime preparation which enabled the beard to be removed by a simple rubbing action. Besides a modest piece of land he possessed a small shop to which he brought goods on a wheelbarrow from the nearest station; subsequently he acquired some horses and used occasionally to go out trading in a basket-covered cart. I used to see him in the morning tying on his phylacteries; as might be expected, he was perfectly familiar with all the Hebrew prayers which are recited as the phylacteries are put in place; he was even able to write Hebrew. He spoke German reasonably well and his Czech showed the same mountain accent as that of the rest of the villagers. For the services on Fridays, Saturdays

and festivals he would assemble with the Jews from the surrounding neighbourhood in the little township. Grandmother,
of course, used to cook strictly kosher food, having retained all
the practices prescribed by ritual. Grandfather was as poor as all
his neighbours, and apart from his deviations, to which the
village had become accustomed, he used to live as they did and
in good friendship with them. When he died, the entire popula-
tion of the village and many of his friends from the countryside
accompanied him to the Jewish cemetery in scores of carts—a
journey which took the slow funeral procession four hours.

This was the normal pattern of life for Jews in Czech villages
towards the end of the last century. Our fathers moved to the
towns, taking with them their store of religious customs and
their awareness of being Jewish, which they had known at home.
The new environment, the new way of life, the daily bustle, and
all the secular cares and ideas which pressed in upon them provided no stimulus to their religious feeling and made it difficult
for them to keep up some of the old customs. Moreover the
townspeople of that time boasted a religious liberalism, which
rapidly attracted the Jews who had newly joined this society. This
in its turn further weakened their adherence to the faith of their
fathers. I remember how, while I was still a child, I used to watch
Father every morning bind his phylacteries round his stout arm,
but later this ceased to be a regular habit and eventually became
a rare one. I do not know whether or not he kept it up after I had
left home. As he put on the phylacteries he would read aloud
the Hebrew prayers, but he did not understand the words. Fortunately they were accompanied by a good translation. For
many years we kept to kosher food, but this was mainly due to
Julia, a devout Christian, who during her youth had worked for
our aunt, a strict Jewess, and who saw to it that we observed not
only the proper regulations regarding food but also other pre-
cepts of the Jewish religion. Outwardly Father's attachment to
his faith was to be seen in his regular attendance at the luxur-
iously appointed synagogue in our suburb of Prague, Královské
Vinohrady, in his membership of various Jewish charitable
organizations and in the way in which his heart and hand were

open to needy fellow-believers. In order to hold his own against competition in business he was obliged to serve behind the counter on Saturdays, but to offset this—it is said that he gave his grandfather a promise to this effect—he refrained from smoking from Friday evening to Saturday evening, in spite of being a heavy smoker. In consequence he was always on edge of a Saturday and quite impossible to deal with.

Father's family were practical people. Mother's family hailed from the same part of the countryside but were more refined and cultured. Among her forbears had been a revered rabbi. One of our uncles was a wood engraver and among our numerous cousins were several doctors, a mathematician and a poet. We three brothers took after her. Mother herself, poor thing, was deaf, shut up within herself, quiet and gentle, and played a passive, almost invisible role in the life of the family.

On Sunday afternoons Father used to take the whole family out of town. It goes without saying that he sent us children to Czech schools and saw to it that we had Czech books to read from babyhood. He belonged to about ten societies, not excepting the patriotic Sokol movement. Now and again he went to cafés to play cards. In short he lived like all the small shopkeepers in the particular street where we lived in our suburb of Prague. This adaptation to environment was even more characteristic of the younger generation to which we belonged. At school, in our religious education lessons, we barely succeeded in learning to read the Hebrew letters, but with such lack of thoroughness that in later years I have had to be content to admire these magnificent ancient characters without understanding their import. We learnt no more of Jewish history than, for instance, of Roman history, and we imbibed little of the essence and ethics of the Jewish religion. From our homes, too, we acquired little in this respect, and in our particular case almost nothing. My last religious act was reading aloud from the Torah when I became *bar-mitzvah*.

We were surrounded exclusively by rationalistic thought, and the outlook of our entire generation, both Jewish and non-Jewish, was far removed from any feeling for metaphysics. As we were better fed and more hygienically brought up than our fathers, we grew up to be at least a head taller than they and consequently were popular members of a football side or sports team. So long as anti-Semitism did not rear its head too close to us or too noisily, our generation looked upon the register of births as its only link with Jewry. Otherwise it interested itself in all the various questions which stirred the world at that time, or the nation in which it lived, in whose culture it had been brought up and in which it aspired to play a full part. Perhaps our origin helped to endow us with our keen social sense. It was this social sense that made us aware of the suffering of the Jews, wherever it might be throughout the world, just as we were aware of the suffering of all social pariahs.

The Zionists, who at that time were only to be found in small numbers, were radically different from our generation. In their ·dreams they saw Palestine as a Jewish country, the Jews as a nation and their religion as a sign of their nationality, just as in due course they expected Hebrew to be. It goes without saying that in Prague, as in the rest of Central Europe, there were Jewish families which felt themselves to be in varying degrees more religious than our family and those like it. But on the other hand there were others who felt themselves to be less religious; such people went so far as to break with the Jewish community and had no qualms about mixed marriages—which horrified even those who set but little store by their religion. Similarly in Prague, apart from the twenty or thirty thousand who were lukewarm in the faith, there still existed circles of believers who were uncompromising in their orthodoxy and who formed in fact a kind of Jewish religious aristocracy. This was quite inevitable in the city which the old Jewish poets had called the "Pearl of Cities" and "Crown of the World", the city which had been made famous by the Jewish synagogue of the thirteenth century, by the beautiful, poetic, old Jewish cemetery, and which from time immemorial had been a place where countless outstanding Jewish savants had worked. It was in these circles of religious Jews and cultured Judaists that my brother Jiří found a teacher of Hebrew and religious traditions, and an adviser and support in his subsequent study. For this he had to go far away from his family.

Jiří was the youngest of us three brothers. He was born in Prague on the 7th of April 1894. He was six years younger than I, and four years younger than my second brother Josef. Although somewhat of a lonely child in his youth, he was the most robust and healthy of all three of us. He was not a hard worker either at his primary school or at his secondary school. He loved music, at least as a listener, and while still a young student used to go to concerts of serious music. In Prague he had plenty of opportunity for this. He was an omnivorous reader and appreciated a good book. I had just published my first literary work at the time and Jiří looked upon me as an authority who could recommend him what to read. Once—he must have been fifteen at the time—he surprised me by asking which of the Czech poets were mystics. I advised him to read Otokar Březina, one of the greatest of our poets, if somewhat difficult to understand. My brother read all his works and was profoundly taken with them. This could have been my first opportunity of recognizing in which direction his interests were taking him. But it was not until a year or two later, when my brother began to be passionately interested in religious questions, that I was to recognize this to the full. By then, however, it was no longer a matter merely of interest and asking questions; for he was already totally immersed in religion, in the full range of that mystical, abstract, spiritual universe which is called religion.

It was natural enough that it should be the Jewish religion, but it did not have to be. As we saw it, the fact of his becoming caught up in this ecstasy of mysticism was mainly due to the influence of a friend of his, Alfred Fuchs, who like Jiří came of a Jewish family where there was no great enthusiasm for religion. Fuchs was a slim, good-looking fellow, always somewhat of a dreamer but brilliant at his school work. It would seem that it was he who was the first to be attracted to religious mysticism. My brother became infected with his enthusiasm and the two of them turned first to Jewish literature. To this end they learnt Hebrew and it was at this time that I first saw Jiří poring over borrowed Hebrew folios. Subsequently Fuchs came to the conclusion that the Catholic religion had more to offer in the sphere of mysticism, being richer, more varied in form, more inspiring and exhilarating. He set about exploring it with the same ecstatic fervour as he had brought to the Jewish faith. For the most part he studied the old Latin Christian texts. This caused the two young men to part company, a separation which was further emphasized when Fuchs, who was not a man to be content with half measures, accepted baptism. A passionate convert, he became a profound religious thinker and courageous Catholic philosopher. During the German occupation he was arrested by the Gestapo when he was at a monastery. He was cruelly tortured, both on account of his Jewish origin and because of the saintly devotion which he showed to the faith he had embraced. In the years immediately after the war there was even talk of his being canonized.

After some initial uncertainty my brother continued to feel himself drawn towards the Jewish religion. It was not long before he was concentrating all his powers on the study of Jewish teaching, traditional commandments and customs, delving into all manner of ancient rites and preoccupying himself with details that bordered on superstition. It would seem to me that in this earlier stage of his development religious ritual held a greater attraction for him than did the actual content of the religious idea. He only came to understand the latter in the course of his study of the vast folios of the Talmud, which he would sit over night after night, his hat on his head, reading aloud in a low voice. He made a point of observing all religious practices in a very ostentatious way and devoted himself to his new study so completely that he entirely ceased to go to school. He would escape from the family atmosphere around him by shutting himself up in the wrapped silence of the hermit, as though he found worldly things unworthy of his attention. He renounced all the normal pleasures of a young man—friends, sport, and even the Czech Philharmonic concerts. As for me, I was able to consider his behaviour from two different points of view. As a medical student in my final years of study, I could

only suppose that his was a case of belated adolescent .psycho-
pathy, which I hoped was a mere passing phenomenon. As a
writer I had come to think of him as the Dreamer of the Ghetto.
Father would give him a paternal homily every day, entreating
him to think of the practical side of life, of his future, and urging
him to be wise and return to school. Jiří would listen without
making the least murmur of protest, almost craven in his silence.
Father became slightly reconciled to the eccentric behaviour of
his son when on one occasion the latter was greeted with respect
by a wealthy Jew of some distinction, who had been decorated
with all manner of official titles and was moreover the head of
the fraternity of undertakers. This gentleman congratulated him
on his son and declared that the day would surely come when
he would be an eminent Jewish scholar and the pride of Prague's
Jewry. After this Jiří was more free to live his modest, solitary
existence at home.

In 1913, my brother packed a small suitcase with a few essential clothes, some books and his phylacteries, and set out on a
journey. He told no one save Julia to whom he confided that he
was going to Galicia and would be writing home about his
journey. He had always been close to her and she to him, perhaps
because each, albeit in different ways, was a sincere believer. It
was only after a few weeks had gone by that a postcard arrived.
It came from Eastern Galicia, from the town of Belz, and asked
us not to worry for he was quite well and would be there for
some time. This, then, was his first journey to the Chassidim, his
first sojourn among them, as he himself describes it in his
introduction to *Nine Gates*.

In this introduction he also outlines the reasons why he
was at first unable to endure life at Belz, why he returned and
what it was that drove him home: the isolation from the world,
the ignorance, backwardness and dirt which he found there, and
perhaps too the sad, marshy countryside. In other words it might
have been expected that his return to Prague, with its civilization
and other advantages, would be an occasion of great rejoicing
for him. With what abandon he would embrace his parents!
Perhaps on the very first day he would want to go to gaze on

the Vltava and the magnificent panorama of the Hradčany. Perhaps he would travel to the mountains and the forests, fragrant with the scent of resin, so different from the plains of Galicia with their swamps and stench of stagnant water. On Friday evening he would visit the glorious synagogue at Vinohrady, with its thousand lights shining on the ornaments which his own uncle had gilded and its five hundred silken top hats on the heads of worthy, well-to-do believers, with the organ playing in the choir and the solo sung in Hebrew by a Christian singer from the German theatre.

His return, however, was not on this wise. Father told me with a note of horror in his voice that Jiří had returned. I understood what had filled him with dread as soon as I saw my brother. He stood before me in a frayed, black overcoat, clipped like a caftan, reaching from his chin to the ground. On his head he wore a broad round hat of black velvet, thrust back towards his neck. He stood there in a stooping posture; his whole face and chin were covered with a red beard, and side whiskers in front of his ears hung in ringlets down to his shoulders. All that remained to be seen of his face was some white, unhealthy skin and eyes which at moments appeared tired and at others feverish. My brother had not come back from Belz, to home and civilization; he had brought Belz with him.

Now he added a sharper edge to the customs which he had been in the habit of observing before he went to the East. To some of these he gave a different significance, and there were other new ones which he had brought back with him. He no longer washed his hands before every meal, as any god-fearing and hygienically-minded person would do. Instead he made this a mere symbolical act, pouring water alternately on to his two palms from a cup. He would not shake hands with women—I do not know if he made an exception to this rule when he was welcomed by Mother—and whenever he spoke to a woman, even our old Julia, he would turn his back on her. He said his prayers aloud, in a sing-song voice, running round the room in a sort of trance. Now even the kosher food provided at Prague's restaurants was suspect, as far as he was concerned. He used to cook various mashes at home on a spirit stove, but his staple diet was bread and onions which could be smelt all over the flat.

It was both possible and necessary to adopt a tolerant attitude towards what happened within the four walls of our flat. But the situation was more difficult when he left the house, for his attire, his way of doing his hair, and his gait, which resembled a vigorous double, drew people's attention to him and made him the laughing-stock of the street, the effects of which were felt by our entire family. For the last three generations, when the Jews had been allowed to live outside the confines of the ghetto, those in our part of the world had not looked in any way different in their outward appearance from other citizens. On the other hand the Jews who lived in the eastern part of the Austro-Hungarian Empire, in territory occupied by the Poles and White Russians, used still to wear the gloomy caftan, hat and other items peculiar to their folk costume. In Prague one only occasionally saw a Galician Jew wearing this outfit—usually in a very shabby state—when he was on his way through the city or had come to beg. On the other hand it was far from being a rare sight in the luxury Bohemian spas of Karlovy Vary and Mariánské Lázně where in the high season they were to be seen in large numbers. These however were rich Jews, their black caftans were of silk and flowed like robes, their side-whiskers were decoratively curled down their cheeks, and their beards, which varied from reddish and black to ermine white, were beautifully combed and wavy, like those of the biblical patriarchs in the churches. These people went to receive treatment for livers upset by heavy kosher food, with its goose delicacies. At the Czech spas they were welcomed as good-paying, exotic guests, albeit not so rare and substantial as the Maharajahs from the Orient. But the appearance of a solitary Polish Jew on the streets of Vinohrady in 1913, belonging to a well-known Vinohrady family, positively cried out to be noticed.

Needless to say, such exhibitionism, whether religious or otherwise, was exceedingly embarrassing to all of us at home. Like the rest of the Jewish community, our family had completely assimilated itself to all the outward signs and customs of our neighbourhood. Would not Jiří's appearance now make us all seem guilty of pretence and hypocrisy? I do not know what interpretation our neighbours put on his behaviour but I rather presume that they tapped their foreheads knowingly. It seems to me that my brother's get-up scared my father and his strata of society in yet another way. It disturbed his feeling for security and permanence; maybe it aroused in him memories of stories, long since forgotten, about the misery and congestion of the ghetto, of a life without rights and freedom, of an existence full of humiliation and injustice. This was no mere concern about the conventions or business interests. It was a spectre from the past that had come among us; somebody risen from the dead had come to warn us. I can well imagine all these feelings which his presence aroused. A quarter of a century later millions of Jews were to experience this when they had to wear on their coats the yellow badge prescribed by Hitler.

The attitude of our family to Jiří seemed to us at the time to resemble the situation in Kafka's novel, *Die Verwandlung*, in which an entire family finds its way of life completely upset when the son of the house is suddenly changed into an enormous cockroach, and consequently has to be hidden from the rest of the world, while the family strive in vain to find some place for him in their affections. At least Father tried to find a practical solution. He requested a rabbi in Vinohrady, a sensitive, erudite doctor of philosophy, to talk to Jiří, hoping that a religious authority of such consequence would lead my brother to modify his ways. But Jiří refused even to speak to this man; he looked upon him as an atheist who read the daily newspapers and other matter not printed in the Hebrew alphabet. However, after some time, he did make some modifications in his behaviour to suit the requirements of Prague. He had his coat cut somewhat shorter, so that it was not very different from an overcoat, he started wearing an ordinary black hat which he no longer placed far back on his head, he plaited his side-whiskers and smoothed them behind his ears. It is probable that he was advised to do this by his Jewish friends in Prague, whom he once again sought out and who supplied him with the cabbali-

stic literature which he had come to know among the Chassidim. But he made no change in his habits at home and hardly
even came into contact with the rest of us. He would answer
when we spoke to him, but he would not start a conversation
himself. Perhaps his isolation was our own fault in that we did
not know how to cope with it. Sometimes we would express
sympathy in what we said to him, sometimes we would make
appeal to reason, often impatiently and forcefully, whereas Jiří
would probably have wanted us to behave as though his behaviour was quite natural. No doubt our behaviour in his eyes
was below the level of naturalness. Under such circumstances, of
course, it was difficult for us to find a common meeting ground.
Not even many years later would he explain to me what he felt
and thought at that time. He would not admit that being a
mystic and visionary, who had renounced all that this world has
to offer and had soared aloft into higher spheres, he felt the
pride of one who is merely waiting for the call to sainthood, and
had a fundamental contempt for us ignorant, coarse individuals
who were tied to material things. Years afterwards he would
merely wave his hands with a smile as if he did not wish to disturb a dream of the past.

He stayed on at home for a short time and then prepared
his suitcase for a second journey to his Chassidim. This time his
exultation was so intense that it communicated itself to those
around him. He bade a very warm farewell to us all. He was
overcome with joy—but I was not to learn this until I read his
book—for the rabbi of Belz had appeared to him in our kitchen
and had invited him to come to him.

He had only been a few months at Belz when the first world
war broke out in 1914. The rabbi of Belz and his entire court
found themselves in the midst of a battlefield, but fortunately
were able to escape to Hungary. Here Jiří received his call-up
papers. Subsequently he had to go to Prague to join up in the
Army. At that time I was on the Eastern Front as a doctor. In
1915 I happened to have my first leave. I came home and found
that Jiří had but recently been sent to the Army prison. He had
made life in the Army very difficult for himself. In the barracks

he used to get up an hour before reveille, while it was still night, so as to be able to say his prayers properly and eat his bread and onions, since he would not allow anything from the Army kitchen to pass his lips. All this the Army would have allowed him to do. But since a strict Jew is not permitted to carry anything on a Saturday, he refused to handle his rifle on that day or do any work at all. Naturally the court martial took a very serious view of this and my brother made things all the worse for himself by declining to answer their questions, or indeed to speak at all. I arrived just in time and was able to furnish the doctors responsible for examining the state of his mind with first-hand information and evidence as to his previous behaviour, with the result that they sent him home as a mental case. But Jiří was convinced that the rabbi of Belz had performed a miracle and delivered him from military service. When I told him of my part in his deliverance he declared that the miracle might have consisted in the fact of my having succeeded in getting leave from the front—which could of course have been true.

After this the war kept us apart from each other for five years. I spent the first part of this period in those regions where Jiří had previously lived. The war swept through the Galician villages, churning them into mud or sending them up in flames. I saw the Jewish, Chassidic settlements, and the infinite misery, agony and despair of their inhabitants who had no idea why all this destruction and murder was going on and why, in particular, it should have fallen on their heads. They fled in desperation, on foot, with bundles on their backs, or pushed before them, on wheel-barrows, a few bed-clothes and cooking utensils. A few of them made better pace on carts pulled by emaciated horses, loaded up with children and some miserable personal possessions. Years later it was difficult for me to compare these heart-searing pictures of frenzied horror with that naïve, carefree, almost childish state of bliss in which they had lived before this catastrophe and which was the underlying feature of the entire life of the Chassidim, as my brother has shown in his book.

After his discharge from the Army, Jiří returned to the rabbi of Belz and spent the rest of the war with him, far removed from the front. In the autumn of 1918, when the Austrian Monarchy fell, my brother's friends at Belz became subjects of the new Polish Republic and my brother of the new Czechoslovak Republic. Each returned to his home, henceforth separated from each other by new State boundaries. I did not meet Jiří until 1920, when I returned from the Army. To my surprise his outward appearance was, one might say, entirely European. His attitude to his family had also become more or less normal. He asked with great interest about my adventures during the war and told me of his experiences. But he had in no wise given up his feeling for religion, nor had he relinquished any of his former religious practices or those which he had taken over from the Chassidim. When speaking to a woman, for instance, he always faced sideways and would on no account shake hands with her. But he no longer wore a hat all the time; at home he wore the velvet rabbi's cap instead, and there was no longer any sign of side-whiskers. For food he went to a Chassidic restaurant in Prague—some groups of the Chassidim had succeeded in re-establishing themselves—and at home, as before, he cooked himself mash on a stove. He was no longer so obstinate as before the war. He would often call me to come and see how tasty his food was.

I received my greatest surprise, however, when I saw what was now occupying his attention. The books he was studying were not printed in Hebrew, but in Czech and German, and he was studying something other than the Talmud. This time it was the writings of Sigmund Freud and his disciples. He had collected all their works so far published and everything that had appeared in *Imago*, the official psycho-analytical journal. We now had in Freud plenty of material to discuss together, except that I was at the time more interested in Freud from the literary point of view. For me his teaching was in the nature of an utterly fantastic hypothesis, whereas my brother accepted Freud's discoveries as axioms with scientific validity. He began to use Freudian methods in analysing the essential meaning of the practices observed in Jewish ritual and in Jewish cults, applying them to his search for the subconscious sources of Jewish mysticism and the actual origin of the religious idea. It was a most remarkable spectacle to see him studying, a scientific work of the great psycho-analyst open in one hand and at his other hand an open folio of the Talmud, or more often some mystical work such as the *Zohar*.

He published the results of his new interest in 1923, in a book called *Die Erotik der Kabbala*, and subsequently in various articles printed in *Imago*. These appeared in German. Up to that time little had been known about Freud in Bohemia. Still less had any one concerned himself with any special connection that might be traced between psycho-analysis and Jewish religious teaching. It surprised me that in his writings Jiří did not hesitate to link the Jewish religion, and its origin, with the archaic phenomena of fetishes, totems and taboos in which Freud had traced the pre-historic consciousness of human social relations and laws. He did not hesitate to mention quasi-sacred Jewish symbols, such as the phylacteries or *mezuzehs* (doorpost signs), in connection with the most primitive idols in the form of sexual symbols which had figured in the cults of prehistoric man. Like Freud he even went so far as to ascribe an erotic derivation to the most spiritual laws and the supreme ethos of the Jewish faith. It seemed to me as a layman that any orthodox Jew would find much that was heretical and blasphemous in these inferences. And yet I saw that Jiří came to these conclusions in total innocence, that he received as much pleasure as the old commentators from each discovery he made in his study of the Talmud. I do not doubt that it was his unrealizable ideal that he should be permitted to write down these notions, that is, to print them in small letters at the side of the Talmud text and win thereby honour and glory as his pre-decessors had done.

I do not remember how his book was reviewed or whether in fact it attracted any attention at all in Prague. At all events his work did not cause him any difficulties, and his piety and reputa-tion for learning led to his being appointed as a teacher at the Jewish College in Prague. Father above all was delighted that his son should at last have obtained permanent employment.

With his pupils, I am told, he was a great favourite since he was easy-going and always full of humour. He was less liked, however, by the school's Board of Governors since he was very off-hand and unpunctual. His lessons never started on time, and if his attention was taken up with something that he was working on privately, he might even fail to put in an appearance for several days on end. In consequence he frequently had differences with the school authorities and on several occasions was given notice; however the authorities invariably had pity on him and took him back. On one of his enforced holidays he made a journey to Palestine. He went more as a historian than a pilgrim or would-be settler. He returned deeply affected by the beauties of the country and the efforts being made by the pioneers of a Jewish homeland, but it was clear that the roots he had put down in Prague would hold him fast. He made another journey to Paris where he stayed for several weeks. It is to be presumed that he spent most of his time in museums since he said nothing of the other delights of the city. Finally he gave up teaching altogether. This involved him in no hardship for he could live with his parents. Moreover I had a decent income from my plays and my brother Josef was well enough off; consequently we were able to provide for his needs reasonably generously. He also earned some money himself on his articles and translations. He had great talent as a linguist. Besides his mother tongue he was completely at home in Hebrew and Yiddish. He had an excellent knowledge of Aramaic, Arabic, German, French and English and was able to read a number of other languages without the aid of a dictionary. On one occasion I remember seeing him leaning over some large photographs of stone slabs covered with cuneiform writing which he was in the process of decipher-ing. He wrote Hebrew and published a book of his verses in Prague under the title *Pijjutim ve-Shire Jedidut* (Poems and Songs of Friendship) and I understand that he was able to speak in the classical language of the Bible. It is interesting that this was the first book of Hebrew verses to be printed at the Jewish printing-works in Old Prague for a whole century.

All this time he remained as deeply religious as before and there

is no reason to suppose that he infringed any commandments
of his faith. Such practices as he allowed himself to give up were
those which savoured of bigotry or were of minor importance.
Thus, for instance, after many years, he ceased to look upon a
bath merely as a ritualistic rite and saw it as a hygienic necessity.
He not only shook hands with women but acquired a reputation
for being very courteous, especially to old ladies. He even took
great pains with his clothing. However when he came to visit
me he would only drink coffee and never stay to supper. He
continued to eat at the kosher restaurants in Prague, some of
which were excellent. He read a great deal and was familiar with
all the latest works of any consequence in world literature. He
went to the theatre and never failed to come to my first nights.
It goes without saying that he often went to concerts. He even
started playing the violin; he had a teacher to instruct him in the
basic principles and then went on to teach himself. He must have
had remarkable talent. I never remember him playing from
music. Above all he liked to walk about his room and improvise
highly inventive variations on themes from the classical com-
posers, from Jewish and Negro hymns, Czech music and Slovak
songs. He played with a pure tone, with ease and passion, showing a marked fondness for stormy rhythms which he picked out
with his bow like a gypsy. In summer he liked to go for a swim
in the river, and in winter he would go skating. The latter was a
sport in which he excelled and I often used to go with the
children to the frozen Vltava to watch their uncle skating,
dancing on the ice and showing off his skill. I understand that he
even wrote an instruction book on figure-skating. He said nothing to me about this and I have not been able to find a copy
since, which leads me to suppose that it was written under a
pseudonym. By this time he no longer lived a hermit existence.
He had a number of friends, whom I did not meet, and sometimes he would come home in high spirits in the early hours of
the morning. During the war he had made friends with Franz
Kafka, and the two men used to go for walks together in
Prague. Kafka evidently found Jiří a kindred spirit; his diary
contains several Chassidic myths and legends which he had

heard from Jiří. He retained his former equable and patient nature side by side with the carefree attitude towards material things which he had taken over from the Chassidim. He seasoned all these good qualities with humour and accepted his lack of success as a teacher and frequent unemployment with equanimity.

After 1930 he began publishing some of his Chassidic stories and legends. They came out in the Jewish Calendar, one each year. Written in Czech, they were very different from the learned cabbalistic literature, destined for a handful of experts, such as he found at home. These stories were written for the ordinary reader, especially the Czech reader. Their purpose was to tell him something different about the Jews from that which Nazi anti-Semitism was endeavouring to smuggle across the Czechoslovak frontiers. Finally they were a work of the heart and not of the brain; they had their roots in personal experience, relationships and love. They required the full poetic resources of the language and it was therefore natural that my brother should tell them in the language which came most easy to him, his mother tongue.

It was not until the year 1935 that Jiří brought me the bulky sheaf of pages which first bore the title 'Nine Gates'. His sketches had grown into a complete book, he told me, but he was afraid that his style was far from perfect. As an experienced writer I should be able to put right what was clumsy in his work.

No sooner had I started reading than I forgot all about any idea of improving the style. I was caught up by all the different events and happenings described in the narrative and was completely carried away by the exotic fantasy and originality they revealed. I read on and on. There was nothing misty or difficult to fathom in the mysticism of the book, and far from the various miracles and wonders, which were knitted into the story, being overcharged with pathos and unduly removed from reality, they were, so to speak, tailored to human proportions; they made an endearing appeal. The legends told of saints, wonder-working rabbis, capable of performing such miracles

but at the same time living in an almost intimate relationship
with the Lord, so much so that they could even afford to be in-
solent to Him. In this setting any miracles that God might perform seemed to be nothing more than a little neighbourly
assistance. The stories told of the little Chassidim, the special
children of God, who by virtue of their infinite piety had the
rare privilege of being allowed, through their saints, to ask for
anything they needed for life from a favourable heaven. But at
the same time their lives were so humble and their requests
were in the same character; in consequence the little things they
asked could be granted to them without any miracle; it was
all beautifully human and earthly.

It was only when I had had my fill of the content that I began
to give some thought to the style, as my brother had requested.
Could it be that he had any doubts on this score? It seemed to
me in every line that the magic effect of his legends lay precisely
in the fact that they were told in such a bewitching way. The
least change in tone or cadence, in the light touch and artless
simplicity of the book, in the choice and arrangement of the
words, would have taken away something of the appeal. The
author had combined deft naïvety, which is the basis of all
Jewish anecdotes, with that refined simplicity which is a
characteristic gift of the greatest Jewish artists, such as Heine or
Chagall. Jiří had laced his narrative throughout with two
threads. One was the smiling scepticism of a very adult human
being narrating to children the unbelievable miracles performed
by fairy-tale rabbis. The other, contemporary thread was that
of the trusting listener who with the gullibility of a child be-
lieves absolutely in every word he hears. The stories were told
naturally, vividly, personally; you could almost see the author's
mimicking, gesticulations and smiles, and the roguish wink in
his eye, as he spoke direct from mouth to ear, with all the
pauses, cadences, pianissimos and fortissimos; it was as though
the story-teller were sitting immediately in front of his listeners
in some oriental bazaar. Moreover the manner in which the
book was put together corresponded to its content; naïve verses
with assonances stood at the head of each set of stories and served

as a sort of musical intermezzo. The book formed a complete whole and had all the atmosphere of a Chassidic *Thousand and One Nights*.

In other words, no need for corrections. What was necessary was a suitable publisher. It was some time before we could find one, so that the book did not appear until 1937, in the midst of the disturbances which had already begun to shake Europe. It aroused great interest among Czech readers. At a different period its original theme and superb narrative skill would have ensured its running into further editions and it would certainly have been translated into other languages. As it was, the impending events, which shortly became actual events, caused it to be limited to the original edition. Eighteen months after publication, during the Nazi occupation, the book was classified among the monstrosities of art, and the edition was destroyed. Only a few copies survived, hidden away by their devoted readers from the house-to-house inspections. Today each copy of *Devět Bran* (*Nine Gates*) is a much prized rarity.

Another way in which Jiří met the need to tell his compatriots, at such a crucial period of history, something truthful about the Jews, as he had done in *Nine Gates*, was by writing a popular book about the Talmud and its origin. He selected and translated into Czech a hundred examples of old Jewish wisdom from the Talmud, the humanism of whose commandments was so directly opposed to the brutalities of Nazi racialism. To acquaint the Czech reader with the great literature of the Jews he translated into Czech a selection from the Hebrew poets of the eleventh to the eighteenth centuries. All verse is extremely difficult to translate, and these ancient Jewish poets with their numerous archaisms and many departures from classical forms presented exceptional problems. Nevertheless it seems to me that Jiří, who was intimately acquainted with the subtleties of both Czech and Hebrew and who wrote poetry in both languages, has succeeded in preserving in his translation the beauty of the old poetry and has also retained that specific Jewish quality which differentiates the Hebrew lyric poets and minnesingers from their Christian contemporaries. This book of poems, called *Songs of the Rejected*, first appeared in 1937 and was republished in February 1939. The selection includes a translation of the mournful elegy written by Avigdor Karo, a Prague doctor who was one of the few Jews to survive the bloodshed in the Prague ghetto in 1389. This elegy is recited to this day at the oldest of Prague's synagogues on the Day of Atonement. The tragic title which my brother gave to his songs was no random choice, and after nearly six hundred years Reb Avigdor Karo's elegy has a prophetic ring about it.

The prophecy was fulfilled in the early spring of 1939 when the German Army occupied the Czechoslovak Republic. For the nation it meant the end of all freedom and rights; for the Jews it meant in addition the Nuremburg Laws, the first step towards the subsequent slaughter at Terezín and Auschwitz. At the beginning of July, I fled across the Polish frontier to France. My brother Josef chose suicide in preference to a slow death in the concentration camps. My parents had died while the times were still peaceful, in an age when it seemed that the world would enjoy peace, if not for all time, at least for long, long years.

In the autumn of 1939, Jiří left for Slovakia which still offered some prospects of escape. In return for bribes the Gestapo turned a blind eye when the Jews began to organize a route along the Danube to Istanbul and on to Palestine. The Danube passage was still to some extent neutral. More than a thousand refugees of all ages, from new-born babies to old people, found their way along this route at the beginning of November, in river steamers and subsequently in iron cargo barges pulled by tugs. Even at the slowest rate of sailing they were able to reach the Danube estuary within three weeks. Once in the Black Sea they were out of reach of the Gestapo. But on the river itself they were not safe. Their sluggish rate of progress was continually held up on all manner of pretexts. It was as though there was an outside force directing the movement of the ship. Even when the refugees reached the Danube delta, they were still not safe from Nazi fingers which might hold up the ship at Sulina harbour, a mere stone's throw from the freedom of the seas. To add to their misfortunes the fugitives encountered frosts that were unusually early for this part of the world. River and ship were held in the tightest grip. The iron barges became a prison and the refugees had sometimes to endure up to fifty degrees of frost without even the most primitive heating arrangements and with insufficient food. Dysentery, severe influenza and pneumonia, with all manner of complications, were rampant and occasioned innumerable deaths.

My brother wrote to me in Paris to tell me about the journey —it was something of a miracle that I ever received his letters— and to ask for help for all concerned. As it was the beginning of the war, the various international contacts and institutions were still functioning quite efficiently—the Red Cross, the Y.M.C.A., the Danube Transport Commission and a number of Jewish, Catholic and Quaker charitable organizations—and I got my friends busy on the matter wherever I could. But the most effective assistance came from our fellow-countrymen in Roumania, initiated by my brother-in-law, and from Jan Masaryk who prevailed upon the British Government to send out a relief ship. However, it was not until half-way through February that the refugees were delivered from their prison of ice and taken to Istanbul.

Jiří was among those rescued—if one can talk of rescue! Always a dreamer in everything he undertook, he had made no proper preparations for the voyage. His suitcases were filled with his favourite books—two hundred he took with him; consequently he had neither thought nor room for any warm clothing or a supply of food. He suffered even more than the other passengers from cold and starvation, and his pneumonia was early complicated by a severe inflammation of the kidneys. When at last he was carried on to the relief ship he was at the end of his strength. His nephritis soon became chronic and in due course brought about his death.

I learned of his life in Palestine from the letters he wrote to me in England. His health picked up somewhat after he had landed on the shores for which he had yearned so long and had spent some time receiving treatment in hospital at Tel Aviv. Life was far from easy. Like all the refugees from Czechoslovakia who were unable to work, he received a small grant from our authorities. But it was not long before his condition worsened and he had frequently to be readmitted to hospital. Fortunately, after the first difficulties caused by the war in this part of the world had been overcome, I was able to send him assistance from England. He translated his Chassidic legends into Hebrew and planned to write a further series of stories about the Chassidic saints in Czech. To bring himself some relief and a measure of joy amidst his gloomy reflections, he turned once again to Hebrew poetry and published his verses in various magazines. Among these was his poem about Prague and the Old-New Synagogue. The reception given by the public was warm and lively.

At times my brother was so weakened by illness that he was unable to read. The letters in which he described his suffering, often with a brave touch of humour, made a deeply moving effect on me, especially in the passages where he wrote of his hope of recovery and subsequent return to Czechoslovakia; he told of how he was looking forward to meeting me and my children, but as a doctor I was well aware that ... At least he had the advantage of living the last days of his life in the beneficial dry climate of Palestine and in a little piece of his long-cherished dream. He loved to get out of Tel Aviv into the country, he loved to make the journey to Jerusalem. Whenever he mentioned the beauties of the Palestinian countryside his writing became rapturous with adoration. He did not write a great deal about people, although he was held in much affection and both friends and strangers brought him flowers when he was in hospital. Among his closest friends were the writer, Max Brod, and his wife. Jiří had a great deal in common with Brod, and the two men were linked by their nostalgia for Bohemia and Prague. After Jiří had been laid to rest in the cemetery at Tel Aviv, Brod made all the necessary arrangements regarding his grave and literary estate, in particular his books which my brother had bequeathed to the Tel Aviv library. Jiří died on the 12th of March 1943. As he lay dying, though still in full command of his faculties, Max Brod brought him the proof-sheets of a book containing my brother's collected Hebrew poems, written in Palestine. It was plainly printed on plain paper. The title he had chosen for it indicated how great was the comfort and how soothing the balm which he derived from that meagre measure of poetry that life had vouchsafed to him in spite of all his tribulation. The name he gave to the book was *Me'at Tsori*, which means 'A Little Balsam'.

His grave at Tel Aviv is marked by a modest stone, erected by his friends. But in his *Nine Gates* he has created for himself a noble memorial. The book is a remarkable, original work which will bring glory to Czech literature. It is also a very authentic document in the history of the Jews and thus shares the two-fold excellence of the work of Israel Zangwill—certainly a significant analogy.

But it is as though *Nine Gates* has been endowed by destiny with still further significance, as though history has appointed an additional mission for it after its birth. For it has become an infinitely tragic memorial erected over the vast, sorrowful graveyard of the Chassidim. Since the time that my brother lived there, the towns, villages and countryside of the Chassidim—Belz, Ropshitz, Lizensk, Kotsk and many another place—have been submerged under more waves of war than anywhere else in the whole of Europe. Such was their destiny during the First World War, and even after the end of that war, when everywhere else there was peace. Defenceless Jewish quarters, albeit poor, have always been the easiest of trophies for armies and marauding hordes. During the Second World War the destruction began when the Germans invaded Poland and started murdering the Jews with the horrifying thoroughness of Nazism. There can be no doubt that, as with the other parts of Central Europe, more than 90 per cent of the Jews in these isolated areas perished in the concentration camps. And if some of them escaped, they were caught up in the death-dealing inundation of war which spread twice over these desolate plains. Today we are entirely without first-hand accounts of the fate that befell the Chassidic settlements. All the tiny villages, each like a little kingdom on its own, in which the rabbi-saints ruled in the name of God, all the synagogues and universities in the mean, squat cottages—everything was transformed into a scene of ruin or conflagration. All those poor, humble, happy little people, the most defenceless of all the defenceless, the most peace-loving community in the world, all these perished in war.

It may be that among the Jews in Israel or New York there are a few handfuls of the old Chassidic believers still adhering to the customs which they have brought from their old homes. But these are merely so many reminiscences of the past. The mystical reality of the Chassidim cannot last under the blue sky of Israel or amidst the bustle of the streets of Brooklyn. It could only exist in that utter isolation from the world and time which it enjoyed in Galicia, in that poverty in which all were equal, in that freedom in which they were subjected to nought save the will of God, and in that spiritual grandeur which came to dwell in their villages through the wisdom and miracles of their saintly rabbis. And thus it was that my brother Jiří depicted it for the last time in his sweet and smiling book, thereby erecting for the Chassidim an eternal monument to preserve their memory for all time.

WORKS OF JIRI LANGER

Die Erotik der Kabbala. Prague, 1923.
On the Function of the Jewish Doorpost Sign (Zur Funktion der
    jüdischen Türpfortenrolle). Vienna, 1928 (Imago XIV, 4).
Pijjutim ve-Shire Jedidut. Prague, 1929.
Jewish Phylacteries (Die jüdischen Gebetriemen-Phylakterien).
    With addendum: Affinity with African Ritual Circles.
    Fire. The Snake. Vienna, 1931 (Imago XVI).
Nine Gates (Devět Bran). Prague, 1937.
Talmud (Extracts and History). Prague, 1939.
Songs of the Rejected (Zpěvy zavržených). Prague, 1938.
Me'at Tsori. Tel Aviv, 1942.

ACKNOWLEDGMENTS

I should like to thank the translator, Mr. Stephen Jolly, for
having undertaken this difficult work and for having devoted so much care to my brother's book. I should also
like to thank Mr. A. D. Millard, of James Clarke & Co.
Ltd., for deciding to publish it. I have always believed that
this work by my brother was predestined to become part
of the world's literature, and I am therefore convinced
that public interest in the book will fittingly reward them
for what they have done to help it to achieve its rightful
place.

FRANTIŠEK LANGER

I. I. 59

CONTENTS

CONTENTS

Nine Gates

to the Chassidic mysteries

THE AUTHOR TO HIS READERS

When you have read my book seven times, you will say, perhaps with justice: "It is a bad book; however, one incident in it pleased me." Which?—Each of you will say something different. . . . Each according to the roots of his soul and the glimmer of the worlds through which his Earth flew on that night.

INTRODUCTION

I

A Youth from Prague Among the Chassidim

Scenes from everyday life are scarcely to be found in these
pages. Rather you will feel that you have been transported
for a while to some far-off, exotic country where different
flowers grow and different stars shine, to some primeval age in
which reality was a dream and a dream was reality.

Yet that is not quite how it is. Everything happened in our
immediate neighbourhood and not so very long ago; almost, one
might say, only a moment ago. For in literary creation, which
can survey more than three thousand years in the mirror of
history, seventy years or a hundred and fifty years are nothing
more than a moment!

It is an impassable road to the empire of the Chassidim. The
traveller who pushes his way through the thick undergrowth of
virgin forests, inexperienced and inadequately armed, is not
more daring than the man who resolves to penetrate the world
of the Chassidim, mean in appearance, even repellent in its
eccentricity.

Only a few children of the West have accomplished this
journey, hardly as many—when I come to think of it—as there
are fingers on the hand that writes these lines.

One summer's day in 1913, a nineteen-year-old youth,
brought up like all the youth of his time in the dying traditions
of the pre-war generation, left Prague inspired by a secret longing which even now after the passage of so many years he still
cannot explain to himself, and set out for the east, for strange
countries.

Had he a foreboding of what he was losing on that day?

European civilization with its comforts and achievements, its
living successes called careers? Had he a foreboding that his soul

would no longer be capable of feeling poetry which up to that time he had been so fond of quoting, that, from the first moment when he heard the rhythms of the Chassidic songs, all the magic charms of music would be swamped once and for all, and all beautiful things which his eye had ever conceived would in the future be half hidden by the mystic veil of the knowledge of good and evil?

He hardly suspected that, at the very moment when he believed he had reached his goal, the most impassable part of his journey was only beginning. For the gate to the empire of the Chassidim never opens suddenly for anyone. It is closed by a long chain of physical and spiritual suffering. But he who has once looked inside will never forget the riches he has seen.

The rulers of this empire are hidden from the eyes of the world. Their miraculous deeds and all-powerful words are only, as it were, of secondary importance—they are merely the hem of the veil in which their being is wrapped, while their faces are turned away from us towards the distant calm of the Absolute. Only a faint reflection of their souls falls on our too material shadows. Yet, even today, years afterwards, these shapes haunt me one after the other. Not only those I knew personally but also those I have heard so much about and read about in the old Hebrew books; they rise again before me in all their greatness and strength. I feel overcome. Something compels me to take up my pen and faithfully write down everything as best I can.

It is a Friday afternoon. The small town of Belz, the Jewish Rome, is preparing to welcome the Sabbath.

Small towns in eastern Galicia have all had the same character for centuries. Misery and dirt are their characteristic outward signs. Poorly clad Ukrainian peasant men and women, Jews wearing side-whiskers, in torn caftans, rows of cattle and horses, geese and large pigs grazing undisturbed on the square. Belz is distinguished from other places only by its famous synagogue, its no less famous House of Study and the large house belonging to the town rabbi. These three buildings enclose the square on three sides. They are simply constructed. But in this poor, out-of-the-way region of the world they are truly memorable. Belz has somewhat more than three thousand inhabitants, half of whom are Jews.

It is a long summer afternoon. There are still six or seven hours before dusk, when the Sabbath begins and even the lightest work is strictly forbidden. In spite of this, the shops are already shut, the tailors are putting away their needles, and the casual labourers—wearing side-whiskers like the rest—their hoes and spades. The housewives in the cottages are adding the last touches to their preparations for the festival.

The men hasten to the baths. After a steam bath we dive—always several of us at the same time—into a small muddy swimming-pool, a *mikve*, or special ritual bath. As though in mockery of all the rules of hygiene, a hundred bodies are 'purged' from the spirit of the working day. The water, like all the water in Belz, smells of sulphur and petroleum. . . .

Although everybody is in a tearing hurry on this day, the whole community already knows that a *bocher*, or young lad, has come to Belz all the way from Prague. A hundred questions are fired at me from every side. I am embarrassed because I do not understand a single word. I have never heard 'Yiddish' spoken before, that bizarre mixture of mediaeval German and Hebrew, Polish and Russian. It was only later that I gradually began to learn it.

The Sabbath candles are already lit in the rabbi's house. I enter with the other guests—there is a long queue of them—to greet the saint for the first time. He has been told that I am the lad from Prague; indeed they have told him a very wonderful thing—that I have succeeded in plaiting (in the prescribed fashion, of course) four fringes to my *Leib-zidakl*, or vest, with my own hands. For this work of art he calls me to him once again. Once again he shakes my hand, this time lingeringly, and regards me kindly. He looks at me with only one eye. The other eye is blind. It seems to me that a ray of light shines from his seeing eye and pierces me to the heart.

He is a sturdy, tall, old man, with broad shoulders and an un-

5

usual, patriarchal appearance, dressed in a caftan of fine silk, wearing, like all the other men, a *shtreimel*, a round fur hat worn on the Sabbath, on his head, round which hang thirteen short sable tails of dark brown colour. (On weekdays, he wears a *spodek* which is a tall, heavy velvet cap, worn by rabbis, similar to a grenadier's cap.)

Such is the welcome the youth from Prague receives from Rabbi Yissochor Ber Rokach—may his memory be blessed—the grandson of the holy Rabbi Sholem and perhaps the only person still living who can remember the old man. He addresses me in a kindly voice. I realize that he is asking me about Prague. Many years ago he was there with his father, to pray in the Old-New Synagogue and to visit the grave of his famous ancestor, the Great Rabbi Loev.

The spacious Belz synagogue has meanwhile filled with people. There are a hundred lighted candles. In a way the interior reminds me of the Old-New Synagogue in Prague. The men, for the most part tall and well-built, old and young, await the arrival of the rabbi, talking quietly among themselves. In contrast to their weekday appearance, they are all absolutely clean. Their festive caftans of black silk reach down to the ground. On their heads the older ones wear *shtreimels*, which smell of the perfumed tobacco they carry in their tobacco pouches. Some are from Hungary, others from far away—from Russia. Owing to the bad state of the roads they have journeyed for weeks on end to get to Belz, and it may be that they will not be staying there more than a single day. The next day, Sunday, they will set out again on the wearisome journey home. Next Sabbath others will come in their place.

Dusk is already well advanced when the rabbi enters the synagogue. The crowd quickly divides, to let him pass. Perhaps the waters of the Red Sea once divided in the same way before Moses.

With long, rapid strides he makes straight for the *bimah*, or reading desk, and the strange Chassidic service begins.

"*O give thanks unto the Lord, for He is good; for His mercy endureth for ever.*"

6

These words from Psalm 107 are used every Friday by the Chassidim when they greet the coming Sabbath. So it was ordained by the holy Baal-Shem when he was delivered out of the hands of pirates on his abortive journey to the Holy Land.

"O give thanks unto the Lord, for He is good; for His mercy endureth for ever."

It is as though an electric spark has suddenly entered those present. The crowd which till now has been completely quiet, almost cowed, suddenly bursts forth in a wild shout. None stays in his place. The tall black figures run hither and thither round the synagogue, flashing past the lights of the Sabbath candles. Gesticulating wildly, and throwing their whole bodies about, they shout out the words of the Psalm. They knock into each other unconcernedly, for all their cares have been cast aside; everything has ceased to exist for them. They are seized by an indescribable ecstasy.

Do I dream?—I have never seen anything like this before! Or maybe I have? . . . Have I perhaps been here before? . . . Everything is so peculiar, so incomprehensible!

"O give thanks unto the Lord! . . . whom He hath redeemed from the hand of the enemy; and gathered them out of the lands, from the east, and from the west, from the north, and from the south."

The voice of the old man at the *bimah* is heard clearly above all the rest. It expresses *everything*—in immense, joyous humility, and at the same time in infinitely sad longing, as though it would flow into the Infinite, as though the king's son, after being cast out for six days, were returning to face his royal Father. With deep sobs he does penance for our sins.

"They wandered in the wilderness in a solitary way; they found no city to dwell in. Hungry and thirsty, their soul fainted in them."

At this moment the power of the saint's prayers brings deliverance to the souls of those who for their great sins have found no peace after death, and been condemned to wander through the world. The *sparks* of the holy Wisdom of God, which fell into Nothingness when God destroyed the mysterious worlds that preceded the creation of our world, these sparks are now

7

raised from the abyss of matter and returned to the spiritual Source from which they originally came.

"Then they cried unto the Lord in their trouble, and He delivered them out of their distresses. And He led them forth by the right way, that they might go to a city of habitation. Such as sit in darkness and in the shadow of death, being bound in affliction and iron. Because they rebelled against the words of God, and contemned the counsel of the Most High. Then they cried unto the Lord in their trouble, and He delivered them out of their distresses. O praise the Lord for His goodness, and for His wonderful works to the children of men!"

The old man at the *bimah* raises his right hand as though to bless an unseen stranger. It is as though healing balsam flows from his quivering fingers.

"They that go down to the sea in ships, that do business in great waters. He raiseth the stormy wind which lifteth up the waves thereof. They mount up to the heaven, they go down again to the depths. They stagger like a drunken man, and are at their wits' end. Then they cry unto the Lord in their trouble, and He bringeth them out of their distresses. Then they are glad because they be quiet; so He bringeth them unto a haven of hope. Oh that men would praise the Lord for His goodness and for His wonderful works to the children of men! . . . Come then, Beloved, come to meet thy Bride, let us hasten to greet the Sabbath! . . ."

The old man throws himself about as though seized by convulsions. Each shudder of his powerful body, each contraction of his muscles is permeated with the glory of the Most High. Every so often he claps the palms of his hands together symbolically.

The crowd of the devout swirls and streams, hums and seethes like molten lava. Suddenly, as though at a word of command, all remain with their faces towards the west, towards the entrance of the synagogue, bowing their heads in expectation. It is at this moment that the invisible Queen of the Sabbath comes in, and brings to each of us a priceless heavenly gift: a second, new, festive *soul*.

"Come in peace, oh crown of the Lord, in the joy and exultation within the true ones of the chosen people! Come, oh Bride, come, oh Bride, come, oh Bride, Sabbath, Queen!"

8

Once again we raise our heads.

"Come, Beloved, come to meet thy Bride. . . ."

The service ends. The ecstasy is over, the mystic vision has melted. Gone is the ecstasy. Now we are again in this world. But the whole world has been made sublime. Joy sparkles in the people's eyes. There is a festive, carefree atmosphere—the peace of the Queen Sabbath.

We walk past the saint in single file and wish him "good Sabbath!"

How hungry we all are!—That is because of the "second soul" that comes on the Sabbath. . . . We hasten to the inns to have a quick meal, so as to be in time at the saint's table. The stars have long since come out in the deep sky above the Ukrainian steppe. They are large like oranges.

The women are not in the synagogue. Their duty is to light the sacred Sabbath candles at home and wait for the return of their husbands and sons. They do not come out till the Saturday morning. We run into groups of them on the square—wearing traditional costumes in which the predominant colours are green, yellow and white.

Let us not look at them too closely—neither the old women in their aprons and hoods, nor the girls, fair and dark, bareheaded! They might wrongly interpret our attention, and that would cause no small scandal!

. . . On weekdays I spend most of my time at the *Bes Hamidrash*, or House of Study. It is open day and night for all who thirst after knowledge. The high shelves round the walls are stuffed full of books from the floor to the ceiling. The tables are littered with a jumbled mass of folios. Anyone may take out any book he likes and study in the *Bes Hamidrash* whenever he wishes. Here of course there are only holy, theological Hebrew books. A devout man would not touch any other. Even to know a single Latin or Russian letter is an indelible stain upon the soul. I sit and study the books from morning till evening, leaving them only for a short while to go to evening prayers or meals. Yet even the nights are not made for rest but—as the Talmud says—

for the study of the Law of God. Spiteful insects remind me of this impressively enough as soon as I lie down. It is forbidden to kill insects. I already know that it would be a sin, so I prefer to go to the House of Study. I either study or listen to someone else, in another corner, reading aloud to himself in a drawling, plaintive chant. The *Shames*, or caretaker, hands us round candles. We hold the lighted candles in our hands so as not to fall asleep over our studies.

One afternoon I dive into the ritual bath in the same way as before prayer, for on this day I am going to the saint with my *kvitel*. A *kvitel* is a small piece of paper on which one of the saint's clerks writes the name of the suppliant and the name of his mother—not his father!—the suppliant's place of origin and, in a few concise words, the substance of what he is coming to ask of God. The Chassidim, it must be explained, do not bring their petitions to the saint by word of mouth but in writing. On my *kvitel* are written the words: "Mordecai ben Rikel mi-Prag, hasmodoh be-limud ve-yiras shomayim", which means that I am asking God "that I may persevere in my studies and in the fear of God". Not one word more. That was how the Chassidim advised me to write it. The saint's entrance hall and room are already crowded—in Belz it is always crowded—with scores of suppliants, mostly women. Some come to ask the saint to intercede with God for success in their business, others for recovery from an illness, others for advice for or against a marriage. The needs of the Chassidim are many and varied, and only *he*, the saint, can satisfy them through his intercession with the Most High. After reading some of the petitions, the saint asks for details before beginning to pray or give advice. He reads some petitions with obvious displeasure, especially those asking for cures. He scolds the suppliant and tells him to go to a doctor. But he wishes him a speedy recovery. Some bring a *matbeya*, that is, a coin which the saint will endow with secret power and which can then be used as a *kameo*, or amulet. The saint places the coin on the table and draws three circles round it. He does so with obvious reluctance. But once the coin has been consecrated by the saint's hand, the suppliant receives it back with an expression of radiant joy on his face. Besides the *kvitel*, we place a *pidyen* on the saint's table; this is a small sum of money according to one's means. The saint is *in duty bound* to accept gifts. This custom was instituted by the holy Baal-Shem, and it has a metaphysical background. When the saint intercedes with God on behalf of us unworthy people, the Lord asks him: "Of what importance is this sinner to you? Have you any obligation towards him, dearly beloved son?" And the saint can reply to God: "Yes, I have an obligation towards him. He has assisted me and my family." Our money offering is thus the only link, mean as it is, between us and the saint; it is the necessary prerequisite for our prayers to be heard. Hence the saint accepts gifts. But he returns the gifts of poor people immediately. From declared unbelievers he will not take any gifts at all. The devout who live outside Belz send their petitions and contributions to the saint's office by post, or if the matter is urgent, by telegram. The suppliant obtains relief as soon as the clerk unsticks the telegram even though the saint has not yet received the remittance. Those who come to Belz from Hungary kiss the saint's hand. The Poles do not. I am last in the queue. The saint reads my *kvitel* with undisguised delight. When I come out of his room, the Chassidim are waiting for me outside, to wish me luck: "Git gepoilt!"— "Well done!"

When the moon is full, the saint cures mental maladies. The people stand in a sad queue in his room while the saint pores over the Talmud by the light of large candles. I once knew a girl who was completely cured of melancholia in this way.

The saint never looks on the face of a woman. If he must speak to women—as, when he receives a *kvitel*—he looks out of the window while he speaks. He does not even look at his own wife, a somewhat corpulent woman, but still beautiful. On a later occasion, when the holy man was alone with his wife, it was only natural that the lad from Prague should seize this rare opportunity of peeping through the keyhole when no one was watching. She had come to ask her husband's advice about their domestic worries, of which they had their full share. Even on this occasion the saint looked out of the window, with his face turned away from her, as though he were talking to a strange woman, not his wife. The Talmud tells of one devout man who did not notice that his wife had a wooden stump instead of a leg, until her funeral. . . . That man was a teacher. Thus far the Talmud.

From the window of the entrance hall to the saint's apartment one can see far out across the Ukrainian steppe. For miles round there is nothing but a flat plain, without a single tree or hill to be seen. It is a fen with a narrow path made of boards running across it. In the distance a small bridge leads into a barren little field; then the path leads on across the bog into the unknown. When I am weary of the House of Study, I cross this bridge and lie down in the little field. This is the only bit of nature where one can find spiritual refreshment in all this wilderness!

I can endure it no longer. This life of isolation from the rest of the world is intolerable. I feel disgusted with this puritanism, this ignorance, this backwardness and dirt. I escape. I travel back to my parents in Prague. But not for long. I must perforce return to my Chassidim.

One night I cannot sleep. I am lying down, facing the kitchen door, which looks towards the East. I have left the door ajar. I have just been reading some holy Hebrew book in the kitchen. The kitchen windows are open, open towards the East, the East where Belz lies at the end of a train journey of a few hours more than a day and a night. . . . It is useless for me to close my eyes to induce sleep. Suddenly I am dazzled by a bright light penetrating into my dark bedroom through the half-open door. What is it?—I know that I have put out the lamp, and there is no one in the kitchen. I stare at the light, and in the middle of it, a few steps in front of me, I can see quite clearly through the half-open door—*the saint of Belz!* He is sitting in his room at Belz looking fixedly at me. On his expressive countenance shines that barely recognizable, sublime smile of his, full of wisdom. I have no idea how long the apparition lasts, but it is long enough to shake me.

So I travel to Belz a second time, this time firmly resolved. I am no longer alone as on my first pilgrimage. This time I have a companion, a Prague lad like myself, who has also decided for Chassidism.

My vision of the saint of Belz that night was a great favour. So the Chassidim said when I told them about it. To behold a living saint from far away and, moreover, while still awake, is not indeed an absolutely isolated phenomenon among the Chassidim, but it is a greater expression of God's favour than, for instance, a conversation with someone who is dead or with the prophet Elijah.

We "who are really in earnest" do not board at the inn like those who "merely journey" to the saint of Belz. We belong to our own society, or *chevre*, the members of which are called *Yoshvim*, or *sitting ones*, because they live, or sit in Belz permanently. Our society lives on small contributions earned with difficulty from the more wealthy visitors to Belz. We cook for ourselves. The dining-room is small. Deep holes yawn in the unplaned boards of the dirty floor. We crowd together round the table on a narrow bench. There is a great shortage of crockery. We young people often eat two out of one dish, with our hands, of course. To use a fork would be an indecent innovation. The menu is not very varied. For lunch we get a slice of heavy rye bread, a plate of vermicelli or potato soup, which of course we eat with a spoon, and a tiny piece of beef to which a large portion of broad beans must always be added. The older men drink vodka, all from the same bottle (though the Talmud, or rather the Shulchan Aruch forbids two people to drink from the same vessel on hygienic grounds). We often have the famous Belz *purée*, made from sweet-smelling brown buck-wheat flour, called *grapel*, which is remarkably tasty. Sometimes we have fish, small white fish full of treacherous little bones. It is my duty to help to scrape the fish in the kitchen when it comes to my turn.

On the Sabbath the crowd is even greater. It is a real squeeze. We do not eat in our mess, but press round the rabbi at his table, quite regardless of each other's comfort in our anxiety to obtain straight from his hands some morsel of food which he has first touched and tasted. Each little titbit of his sweet *kugel* (a hot pudding), each piece of his greasy *chaulnt* (chaud lit), each drop of his home-made raisin wine contains a complete paradise with all its accompanying celestial delights. He who eats of food which the saint has blessed is sure to obtain both earthly and eternal bliss. At the table the Chassidim sing their Sabbath songs in praise of Belz, songs whose changing rhythms are a dance of gaiety and sorrow, chaos and desire. Before the grace after the meal the rabbi expounds the Word of God. Every new truth which the saint brings out from the depths of the Law is fashioned by God into a new heaven. The saint's exposition is at the same time a sermon. I hear his deep mystic voice, but I cannot distinguish the words.

On festivals there is dancing. A hundred men take hold of each other's hands, or put their arms round each other's necks and form a large circle that rotates with a rocking dance-step, slowly at first and then faster and faster. The dancing begins in the *Bes Hamidrash*, but after a while the whole crowd spreads out on to the square and dances under the rabbi's window. A dance lasts uninterrupted for an hour, or maybe more, till the dancers are exhausted, intoxicated by the endless repetition of the same, mystically coloured, dance melody. In the same way the celestial spheres dance eternally round the glorious throne of the Lord. We young people are not allowed to take part in the sacred dance of the Chassidim. We look on and sing, clapping our hands in time to the rhythm. The rabbi dances only a short while during the morning service on the autumn festivals. He dances alone. In his hand he holds a palm branch or a parchment scroll of the Law. The sight of the saint's mystic dance fills us with godly fear.

We take very good care not to catch the saint's eye during a service. As he enters the House of Study we press together in one confused mass, to leave him as much free space as possible. No true Chassid comes within a distance of *four ells* (about eight feet) of him either during prayer or before it. If we are not sufficiently careful and agile he shouts at us—using words like "cattle!" or even "robbers!"—and sometimes he slips off his *gartel* (belt) and belabours the careless individual who has got in his way. But, surprisingly enough, his blows do not hurt in the least. Nor do his words. We laugh quietly to ourselves with joy, because we know that they are not insults but a high mark of honour, a secret blessing which he disguises with blows and rough words. For the Devil must not recognize them, or he may stop them from ascending to the throne of the Most High. Nevertheless we try to keep our distance from the saint; the farther we get away from him the better it is. Why?—Why do we take such care not to come close to him? Why does he warn us so sternly to keep away? After all he is well aware that not even with a whisper would we interrupt him but would only pray in the most devout fashion. It is not because we might say anything we ought not to, or knowingly disturb him, but because our *thoughts*—all those silly thoughts we carry in our heads, even though not expressed, even the most devout— would upset his spiritual, mystic concentration. For our thoughts are so material that they would sully his pure, mystic concentration and detract from the splendour of his thoughts, each of which is a glorious, living angel. Some Chassidim hide modestly behind the backs of those who happen to stand in front of them. That is foolish, for the saint knows about everybody—even those who are hiding or are far away.

The weekdays slip by monotonously. I continue my study of the Talmud. I have long been fond of these interminable discourses of the ancient Palestinian and Babylonian rabbis on ritual and law, their legends, moral teachings, proverbs, anecdotes, paradoxes, that go to form the Talmud. The Hebrew and Aramaic languages, with their ancient elegance and terseness, have never lost their charm for me. Those picturesque signs in Hebrew writing which even to this day are half hieroglyphic, without vowels or punctuation, have been my favourite reading matter almost from childhood. Now for the first time I can give myself up to this pleasure completely. I sit and learn. When I do not understand one of the complex Talmudic problems, I ask an older person to explain it for me. But mostly I study alone. I repeat each page at least six times as I have been recommended

to do. I memorize the actual Talmudic text; I learn the remarkably exact mediaeval commentaries which are printed round the
text on each page like a wreath of tiny flowers, the diminutive
letters of a mediaeval rabbi's handwriting. Sometimes I use
other large volumes containing notes about these commentaries
to help me along.

Books are greatly respected here, worshipped in fact. Nobody, for instance, sits on a bench if there is a book anywhere on
it. That would be an affront to the book. We never leave a book
face downwards or upside down, but always face upwards. If a
book falls to the ground we pick it up and kiss it. When we
have finished reading we kiss the book before we put it away.
To throw it aside, or put other things on top of it is a sin. Yet
the books are nearly all woefully dilapidated by constant use.
When a book is so badly torn that it cannot be used, the caretaker takes it to the cemetery and buries it. Even the smallest
scrap of paper with Hebrew characters printed on it must not be
left lying about on the floor, or trodden on; it must be buried.
For every Hebrew letter is a name of God. We never leave books
open except when we are actually learning from them. If we
are obliged to slip away for a moment, and do not wish to close
the book, we may leave it open so as not to lose the place, but
we must cover it with a cloth. It anyone notices another person
going away from a book without closing or covering it, he goes
over and shuts it himself; but first he will look at the open page
and read a few lines out of it. If he were to shut the book without
reading it at all, his act of closing it would weaken *the power of
memorizing* in the other person who left the book open. The
parchment scroll of the Law, which is hand-written, is held in
even greater respect than printed books.

I am gradually becoming acquainted with *Chassidic* literature.
The first book I read is called "The Beginning of Wisdom"
(Reshit Chochmah), a cabbalistic book of exercises for the ascetic.
It inculcates humility and self-denial and is full of beautiful
quotations from the mystical Zohar and a book called "The
Duties of the Heart" by Bachya Ibn Pakuda. "Reshit Chochmah"
is the work of a famous cabbalist named Elijah de Vidas who

lived in Palestine at the end of the seventeenth century. Another book I read is "The Joys of Elimelech" (Noam Elimelech) by the "Rebe Reb" Melech of Lizensk (Elimelech). I shall be telling you something about this book and its wonderful author later on. The first of these books was recommended to me by the saint of Belz himself; the second was brought to my notice by the Chassidim. I early got to know other books, Chassidic, old Hebrew and, after a while, modern ones (see the note on Literature). But the first two are the dearest of all to me. They accompany me on all my journeys; I had them with me even when I was a soldier. When I am alone and no one can see me, I dip into cabbalistic writings which we young people have been forbidden to study.

My health is affected and I am conscious that I am becoming physically weaker every day. The daily bath before morning prayer, the bad food, the all too frequent voluntary fasts, the loss of sleep, and the lack of movement and air, considerably weaken the otherwise strong constitution of a youth who is not yet physically mature. But I force myself to face up to things. I will not give in.

Why in fact are we here at all? Why not serve God at home? Is it perhaps because we want to become rabbis, or perfect saints like the saint of Belz? No, not at all. Nothing like this ever occurs to us. We have no desire to be rabbis and we shall never become saints. We are quite convinced of that. All we want is to enjoy the glory of God's majesty which the personality of the saint sheds around him. We want to enjoy it throughout our lives, continuously and unceasingly. We know that when the day comes for him to bid us his last farewell, he will leave us his first-born son, no less a saint than himself and perhaps even greater. Many people are convinced of this already. Perhaps the future has proved them right; I cannot allow myself to decide about that. I would prefer to sketch another picture of Chassidic life.

. . . On weekdays, at Belz, we do not say morning prayers until noon when the rabbi comes into the House of Study with his sons. We pray at the synagogue only on the Sabbath. The weekday service, which in other places lasts nearly an hour, is completed in an almost miraculously fast time at Belz—fifteen or twenty minutes. This speed is very important for "no pig can penetrate a fence if the stakes are set close together"; in other words, no sinful thoughts can steal into prayers if the words are spoken quickly and without any pauses. "A person who cannot say a thousand words with one breath has no right to be called a saint."

(*Speed and agility* in bodily movements—especially, of course, in the performance of religious duties—are a great virtue and an excellent means of ennobling the soul and making the mind supple. This was emphasized by one of the *predecessors* of Chassidism, the Italian cabbalist and poet, Rabbi Moses Chayyim Luzzatto, in his ethical work, "Mesilat Yesharim". This ray of sunlight from Renaissance Italy has to this day given Belz Chassidism a particular character of its own, making it a striking exception in this somewhat dull-witted northern region. Indeed the other Chassidim cannot tolerate the brisk way we do things at Belz. They see something grotesque about it.)

I am still a foreigner. People are very polite and full of respect when they talk to me, but they are mistrustful. The mere fulfilment of religious injunctions, however precise and conscientious, is as little adequate to inspire confidence here as is the utmost zeal over one's study. Excessive religiosity is not welcomed. But now that my beard and side-whiskers are well grown, now that I am able to speak some Yiddish and have begun wearing a long *shipits* (an overcoat similar to a caftan) instead of a short coat, and ever since I have started wearing a black velvet hat on weekdays, as all the other Chassidim do, this ice-wall of mistrust has gradually begun to thaw. But why even now am I not completely like the others? For example, why am I not gay, all the time, as a true Chassid ought to be? . . .

At last, when my face is pallid from undernourishment and illness, and my emaciated body has acquired a stoop, it is clear to nearly all of them that "I am really in earnest". No longer will the gates of Chassidism be closed in front of the youth from Prague.

Meanwhile I have come to know a number of Chassidic truths. For example I already know that "the whole world hates the Jews, that all Jews hate the Chassidim, that all foreign Chassidim hate the Chassidim of Belz and that the Belz Chassidim (that is, those who 'merely journey' to see the saint of Belz) hate *us*, the true *yoshvim*, but that we, the *yoshvim* of Belz, are the pillar on which the whole world rests". I assimilate the mysteries of humility and modesty. Nothing can now deprive me of these fundamental Chassidic virtues. Nothing can tempt me away from them. My Hebrew name, Mordecai, prompts one of the *yoshvim* to quote some words from the book of Esther and apply them to me: "And Mordecai sat in the king's gate." It is meant well. It is a discreet form of praise for my having advanced so far as to sit in the gate of the King of kings, for my having become a real *yoishev* (*yoishev* means: sitting). But to me it does not seem to be any great compliment. I prefer to interpret it as a gentle reproach: I am only in the *gate* of the King; I have still a long way to go before I get to the chamber....

The Chassidim are becoming kinder to me every day. My lot is being improved in every possible way. Better bread, and milk. But my weakened stomach resolutely refuses all these extra comforts. Moreover, the insects are becoming crueller all the time. They have absolutely no pity on me. The mice nibble at my clothes. I sleep on the ground on a heap of old straw. My whole outward appearance testifies that I am gradually turning into a complete *chnyok* and *katcherak*. These two words are untranslatable nicknames used by the Chassidim to mock any of their fellows who are totally indifferent to their outward appearance.

Meanwhile the scene itself has long since changed. But the difference is not very great. Instead of the Ukrainian steppe, there is now the Hungarian puszta. We are no longer in Polish Belz but in the no less dusty Hungarian town of Ratsfert (Ujféhérté), near Debrecin. The Belz rabbi came here for refuge with his entire court at the beginning of the war.

At this time, however, we do not even need to travel to Ratsfert to quench our thirst at the fount of Chassidism. Gunfire has swept the villages and towns, and thousands of bearded Jews are fleeing westwards, arousing contempt and disgust wherever they go. Some have succeeded in saving their holy books and old manuscripts. Prague is flooded with Jews from the east who have set up their own synagogues and schools. Among the thousands of refugees are a few dozen genuine Chassidim who have come from a great variety of places and from all possible directions. For the time being, Prague is part of the Chassidic Empire.

The saint of Belz has fallen ill. After a great deal of persuasion he has decided to visit Mariánské Lázně (Marienbad). We are carrying him there along the paths through the forest. At other times he is separated from us by his secretaries and servants, as God is separated from our souls by myriads of spheres and worlds. But here among the forest trees we can all approach him. Although he is seriously ill, he talks cheerfully to everybody. We are conscious that his are no ordinary words even when he is talking about things which appear to be everyday matters. All his words, however small, are to be understood metaphorically. The whole time his thoughts are concentrated exclusively on supernatural matters. He talks to us, but we are aware that we understand his words no better than the wooden gnomes adorning the forests of Mariánské Lázně. He converses with these distorted little figures as gaily and unconstrainedly as he does with us living people. When he is not speaking to anyone, he repeats the Talmud to himself, which he naturally knows by heart in its entirety—all thirty-six tractates in their twelve mighty volumes! Once, as we were walking through the forest, he remarked: "If I didn't have you, I would pray with these trees here." He has never made a secret of his pacifist opinions. We have often admired his outspokenness. Once, when he noticed a public collecting box for war contributions on one of the forest roads, he called out with passion: "Is that what we've got to do with our money—so still more people can be murdered?" And on another occasion he said: "The German says: The whole world belongs to me! The Englishman says: The whole sea belongs to me! But my Yossele—that was the name of the Chassid who led the prayers in those days—my Yossele sings so sweetly: The sea belongs to God, for He made it; the dry land belongs to God, for His hand created it."

Ever since this time I have felt profoundly indebted to the saint of Belz. I know that it is he alone whom I have to thank for my miraculous deliverance from Austrian military service. It was his intercession with God that brought this about. Everything is again as it used to be. My beard and side-whiskers, which I had to shave off whilst on active service, have grown again.

It is now quite a time since I last saw Gavril, my friend from Prague. He is settled at Hivnev, near Belz, and is making good progress with his studies. He is sure to be enjoying himself, having recently got married.

We are at Ratsfert again. The autumn holidays are over. It is 1918. All of us are very run down. Influenza is taking its toll. But a magic word is going through the world: Armistice—peace!

The woebegone lad from Prague is strangely excited. He does not himself understand what is happening to him, as on that day five years ago when he started out on his first journey to Belz. He bids farewell to the saint and the Chassidim. They do not try to hold him back. Everyone is excited, everyone is looking forward to getting home. They wish him every success and hope he will soon return to them in good health. Some of them go with him a short way. Mechale of Baiberk accompanies him to the station. They eat out of the same dish. A final warm handshake, and the youth from Prague leaves for Budapest and thence on to Vienna. Since then he has not returned to his Chassidim. Europe has not let him go. He returns to them only in this book. . . .

The heroes of our story are the *Tsaddikim*, the rulers of the Chassidim. The word *tsaddik* means a perfect and just person, a saint. The word *chassid*, which becomes *chassidim* in the plural, means a deeply devout person who is wholeheartedly devoted to a particular *Tsaddik*. The founder of Chassidism was Rabbi Yisroel Baal-Shem-Tov who lived and worked in Poland in the middle of the eighteenth century. (He died about 1761.) To this day hundreds of thousands of Chassidic communities live almost totally isolated from the surrounding world, faithful to their unique traditions, and it would be true to say that in Eastern Europe they form states within states. Their *real* rulers are the grandsons and great-grandsons of the saints whom I shall be writing about in this book.

To relate stories from the lives of the saints is one of the most praiseworthy acts a Chassid can do. He will tell of them at every opportunity—during a meal, during his studies, on a train journey, but especially on the anniversary of a saint's death. He must never forget to add the word "holy", or the phrase, "May his merits protect us!", whenever he mentions the name of a saint. Woe to the listener who protests that he has already heard .this or that episode before! Everybody is in duty bound to listen patiently to each story even if he has heard it a hundred times already. In this way, over the course of years, everything becomes imprinted on the memory—the heroes' names, their wives' names, the characters connected with them and the place where the various events took place.

Anyone can be a narrator. If you know a nice story about a saint, it will be gratefully accepted, and one of your listeners will immediately reward you with another story about the same saint, or a similar anecdote about another saint, or something a saint has said. If you make a mistake in any detail, you will immediately be corrected by your listeners, for of course they know it much better than you do! . . .

The story-teller does not speak with words alone. If his vocabulary proves inadequate, he can help himself along with gestures, miming or modulations of the voice. When relating something gloomy, he will lower his voice to a whisper. If he has a mystery to unfold he will content himself with hinting, breaking off in the middle of a sentence with a meaningful wink or squint. If he has to describe some supernatural beauty he will close his eyes and roll his head about in genuine ecstasy. In this way the listener can understand much more than if we were to paint everything in detail with the choicest and cleverest words. The narrator's style is absolutely simple, without any special pathos, and completely inconsequent. He often wanders from one saint to another—so do not be surprised if I sometimes do the same.

The Chassidim are aware that by no means everything they relate about their saints actually happened; but that does not matter. If a saint never really worked the miracle they describe, it must still have been one such as only he was capable of performing. Rabbi Nachman of Brazlav goes out of his way to point out that "not everything related about the holy Baal-Shem (for instance) is true, but even the things which are untrue are *holy* if told by devout people. The fact is (says Rabbi Nachman) that man is perpetually sunk in a magic sleep throughout his life and is unable to rouse himself except by narrating anecdotes about the saints."

It is as though the Chassidic saints had breathed their soul into the legends which the people tell of them. In consequence these Chassidic legends are perhaps more faithful in depicting the characters of their heroes than in recording the actual deeds performed or the actual words spoken.

If I do not use a tearful voice when telling about the Chassidic saints in this book, that is fully in keeping with the style of the Chassidic story-tellers who never avoid humour if it befits the occasion. May I be forgiven if in presenting the various stories I follow a different order than the chronological sequence. By way of excuse I would recall what the Talmud says, that "there is neither *before* nor *after* in the word of God". The verses at the head of each section of the book are modelled on the practice followed in old Hebrew books which used to have similar verses in praise of distinguished rabbis. No chapters in this book are specially devoted to the actual founder of Chassidism, Baal-Shem, whose spirit pervades all our stories. There is of course a purer strain of poetry in the legends about the Baal-Shem, and the truths revealed to him are deeper than the aphorisms of his successors. Above all I have aimed to introduce my readers to some of the more recent representatives of the Chassidic movement.[1] Furthermore I have been lured on by the realization that

[1] Literature (A). *Hebrew:*—Anonymous: Or 'Olam (Lvov s.a.)—Deutsch, Shimon: Hakme ha-Razim (Mukajevo 5696)—Horodetsky, S.A.: Ha-Hasiduth ve-ha-Hasidim (Berlin 5683)—Israel ben Simha: Eser Oroth (Pietrokov 5667)—

I have an opportunity in this book of publishing various stories which have possibly never been written down before—not even in Hebrew—and which I have learnt only from verbal tradition.

It is not the purpose of this book to present a philosophical analysis of Chassidic learning. Certainly it is easy enough to bore one's readers and misuse their patience, but it is not godly. My aim is rather to entertain the reader and at the same time to give him a truthful report. The remaining part of this chapter is not primarily intended for the ordinary layman. It is written more particularly by way of anticipating the ill-will of the learned philosophers and the most esteemed critics.

Chassidism is the Cabbala made accessible to the people. It is a particular type of pantheism with a popular appeal of its own and at the same time partly dogmatic, a pantheism which is shot through with the mystic magic of the *idea* of rabbinical Neo-Platonism and subtly interwoven with pseudo-Pythagorean threads, the whole ingeniously grafted on the old stock of Old Testament Talmudic Judaism. It grew up long, long ago in Palestine, Egypt or Mesopotamia, like a hardly discernible plant in the semi-darkness of unknown circumstances. It was then transplanted to the romantic environment of Catholic and Arab Spain and subsequently returned to Palestine. But it was not until the last two centuries, on the fertile soil of Slavonic north-eastern Europe, in the shade of the Carpathian forests and on the Ukrainian plains, that it developed into the present

Kaddish, Yo'es Kayyam: Siah Sarfe Kodesh (Lodz 5686)—Kahana, Abraham: Sefer ha-Hasiduth (Warsaw 5682)—Kahana, Abraham ("Abrech"): Deyoknaoth ve-Ikunim (Przemysl 5695)—Walden Aharon: Shem hag-Gedolim he-Hadash (Warsaw 5624)—Zeitlin Hillel: Ha-Hasiduth (Warsaw 5682). (B) *In other languages:*—Aescoly W. A.:—L'introduction à l'étude des hérésies religieuses parmi les Juifs. La Kabbale—Le Hassidisme (Paris 1928)—Bloch C.: Priester der Liebe (Vienna 1930)—Buber M.: Die chassidischen Bücher (Hellerau 1928)—Dubnow S.: Die Geschichte des Chassidismus (Berlin 1931)—Klein G.: Bidrag till Israels religions-historia, sex föredrag (Stockhom 1898)—Lehmann E.: Illustrerad religions-historia (Stockholm 1924)—Mosbech H.: Essaeismen et bidrag til senjdendommens religionshistorie (Copenhagen 1916)—Oesterley W. O. E.: The sacred dance, A study in comparative folklore (Cambridge 1923)—Ysander Torsten: Studien zum B'eshtschen Hasidismus (Upsala 1933).

fabulous, many-branched tree whose blooms are so remarkable in their variety. Not many reliable dates can be given. A fundamental problem is presented by the "Zohar", that most important of the cabbalistic books, in that it is not known when and where it was set down in writing. The book appears in Spain at the end of the thirteenth century, when it purported to be an ancient work of Palestinian origin. The dispute about this question—which has a certain analogy in the controversy over the Králové Dvůr and Zelená Hora manuscripts in Czechoslovakia —is not yet at an end. Yitzhak Luria Ashkenazi, who is designated in our stories by the sign *Holy ARI*, the great promulgator of cabbalistic doctrines, was born in Jerusalem in the year 1553 and died at Safed in 1572. His teaching, which was edited by Chayyim Vital Calabrese, a disciple of his, was of particular importance for the rise of Chassidism.

The Chassidic Cabbala is linked with Platonic and Neo-Platonic philosophy in a number of aspects—in its conception of "spheres", in its doctrine of the contraction of the Infinite before the creation of the world, its understanding of all phenomena in a symbolic way (likewise its allegorical interpretation of the Scriptures) and so on. The similarity with Pythagorean philosophy is to be seen in the cabbalists' belief in the creative power of figures (and letters) and in their teaching about the transmigration of souls. On the latter point there is a striking similarity to both Brahmanism and Buddhism. Unlike these two systems, however, the Lurian Cabbala teaches that the human soul can be incarnated not only in animals but also in plants, waters and minerals. The connection with the Indian Upanishads is to be seen in the doctrine of the worlds that preceded the creation of our world, while in its emphasis on the world-creating principles of manhood and womanhood the Cabbala reminds one of Chinese mysticism (Lao-Tse). The idea that man is created in the image of God leads the cabbalists to views about the microcosm similar to those found in Aristotle and Plato, or, for instance, in the Catholic mystic, Nicholas of Cusa. The emphasis on permanent joy as being the most important ethical principle of life links Chassidism with the mysticism of the Mohammedan Sufi, while the functional importance which the Cabbala attaches to the secret "names" of God and the angels brings us near to Ethiopian and even perhaps ancient Babylonian magic.

In popular Chassidic mysticism we find these elements so delicately diffused and elaborated that at first sight we are hardly aware of their presence. In consequence we cannot dismiss Chassidism as a mere inorganic fusion, or medley of mystical ideas culled from various world systems. It may be that Chassidism is a sea into which all mystical streams flow, but if this is so then the fusion took place deep in the subconsciousness of history. It would be possible, perhaps, to reconstruct the bridges linking Chassidism with the mystic centres farthest removed from it both in time and place. Nevertheless the overall impression it gives is so individual and particular that any doubts as to its independent growth are to a large extent dispelled. The Chassidim point out of course—and not altogether without justice—that in one form or another the elements of their teaching are contained in the ancient Talmud and also, in part, in the Holy Scriptures. In confirmation of this opinion it is pertinent to observe that some Christian theologians in the Middle Ages considered that certain Greek philosophical systems were actually of Jewish origin. In recent times, only Nietzsche has held the view that there is evidence of Jewish influence on the philosophy of Plato. In ancient times the Jewish Essenes were almost perfect Pythagoreans, as is clear from the records left by Flavius Josephus.

In time and place Chassidism is closer to the Orthodox Church than to any other denomination. To a certain extent this is also true, I think, in a cultural sense. However this opinion must be taken *cum grano salis* even if justified in certain details.

In support of this view I might instance the deification of the saints during their lifetime and the eating of food sanctified by their mouths, which are phenomena to be found not only among Orthodox Christians and in Chassidism, but also, for example, in far-off Tibet. It is clear from certain passages in the Talmud that similar customs have been considerably widespread among the Jews from oldest times.

Boundless faith, joy inspired by other-worldliness, humility, hope and love, but above all simplicity of soul—these are the qualities that form the foundation of the ethics and moral strength of this legendary Chassidic world. The Chassidic saints are filled with these virtues to an extent that is truly superhuman. Simplicity is not of course a primary quality in the complicated Jewish psychology. Nevertheless Chassidism succeeds in cultivating it by means of its rigid discipline. It is this simplicity which is the source of that naïve refinement and refined naïvety that give the Chassidic legend its peculiar charm and attraction. For although Chassidism profoundly respects Talmudic learning, it takes strict care to ensure that not even scholarship shall be achieved at the expense of simplicity and pureness of soul. For this reason the Chassidim have no love for the eccentric sophistry of the average Talmudist and forbid the reading of pseudo-rationalistic works written by mediaeval Jewish scholars under the influence of Aristotle. They do not even make an exception in the case of the philosophical writings of Maimonides although certain Chassidic saints have made a very careful study of them. In this the influence of the Chief Rabbi Loev of Prague is clearly seen. Loev would have nothing to do with the fruitless controversies of learned Talmudists and vigorously rejected the philosophical speculations of the mediaeval Jewish peripatetics. The influence of the Prague miracle-worker is also evident in the warmheartedness felt by the Chassidim towards their saints.

In spite of differences between Talmudic Judaism and Chassidism, both in philosophical outlook and in the manner of studying the Talmud, it should be stressed that nowadays even the Talmudists do not look upon Chassidism as a heresy or as a sect in the usual sense. The differences in ritual are insignificant. Differences over dogma are virtually non-existent. Both consider the Old Testament and the Talmud, with all its annotations and decisions, as equally authoritative. The main difference between them lies in the fact that Chassidism has elevated occult lore, or the Cabbala, with all its implications, above everything else. It has made it accessible to the ordinary people, as we have already said, whereas for the rest of Orthodox European Jewry the Cabbala has, on the whole, a subordinate position and is virtually only of theoretical importance, being at best only one of the religious subjects studied by certain rabbis, and without any perceptible influence on religious life. In its positive attitude towards the Cabbala, Chassidism comes near to oriental Judaism, especially in the liturgical aspect and its doctrine of the transmigration of souls which is totally unknown in western Judaism.

The most beautiful Chassidic doctrine is undoubtedly that of the *spiritual nature* of all matter. According to Chassidism, all matter is *full of supernatural "sparks" of the holiness of God*, and purely human functions such as eating and drinking, bathing and sleeping, dancing and the act of love are dematerialized and considered as the *most sublime* actions *in the service of God*.

The Chassidic legend is not without its cloudy moods. On the whole however it can be said that the mysticism of the Chassidic legends is *bright and joyous*, which gives it a great charm and appeal without in any way detracting from its depth.

Chassidic first names are given in their Chassidic form and not as they are found in classical Hebrew. Thus, for instance: 'Sholem' not 'Shalom', 'Avrum' not 'Abraham', 'Yisrol' not 'Israel', 'Nachman' not 'Naaman'. For the most part the names appear with one or other of the diminutive endings in which the Yiddish language is very rich, for instance, -ele, -el, -nju, -tje, -ke.

The Hebrew word 'reb' has been preserved in referring to the rank of the man concerned. It is always used immediately before a proper name and never as an independent word. If the word 'rabbi' is to be used independently, the Hebrew word is 'rebe' (rabbi) or 'rov' (rab). Titles of works (except where they are used as their authors' names) are written in accordance with academic usage. Well-known biblical names are spelt in the accepted way.

(Where transliteration has been necessary, the following points should be observed: 'ch' is always guttural, as in the Scotch word 'loch', 'tch' is to be pronounced as in the English word 'catch', 'sh' is as in the English word 'shoe', 'h' is always aspirate, 'u' is always to be sounded as in the English word 'put', a final 'e' must always be pronounced as in the Italian word 'niente', 'j' is to be pronounced as a short 'ee' sound. Translator's note.)

How a silken young man was not fitted to go into business, or how the predictions of the Seer were fulfilled—a disputation between the Devil and a Messiah, or how our Redeemer was confounded by a woman—how the holy Reb Sholem built a House of God and how the holy Rebe Reb Shimon of Jaroslav visited it and kissed every stone in it—how the holy Reb Sholem lived with his consort Malkele as in paradise—how the holy Malkele expounded the Scriptures and healed a lame man—then it is related how the holy Reb Sholem was incarnated in a citron (*esrig*) and how a disciple unveiled a mystery—how our Chassidic stubbornness is our greatest virtue—how a sinner was punished by having to eat swine's flesh, and how another sinner was saved by his stubbornness—how the angels sought an intercessor and how they made the holy Reb Sholem their cantor—how the holy Reb Sholem settled a disturbance after his death, or how he tarries among us at our prayers.

All you, then, who wish to live, enter this gate with me, for there you shall read all this.

The First Gate

Of diamonds in the Lord's crown the costliest,
Shining jewel of humility,
In modesty the purest,
Source of peace and loyalty,
In faith the deepest.

To him thousands of Jacob's sheep have hastenèd,
Through him their thirsty souls have quenchèd,
And to his wisdom piously have listenèd,
Our teacher and our master, godly man perfected,
Light of all Israel eternally ahead.

THE HOLY REB SHOLEM OF BELZ

may his merits protect us eternally!

THE FIRST GATE

Old, very old, is the wondrous family of the Rokachs, Rabbis at Belz. We shall not here discuss whether or not it is likely that they are able to trace back their lineage to King David. We are restrained from so doing by our firm Chassidic faith. It is certain that bearers of the name of Rokach were learned Rabbis in Germany as early as the thirteenth century. On the distaff side the Belz Rokachs are descendants of Loev, the great Prague Rabbi, and the no less famous Chacham Tsvi of Amsterdam. Of this there is no doubt.

It was the holy Reb Sholem, the great-grandfather of the present Rabbi, who first started the family on the road to Chassidism.

Reb Sholem was a *silken* man. Silken?—Yes. In other words, he was an exceptionally learned man, perfect in godliness and richly endowed with all the virtues, a rare, exceedingly rare fellow, a silken fellow. *A zadener yinger mantchik*—it really is impossible to express it in any other way.

Reb Sholem did not want to become a Rabbi. Why not?—Out of modesty, evidently. He wanted to be a perfectly ordinary Jewish trader. But there was a stumbling-block, for the holy Reb Sholem—may the Light of his merits protect us—was a man of no mean gifts. Gifts for learning and meditation, of course. It has not been proved if he also had a bent for commerce. All his days he had spent brooding over the Talmud but now the time had come for him to start up in business. How does a person set about becoming a business man? Sholem had no idea. So he made friends with another young man, a trader in the true sense of the word, but an honourable, reliable fellow at the same time, in short, an ideal partner.

To begin with, the two enterprising young men wanted to know what the holy *Seer* would have to say about it because it was he who had been their teacher. So they went to Lublin to see him.

It was strange advice indeed that the Seer gave them. He recommended Sholem to go into business but warned his companion against entering into partnership with him. So the two men reconsidered what they should do, for the mysterious words of the Seer had not left them any the wiser. Finally they decided that at all events they would set up shop together. Sholem put all his small fortune into the concern.

But the business did not prosper. Both Sholem and his partner soon lost everything they had.

"Did I not tell you not to get involved in any business ventures with him?" the holy Seer asked Sholem's partner, when the two men came to Lublin a second time. Then turning to Sholem he said:

"As long as you had money, you did not want to become a Rabbi, even though you were predestined to be one. Now that you have nothing you will have to do so, whether you want to or not, to earn a livelihood for yourself and your wife. Now perhaps you understand why I advised you to go into business...."

And so the good Sholem had to become a Rabbi, as his forefathers had been before him, and take his place at Belz.

Although small, Belz is both ancient and famous. Before the holy Reb Sholem became Rabbi at Belz, the Rabbi's office had been managed by none other than a *Messiah*!

There is a Messiah in every generation. He leads a solitary life and no one knows of his existence. He may not reveal himself to the world because of our guilt. But at that time the whole world knew that a Messiah was there, living at Belz, and that his name was Aaron.

The whole world knew about it and was glad, both those on earth and those in heaven.

Only the Devil did not rejoice. He could not reconcile himself to the idea of having to bid farewell to his rule over the world and hand over his sceptre to a Messiah.

So the Devil changed himself into a woman, a woman of outstanding beauty and—this is what was unusual—wisdom. Thus disguised he set out on his road.

He went from town to town and wherever he came started learned discussions with distinguished Rabbis. No one surmised who this erudite woman could be. But all the savants whom she induced to talk with her were confounded by her arguments, whatever the subject discussed. Her fame flew round the world.

Reb Aaron Messiah also desired to cross swords with this wondrous woman.

Dear me, what an occasion that was, this battle of words between a Messiah and the Devil! It is a wonder they did not burn each other up with the fire of their breath. In their wit and wisdom they overturned rocks by their roots and ground each other to pulp.

Finally the woman produced a question which even the Messiah was unable to answer.

"I will tell you when we are alone," she said. "It's a great secret. No one must know it except us."

Not knowing whom he had before him, the Messiah ordered everyone present to leave the room. Not even a child was allowed to remain, so sublime was the secret!

It was not until he had shut the door after the last person that the Messiah saw his error. In the heat of the learned dispute he had forgotten the words of the holy scholars in the Talmud which forbid us to be alone with a strange woman for a single moment.

It was too late. The Messiah's holy mission had been profaned and his journey on this earth came to an end. It was the sixth day of the month of Tishri. The Devil celebrated his victory.

As a result we have longer to wait for our salvation. It will be a long time yet, a very long time, perhaps.

Only an old tombstone in the Belz cemetery shows us that a Messiah really lived there: Reb Aaron Messiah.

It was the holy Reb Sholem who succeeded the Messiah.

Reb Sholem acquired miraculous qualities through the merit of his wife, Malkele.

Reb Sholem devoted his days to the study of the Talmud. This was no secret and nothing out of the ordinary. In those times almost all devout men did nothing else but meditate on the Talmud the whole day long and leave the care of the family to their patient wives. The latter were well aware that they would be richly rewarded for this in the next world, that for their self-sacrifice they would be allowed to sit at golden tables in paradise with their husbands, in the company of the most famous scholars of Israel, and that they too would rejoice in the glorious light of the majesty of God.

Malkele however was not satisfied with this. She wanted her Sholem to sit on a throne of rubies and pearls among the most holy of the saints and the angels of the Lord, wearing the diamond crown of the purest merits, high, exceedingly high above the husbands of all her neighbours—and she at his side.

For this reason, as soon as everybody had gone to sleep in the evening, Malkele would let her husband out of the house. To make sure that no jealous soul should know of it he climbed out of the window with the help of a ladder. Sholem's new partner would be waiting for him in front of the house. As before with the shop, so now he had a partner with whom he secretly went off to study in the empty *Bes Hamidrash*. There the two young men would search the word of God and its sublime mysteries the whole night long. Night after night—except perhaps the night of the Sabbath—they did not get a wink of sleep. They spent altogether nine hundred and ninety-nine nights in this way.

On the thousandth night there was a terrible storm with heavy rain, hail and thunder, and the Devil himself came to bar their way to the *Bes Hamidrash*. Sholem's companion was profoundly scared and preferred to go home to his wife. But the holy Reb Sholem would not give in. However he did not spend that memorable stormy night alone in the Belz House of Study. The immortal prophet Elijah and the spirits of saints who had long since died came to initiate the dauntless Sholem into the inscrutable mysteries of the Cabbala and give him the keys of the celestial gates.

Such is the way Heaven rewards perseverance. A single night more—and Reb Sholem turned into a saint. A single night less —and his companion remained an ordinary human being!

So the Seer of Lublin was not Sholem's only teacher; there was none other than the prophet Elijah as well. Let us remember him, this wondrous man, let us sing his praises and he will bring us his blessing.

Elijah in Gilead had his place,/Happy the man who but dreams of his face,/Happy the man who has greeted him but once,/Happier still if he returned him his glance,/A leather girdle round his loins is wound,/In the desert his food by ravens was found,/On horses of fire he ascended to heaven, He never knew death nor to the grave was given,/The hearts of the sons he returns to God's word,/And in evil times he is sent by the Lord,/Or when the oppressor is strong./Brothers, to be sure, you know the old song.

The holy Reb Sholem never forgot what his Malkele had done for him.

When he was famous throughout the world for his holiness and for the miracles he performed, and when hundreds and thousands of devout persons journeyed from far and wide to his table at Belz, to fulfil obediently his every word, the slightest nod of his head, he would declare:

"If it were not for Malkele (which means *little queen*), Sholem would not be *king*!"

But when an inquisitive person once asked the holy Reb Sholem if it were true that he had watched through a thousand nights, Reb Sholem opened his holy eyes wide and repeated the words after him in amazement:

"A *thousand* nights?" . . .

Behold! How modest was the holy Reb Sholem!

The ladder by which Malkele let her husband out of the house is exhibited to this day. It stands as an eternal memorial at the Belz House of Prayer, which Reb Sholem caused to be built to a plan of his own. It is a wonderful House of Prayer. Through

its doors the Messiah will come to this earth when His time is
really come.

We ordinary mortals cannot even surmise the holy secrets
Reb Sholem incorporated into the masonry of this House of
God from his precious heart. Only a saint like the holy Rebe
Reb Shimon of Jaroslav could feel their fervour.

One day after a wedding ceremony, a colleague of Reb
Sholem's, the famous blind saint, the holy Rebe Reb Shimon of
Jaroslav, visited Belz. (It was he who wrote the book "Nahalat
Shimon", "The Legacy of Shimon".) The holy Rebe Reb
Shimon entered the new synagogue. He crept along the walls
and kissed each stone, each brick. But at one spot he removed
his holy lips from the wall and started kissing again only when
he had moved a few steps farther on.

"Forgive me, Master," the holy Reb Sholem apologized
modestly, not in the least surprised by the strange behaviour of
the blind saint. And pointing to that part of the wall which the
saint had not kissed, he added: "I happened not to be present
when this piece of wall was being built."

Naturally the Chassidim who built the House of Prayer had
laid stone upon stone with the same piety as when they prayed.
But the good bricklayers did not breathe their soul into the
building nor infuse their hearts into the cold stones. Only their
holy Reb Sholem could do that. But on one occasion this had
not happened, and only the holy Rebe Reb Shimon of Jaroslav
could be aware of that.

If the learned Reb Sholem was a worker of miracles, his devout wife Malkele was no less so. One day there arrived a man
who had something seriously wrong with his feet. The doctors
had been unable to help him. He had therefore travelled to Belz
so that the saint might entreat the Most High to cure him.

"You needn't go to the Rabbi," Malkele told him. "Go to the
House of Study and light a candle!" The cripple limped off and
did as Malkele had advised him. Wonderful to relate, he was
immediately cured. When Reb Sholem heard of it, he asked
Malkele: "Who revealed to you the mystery by which a man
can be made whole?"

"There's no mystery about it," exclaimed Malkele, "It's there for everybody to read in the Psalms of David: 'Thy word is a light unto my feet.' What else should that mean except that the light we use for studying the holy Law is good for feet?"

Such "mistakes" in interpreting the Word of God can of course only be made by the purest and simplest hearts, like the heart of the holy Malkele.

"God gives commandments and the saint breaks them," says the Talmud. Because the pious Malkele was also a saint, she too had something to say when God gave an order. The following incident is evidence of this:

One day a certain Chassid was travelling to Belz from a distant Galician town to see Reb Sholem. On the way he was obliged to spend the Sabbath at Przemysl. Naturally he would have considered it most reprehensible and discourteous not to visit the renowned saint of Przemysl, the holy Reb Mayerl. "You certainly didn't come here intending to see me," observed Reb Mayerl when he saw the Chassid's unfamiliar face. "You're on your way to Belz, I'm sure. When you get there, tell them that Mayerl likes to eat capons."

The holy Reb Mayerl always talked of himself in the third person and—like many other saints—avoided using the arrogant word "I".

The Chassid was unaware of the import of Reb Mayerl's words. However he hastened to deliver the message.

"All right," said Malkele when she heard the message. "Then we shall put it on the unclean birds" (meaning the birds we are not allowed to eat)!

Malkele's words were equally incomprehensible to the good Chassid. It was only later that he understood what they were all about, for soon afterwards all the crows and owls in the neighbourhood began to die off, as though shot by an unseen hand.

What had happened was this: A command had gone forth in heaven that a fatal disease was to attack the poultry that year, which was to exterminate them. However Malkele came to the conclusion that it would be quite enough if only the capons perished because very few people ate them in any case. Clearly she had forgotten the holy Reb Mayerl of Przemysl. Naturally he too knew what plans were being made in heaven and he was also aware of what Malkele had decided. Hence his message— which prompted Malkele at the last moment to intervene in heaven a second time, and so prevent the disastrous decision of the celestial court from descending upon the capons.

Worthy Malkele! Blessings upon you, you thoughtful house-wife!

Reb Sholem never withdrew himself from the company of his excellent wife. Contrary to the custom of all devout men he even ate at the same table with her. At first sight, it might seem that this was at variance with the practice of a real saint. Reb Sholem however was a man of such genuine piety that there could be no harm in it. That this was indeed the case was observed by a saint who once stayed as a guest at Reb Sholem's house: "Reb Sholem," he declared, "lives with his wife in a state of innocence, like Adam and Eve in paradise before the Fall." It was true. They did indeed live as in paradise.

To this day we Chassidim at Belz celebrate the memory of the holy Malkele every year. We observe the anniversary of her death on the 27th of the month of Adar with as much ostentation, if not with still greater piety, as when we commemorate the death of any other saint.

Now let us hear how deeply the holy Reb Sholem loved to fulfil the commandments of God! The Rabbi of Kamionka— also Sholem by name—came to Belz for the Feast of Tabernacles while he was still a disciple of Reb Sholem at Belz. He entered the House of Prayer at the precise moment when our Reb Sholem was saying the Halel prayer at the *bimah* with his Chassidim. The disciple heard the master's voice raised in fervent prayer and rejoiced. Naturally he also wanted to look at his teacher's holy face, where the light of the glory of God was continuously reflected. But his search for his master was in vain. The latter was nowhere to be seen. Finally he found him where clearly no ordinary person would think of looking. In his great humility and his love for God's commandments Reb Sholem of Belz had incarnated himself completely, every little bit of himself, in a citron, an *esrig*, which in accordance with the law of Moses he held in his hand during the solemn prayer (the esrog or ethrog is a kind of lemon imported from Palestine). So completely had he fitted himself into the *esrig* that he, a saint, was not to be seen at all.

Sholem of Kamionka of course was no ordinary disciple. A typical proof of this was the wonderfully prompt way in which he expounded the Scriptures. On one occasion his teacher, Reb Sholem of Belz, asked him:

"It is written (in the first book of Moses, Chapter 8, verse 13): 'And Thou didst say unto me, I will do thee *good, good*. . . .' " These were the words with which our forefather Jacob called upon the Lord, as literally quoted in the Hebrew text. "But is there any passage where we read of God having spoken like this to Jacob on a previous occasion?" the saint of Belz inquired of his disciple. "God never made him a promise that He would do him *good*. As for His having promised to do so twice, that surely is nowhere written in the Holy Scriptures!? How then could Jacob say: 'And Thou didst say unto me. . . ?' "

"It is written," returned Kamionka without a moment's hesitation, "It is written at the very beginning when God created the world. For the seven days of the beginning of all things are an expression of those seven qualities of God which are also represented by the Seven Shepherds: the first day, Sunday, is the Love of Abraham. Monday is the Strength of Isaac, Tuesday the Truth of Jacob. Wednesday is the Might of Moses, Thursday the Humility of Aaron, Friday the Faithfulness of Joseph and Saturday the Rule of David. For each day at the beginning of the first book of Moses it is written: And God saw that it was *good*. The only exception of course is Monday, for on Monday Hell was also created through the Strength of Isaac, and that is not exactly a good thing. We never start on a journey on a Monday since we are aware that it is not a lucky day. Tuesday, on the other hand, is the expression of the Truth of *Jacob*, and so it is written *twice* (verses 10 and 12): And God saw that it was *good*, and once again . . . and God saw that it was *good*. In very truth, then, God did promise our forefather Jacob—whose day is Tuesday—that He would show him good and again only good from the very creation of the world. Jacob therefore was quite *right* when he prayed: "And Thou didst say unto me: 'I will do thee *good, good.*'" He was recalling the actual words of the Creator.

Let it not be supposed that Sholem loved only the more learned disciples. He loved all the Chassidim and took them all under his protection. One day, for instance, some one protested that one of the Chassidim was a great glutton and would eat a whole goose at one sitting.

"Never mind," said the holy Reb Sholem in defence of the Chassid, "Let us not forget that that is the only passion he has." And indeed blessed is the man who has no worse passions!

It is true that no respectable person ought to be a glutton. But you often reproach us Chassidim with not being respectable people at all. How do you make out that we are not respectable? —Well, you say, a respectable man will keep his promise. He looks upon his pledged word as something sacred. But the Chassidim?—They are not put out in the least when they break a promise. Yes, you respectable people, when you promise something, even if it be to Satan himself, you do not hesitate to carry it out. I do not doubt that. And in the same way with us many a *silken* young man lets himself be persuaded now and again and promises the Tempter that he will commit this or that sin. But then he immediately reconsiders the matter, commits no sin and is quite unconcerned at having broken a promise he had made to the Tempter. So we Chassidim are not really respectable people. We gladly acknowledge it.

But to make up for this we have at least one virtue which you cannot boast of. We are obstinate people, as we ought to be, especially when we have some good deed to perform. The same is true of us in all matters of Faith in which no one can dissuade

42

us and nothing can shake our determination. Yes, obstinacy, *akshones*, that is our finest virtue at Belz. Every Chassid must first and foremost be *akshen*—obstinate. This is our highest principle. How we put it into effect will be immediately clear to you from the example of Mordche Pelts.

The Chassidim at Belz had a profound belief in the magic power of the holy Reb Sholem, a belief as boundless as the ocean. One day a *Tsaddik* arrived at Belz who was a stranger to the town. The holy Reb Sholem invited him to go for a drive round the town. The two saints strictly forbade anybody to accompany them on this trip. Why?—Well, so that they could discuss the mysteries of the Cabbala without anybody disturbing them. To be sure, the holy Baal-Shem had also sometimes gone for drives in this way with his most trusted followers, and so had the holy ARI himself.

But such prohibitions had no effect on Mordche Pelts. Not for anything in the world would Mordche Pelts be separated from his master for a single moment. He was incessantly at the saint's heels. And now that he could not ride openly with the saint, he did not hesitate to use guile. He got into the carriage by stealth and covered himself with straw. To such lengths did the Chassidim carry their devotion in those days, overcoming conventions and express commands!

For some time Mordche Pelts travelled unnoticed in the straw, like a lord, until the moment came when he found himself in an unpleasant situation. If you have ever had occasion to hide yourself in straw you will understand his plight and will not be cross with him. Suddenly something began tickling his nose, and although he struggled like a lion, he could not hold out indefinitely. Finally a great sneeze burst forth from his pent up lungs: "He-tishu!" and the straw went flying in all directions.

"Get out!" shouted the visiting saint at poor Mordche Pelts, "Or I shall cast your soul into deepest Hell."

But Mordche Pelts would not give in.

"What if you do cast me into Hell?!" he retorted. "Our holy Reb Sholem will haul me out again immediately."

43

When the holy Reb Sholem—may his merits protect us—
heard this answer, he smiled and said:

"You stay where you are, Mordche!"

And Mordche Pelts did stay where he was. Upon my soul, he
did. What a magnificently obstinate fellow he was, and what
faith he had!

It is a well known fact that a saint will lead his Chassidim all
the way to the Garden of Eden in the other world. Moreover
this will be quite a simple operation. The Chassidim will catch
hold of his *gartel*, his belt I mean, and he will then pull them
all into paradise hanging on to his belt.

There are other ways in which the belt is a very important
instrument for a true Chassid. It is a thick cord of black silk
which we wind round the waists of our *bekish* (caftans). The
ends of the belt are ornamented with handsome fringes. It must
be sufficiently long to encircle the waist three times. We wear it
the whole day long. It is particularly important that we should
not be without it at prayer, when we are studying the Law, and
during meals. The Talmud declares that it is only the upper part
of the human body—the head, chest and hands—which is
created in the image of God. In the lower part, with its functions
of digestion and secretion, a man is similar to an animal. The
belt thus demarcates the boundary between the godly part and
the animal part of a man and prevents *the heart from seeing shame*.
When we put on our belts in the morning we say a charming
benediction: "Blessed be the Lord our God, King of the world,
who hast girt Israel about with strength and power!"

Take care that no one ever makes a knot in your belt! During
prayer the Devil moves round a man's waist at his belt. If it has
a knot in it he could stop there and snatch away your prayer.

Furthermore the letters in the word *sheker*, which means a
lie, are the same as the letters in the word *kesher*, a *knot*.
Everything about a Chassid has to be truthful. Therefore the
genuine fervour of our prayers must not be disturbed, even by
a small knot in our belts.

For a similar reason we Chassidim of Belz walk about with

our chests partially uncovered, both in winter and summer—to help us remember that *the heart must always be open.*

We are also careful to see that in taking our phylacteries off our arms, we do not cover the knot. The knot on the phylactery reminds us not of lies, but of the Truth. By its shape it recalls the first letter of the Hebrew word for God. This letter is called *yod* and looks exactly like a little knot. Similarly the word "Jew" in Yiddish sounds exactly like the first letter of the name of God: *Yod.* That is the reason why we may not cover the knot on the phylactery. For a Jew, a *Yod, has to be open and has always to act without guile.*

The phylactery is wound round the arm seven times. We Chassidim do the winding away from ourselves, away from our bodies. Our adversaries wind towards themselves, towards their bodies. They do it this way because they are selfish, and only think of themselves, whereas we think first and foremost of our neighbours and their happiness. That is the reason why we wind the phylacteries away from ourselves and towards our neighbours.

Phylacteries are an infinitely sacred commandment of God. If we were to place all the other commandments and laws on one side of the scale and put the phylacteries on the other, the latter would outweigh all the other commandments of God. By means of these black phylacteries, we bind on to our arms and heads four little paragraphs from the Holy Scriptures, sewn into little black leather cubes. Their beautifully written Hebrew letters radiate invisible rays which penetrate directly into our brains and hearts. They bring us closer to God and neutralize the harmful outside influences. He who does not bind them on himself incurs the grievous curses of the holy Rabbis. God also has His phylacteries.[1]

The phylacteries of course may only be worn by a person who is perfectly pure in body and soul. Does not each of those little black cubes contain parchment with holy writing wherein the most sacred name of God is repeated twenty-onetimes? When we

[1] Those who desire more detailed information on this subject should read my a rticle on phylacteries in the international *Freudian* psychoanalytical journal *IMAGO*, Volume XVI, 1930, pages 435–85.

are wearing our phylacteries we must concentrate our thoughts totally and unceasingly on the content of this writing. This is not easy. Inside these cubes it is written how God permeates all the worlds with His holy power, how He redeems the faithful from the yoke of evil and how everywhere and for all time He remains undisturbed in His holy oneness. It is also written there that we are to love Him with all our heart, with all our soul and in all circumstances, and that we must faithfully fulfil His sacred commandments. There is also something written there about rewards and punishments. So we have plenty to think about when the phylacteries are on our bodies! If a person does not have all these things in his thoughts the whole time, the phylacteries are of no use to him: *It is as if he had bound stones to his head and arms!* At the same time, of course, we are required to think about the words of the prayers. But then it is only during services that the phylacteries are worn. How earnestly we have to think about the prayers! Before you can read this one page we should have read ten pages in the prayer book. Read them, did I say? No!—we fly through them. We pronounce every sound properly and yet fly from letter to letter, from world to world, like lightning. Our little soul jumps into each precious letter as one might jump into a swimming bath. It dives in with all its love and all its fear —those are its wings—with all its strength and feeling—those are its legs—and once again it jumps out of one letter like a flea and jumps into the next one. (An honest flea has no wings, do you say?—Then you don't know the Chassidic fleas, the little beasts!) And when the soul has flown through all these letters, all these thousands of worlds, it is purged and will be redeemed. That is how we Chassidim serve God every day of our lives. At the same time we do not think merely about the simple sense of the words and sentences! We also remember what the Talmud says about this or that place, and how a saint expounded this or that verse. We do not stop for a single moment. The whole time we keep rushing farther and farther, higher and higher. As for the saints—how much more do they think about during prayers: the sublime mysteries of the Cabbala which are so diffcult that it is impossible to describe them! You only have to take a look at the Holy ARI's commentary to the prayer book! Your head turns as though you were on a merry-go-round.

Through the ocean of substance we creep, useless *drops of evil-smelling drift.* more slowly and lazily than the clumsy shad-fish making its way through the slime at the bottom of deep pools. But prayers that spring from ecstasy—perhaps you too have sometimes experienced such moments—raise us above all worlds, material and spiritual, back to that original point in which everything is contained, all worlds, times and ages, all souls, all spirits, the entire law of God and all its mysteries, everything, every little thing, like the tree in the seed. Everything in one unique indivisible unity! And this original point is the first word of the mystic, sacred Scriptures: BEkESHIS—At the Beginning. From this, from this word, all Creation has crept forth like the snail from his little house, and thither we flee for all eternity when times are at their worst for our souls. Only please do not think that in passing on to you this my cogitation about fleas, shad-fish and snails, these unclean and forbidden animals, I merely want to vex you. Know then that just as God has created us in His own holy image, so He has also created the unclean beasts in a particular likeness—that of mysterious worlds, and for the sole purpose of instructing us. Every animal in its own kind is created in the image of some former world, and before our world was created there was quite a number of these worlds. But do not expect me to tell you about this too because these things are great mysteries.

I do not want to bore you by repeating things that are well known. I have told you that already. But I must say a word about another very important commandment. This will help you to understand the very charming incident which the holy Reb Sholem used to relate. First of all, then, regarding the commandment.

It concerns the washing of hands. We perform this duty as follows: First we pour some clean water into a pot, but before doing so we must make sure that the pot is intact. It would never do to pour the water into a flower-pot—which has a hole in the bottom. Next, there must be no notches on the rim of the pot. The edge must be as even as the knife we use for killing animals. We take the pot of water in the right hand; from the right hand we put it into the left hand, and from the left hand we tip half the water over the right hand. We then take the pot into the right hand and with the right hand we pour the rest of the water over the left hand. We rub our hands together and bless God "that He has sanctified us with His commandments and ordered us to wash our hands", after which we wipe our hands thoroughly. Throughout the entire holy ceremony we carry a towel over the left arm. A proper Chassid always carries a towel in addition to a handkerchief. When wiping our hands we must keep the left hand continuously covered by the towel. Not everybody knows this, but it is very important. Only when we have washed our hands in this way and wiped them really thoroughly and conscientiously can we finally bless the bread and eat.

If you do not cut your nails every Friday before the Sabbath, you must examine them before washing your hands, to make sure they are not dirty; if they are the least bit dirty your act of washing could be considered invalid. When you cut your nails, you must be careful to see that not a single piece of nail gets lost; all the bits must be burnt at once, otherwise you will have to look for them after you are dead. When burning your nails you must not forget to put two small pieces of wood in with them as witnesses.

There are great and sublime mysteries in the washing of hands. Any one who dips into the mystic writings of the Holy ARI will soon realize this, always granting of course that he understands them.

There is one great secret in the washing of hands which you will not find even in the writings of the Holy ARI. In every generation there is only one saint whom Heaven has inspired to know this secret.

If you do not wash your hands before eating in the way laid down by the law you put yourself in dire danger. The Talmud warns us of this when it relates the terrible story of what happened to a certain guest.

This individual came to an inn and ordered dinner. The inn-keeper noticed that he did not wash his hands before partaking of bread and inferred from this that the man was not a Jew but a Greek or Armenian, in short, a Gentile. He therefore gave him pork and green vegetables. This ghastly mistake only became apparent after the meal.

It can thus be seen that every sin leads directly to another, still worse sin.

He who is negligent in the washing of hands will incur grie-vous punishment after death—a punishment inflicted only on murderers who have spilt the blood of an innocent man. The souls of such persons will be spirited away to a waterfall. In summer and winter torrential water will stream down on them without interruption, without relief. Special *malignant* mes-sengers from God will be entrusted with the task of watching over the poor condemned souls, to make sure that they are not able for a single moment to escape their just sentence, until their guilt has been washed away and atoned for.

On the other hand, the man who throughout his life has properly observed the commandment concerning the washing of hands in all its details will obtain rewards in paradise which cannot be taken away from him.

The holy Reb Sholem used to tell the following story: "There was once a great sinner. Throughout his life this sinner did not do a single good deed. He sinned continuously and forgot about God. However there was one commandment which he always obeyed faithfully, as his mother had taught him in childhood: the washing of hands before meals. Strange to relate, he clung to this commandment pertinaciously.

"One day he went on a far journey and became very hungry. He had plenty of bread with him but no water for washing his hands. He knew there was a spring in the forest not far away, but he also knew that this forest was infested with robbers who killed without mercy all who came within their reach. So the unfortunate sinner preferred to continue his journey without having anything to eat. But his hunger pressed ever more cruelly upon him.

" 'Suppose I die of hunger?' he thought. 'How foolish I am, still refusing to eat with unwashed hands at a time like this! After all, it's only a small, unimportant commandment of the Rabbis, and I have many, many worse sins on my conscience. Besides, the Law allows us to eat anything if it means saving our lives.'

"So the poor man took a slice of bread out of his knapsack and was just about to bite into it, but in the last moment his courage failed him and his hand dropped.

" 'No, no,' he said to himself. 'This is the only commandment I have never yet broken. I will not do so now, whatever happens! I would prefer to take the risk and go into the forest. If they kill me—they kill me. But I will not eat bread with unwashed hands!'

"Nor did he. He went into the forest for water and there he was killed.

"Thus it came about that his sinful soul appeared before the court of Heaven.

"When a person leaves this world for all eternity, in that very hour all his deeds go on before him. They say to him: You did this and this on such and such a day, at such and such a place. And he answers: Yes. And they say to him: Sign!—And he signs. So it is written in the holy Talmud.

"So it was with this sinner; all his deeds accompanied him. They were terrible sins indeed. There was no end to them. But because all his life he had observed the commandment about the washing of hands, even to the point of sacrificing his life for it, everything was forgiven him. The gate of Mercy was opened to him and he was received among the righteous."

"If such a hardened sinner as this man was received into paradise," the holy Reb Sholem would conclude, "if such a man was allowed into paradise for no other reason than that he had sacrificed his life for a single commandment, how great is the reward awaiting those who devote their whole lives to the performance of good deeds, as God and His holy men of learning have commanded us!"

I have already had occasion to show how Reb Sholem of Belz never became arrogant on account of his learning which, he said, he had acquired through his faithful Malkele. Nor did his knowledge of the fact that there were so many famous men among his ancestors incline him to become haughty. On the contrary: the very realization of this served him as a source of humility and modesty.

One day he received a visit from a learned man who was himself also perfect—for he was a *Tsaddik*—only his parents and all his ancestors had been simple folk. This "self-made man" had got it into his head that Reb Sholem had cut him, and had ascribed this to his humble origin. In reality, of course, this had only seemed to be the case. The kindly Reb Sholem never cut any one. How much less would he behave so discourteously towards a man who had himself attained such virtues as this *Tsaddik*! Nevertheless the latter still continued to bear a grudge in his heart. With the intuitiveness of his holy spirit Reb Sholem sensed that his guest still harboured resentment. "Our learned men of blessed memory," he remarked to the *Tsaddik*, "have told us in the Talmud that it is always our duty to ask ourselves this question: 'When do my deeds approach the greatness of the deeds of my ancestors?' From this it is clear that a man whose ancestors were neither holy nor learned is happier than a man with distinguished ancestors. The former never needs to feel ashamed in front of his ancestors. For me, however, it is more difficult," continued Reb Sholem, "I did have ancestors of distinction, so I must always feel ashamed in front of them, for I know that I am still very far from approaching their perfection."

If the holy Reb Nachman of Brazlav declares that true humility is only attained by a man who can say of himself with a pure conscience that he is humble, this statement is true in full measure of our holy Reb Sholem. When Reb Jacob Yitzhak, the Seer of Lublin, was still an ordinary Chassid, a saint once came to Lublin to see him.

"Is it true," the saint inquired of the Seer of Lublin, "that one of your disciples is as humble as was our teacher Moses, about whom it is written that he was the most humble person in the world?" "It is so," came the reply. Then Reb Jacob Yitzhak called Sholem and asked him in the presence of his guest: "Sholem, are you as humble as our teacher Moses was?" "Yes!" assented Sholem simply.

In the same way Reb Sholem was undeterred by the fact of a man's humble origin when choosing as his teacher, in addition to the Seer of Lublin, Reb Urele of Strelisk, who was the son of an ordinary coachman and maid-servant.

Yes, great was the humility of the holy Reb Sholem, as it should be with every real saint. He was entirely free of vanity and pride. What I am now going to tell you may seem to be at variance with this virtue, but this is only apparently so. Somebody once asked him if the Chassidim are right in maintaining that we ought to recount anecdotes about the holy Baal-Shem once a week, on the evening of the Sabbath. This habit is said to bring great success in business both to the narrator and his hearers throughout the following week. "They are right," said the holy Reb Sholem. "However it is beneficial not only for material success but also for the fear of God, not only on Friday evening, but on every other day and at all times, and not only if the stories are about the Baal-Shem, but also if they are about any other saint—*me, for instance. . . .*"

Unlike the other Chassidim, Reb Sholem was somewhat abstinent. One day the saint of Lublin wanted to treat him to a glass of vodka. Reb Sholem was embarrassed. He did not want to offend his teacher, but he also did not want to sin against his principles. So he left the glass standing for such a long time that in due course, by the dispensation of God, it snapped asunder and the vodka flowed away. The saint of Lublin immediately filled another glass and placed it in front of Sholem. But the second glass likewise broke and the vodka was lost. The saint of Lublin then poured out a third glass, placed it before Sholem, and said: "Drink it up quickly now! You don't want all my glasses to get broken, do you?" "Thank you," said Sholem, "I do not drink intoxicating liquors." From that day the saint of Lublin never pressed Sholem to drink.

Sholem learnt a great deal from the saint of Lublin. For instance, you know what a *kvitel* is—how when a Chassid asks a saint to intercede with the Most High on his behalf, he writes his mother's name and the place where he lives on a piece of paper called a *kvitel* in the Jewish language (*kvitlach* in the plural) how he brings this piece of paper to the saint who knows better than any one else what to ask God to do for that person. Well, it was the Seer of Lublin who taught Reb Sholem how to read *kvitlach* correctly. This is how Sholem puts it in his own words: "He taught me to read in each person's *kvitel* where the roots of his soul are, in Adam, Cain, or Abel, how many times his soul has been reincarnated, what transgression he has committed to bring about this or that reincarnation, what harm he has done, what vice has taken root in him and what merit has been added to him. He also taught me to recognize which constellations of stars are favourable when one prays for this or that, and which not. If he was given a *kvitel* from a good person it was his holy custom to gaze at it for a long time; but he would quickly lay aside the *kvitel* of a bad person. He did not want to look on human shame."

The Chassidim of Kotsk were opponents of the Chassidim of Belz. Let it be stated in praise of the latter that they at least conducted their struggle with academic decorum. The same cannot always be said of the Chassidim of Kotsk.

Shortly before the *departure* of Rabbi Sholem, he received news of a great invention: carriages that travelled without horses. In other words, the first railways. For a moment Reb Sholem was lost in thought. "I fear," he said, "I fear very much lest salvation should come in a natural way." The reason for his fear was as follows: If salvation were to come by supernatural means, more or less miraculously, like the departure from Egypt, there would no longer be any doubters and unbelievers. Everybody would believe in God and His omnipotence. If, however, salvation came in a natural way, even if it was only an apparently natural way, then doubters would continue to exist on the earth. The holy Reb Yisrul of Ruzhen likewise shared this fear with Reb Sholem. What the two saints foresaw with some trepidation has manifestly come to pass, and in this too, as always, God has heard their prayers. We need now have no fear lest salvation may perhaps come in a natural way. In this modern age it is quite clear that the world will not find any salvation in all these human inventions.

In his old age the holy Reb Sholem grew blind. Thereby God conferred a special favour on this holy man in saving him from having to observe any longer the increasing depravity of the world. It is not surprising that he lived to a great age—he was nearly a hundred years old when he died—but it is a very unusual thing that he should have had to leave our earth prematurely, while still hale and hearty.

The Festival of the New Year was approaching. On this Festival God judges all His creatures, and in consequence each community of believers, in accordance with the wise counsel of the "Shulchan Aruch", seeks out some much loved, perfect man to lead the community in prayer at the *bimah*. If no such person is to be found, it is quite common to call in a man from another community, often from far away. Thus it was in heaven too, in the year 5615 from the creation of the world. All the saints and angels had searched in vain whom to choose from their midst as mediator with God. No angel was so beloved, so perfect and godly, as our holy Reb Sholem of Belz. So the angels of the Lord summoned him to be their cantor on the festival day. On the 27th of the autumn month of Elul, exactly three days before the Festival of the New Year, he left our world for all time.

Even after his departure from this world Reb Sholem did not cut himself off from his Chassidim. Disputes arose after his death as to who should be his successor. Some wanted Sholem's younger son, Reb Shiyel, who was very learned, others following the usual practice in Chassidic Rabbis' families, asserted the

right of the elder son. Moreover the latter was himself determined to defend his sacred right to the bitter end!—When
therefore, conforming to the wishes of his "party", Reb Shiyel
went up to the *bimah*, and the crowded House of Prayer waited
tensely to see in which *way* the new *Tsaddik* would serve God,
his elder brother attempted to force his way through the crowd,
determined to push his younger brother aside, and take his place
at the *bimah*. When he was nearly there he suddenly felt a hand
on his shoulder. As he turned round, behold, he stood face to
face with his deceased father, the holy Reb Sholem, who was
making warning gestures to him to desist from his intention. So
it was that the younger son, Reb Shiyel, remained as Rabbi of
Belz after his father, and the House of God was saved from
shame and violence, and the *desecration of the Name of God*.

Ever since then the holy Reb Sholem has never forsaken his
beloved Chassidic community. He comes to our synagogue
during our common prayer and sits in his old place; and therefore no one else may sit there. On the great festivals his living
descendant and successor gets up from his place and comes and
stands beside the prayer desk where the *baal-tfila* prays. (The
baal-tfila is an exceptionally devout Chassid whose duty it is to
lead the prayers, somewhat like the cantor in western Europe.)
The Rabbi shares his *machzor* (prayer-book) with him. For the
holy Reb Shiyel, who has long since died, comes and sits in the
seat of his living descendant, beside his father, the holy Reb
Sholem. Both saints are of course invisible to the Chassidim.
During the prayer "We adorn Thee with a crown" the *baal-
tfila* must be careful not to raise his eyes from his prayer-book,
for in that moment he is the only one who can see their holy
shapes. Woe betide him if he in any way lets it be known that he
has gazed on Reb Sholem's flaxen beard. A *baal-tfila* who is so
uncircumspect will not outlive the year. To this day, no doubt,
none of those to whom it has been granted to see the departed
saint—and there have been several *baale-tfila* who have seen
him—have been strong enough to keep quiet about it indefinitely. May their memory be a blessing to us and may the Light
of their merits protect us, for their souls have long since been

joined by the bond of eternal life with all the righteous and godly
in the Garden of Eden, AMEN!

*You, then, who wish to live, enter with me into another Gate, for
there you shall read:*
How the cattle at Przemysl fell sick of the plague, but how
they were made well again by a message from Mayerl of
Przemysl—how the holy Mayerl interceded for sinners and how
he defied God—how Mayerl did not wish to sanctify the Sabbath
in wine and how he blessed it in mead—how a Christian became
one of Mayerl's Chassidim and distributed boots—how the holy
Urele of Strelisk wished to deprive Mayerl of Przemysl of his
magic powers—how Mayerl did not know how to eat *kreplach*
—how the saint of Ruzhen gave him wise advice—and finally
how the candles went out in Sadagor—how you know all about
it, let none of you tell me he does not—I tell you truthfully,
devoutly: at sixes and sevens.

The Second Gate

Child of God, our dearest,
Charioteer and war-chariot who for all Israel intercedest

our teacher and our master

THE HOLY MAYERL OF PRZEMYSL

may the Light of his merits protect us evermore!

THE SECOND GATE

Mayerl of Przemysl (Meyer of Premislan) fully deserved to have Malkele as his wife on account of his thrift. He was one of those saints whose prayers God never fails to grant. What miracles he performed! Enough to fill a fair-sized book.

In comparison with Belz, Przemysl is a large town. It has a good few thousand more souls, both Poles and Jews. And what a lot of livestock!

I want to tell you something about the livestock at Przemysl.

One day the cattle at Przemysl caught the plague. With loud lamentation, one of the Chassidim ran to Mayerl. "What am I to do?" he cried. "All the cattle are infected."

"Run round the cowsheds reciting the Sabbath hymn: 'God is the Lord over all creatures. . . .' Mayerl advised him.

The farmer did as he was told, and the cattle recovered.

Then one of the neighbours found that all his cattle had fallen sick. Having seen what the other man did, he too took to running round his cowsheds, reciting prayers. But it was all to no avail. So he ran to Mayerl to ask his advice.

"Run round the sheds and pray: 'God is the Lord over all creatures!'"

"But Rabbi," wailed the Chassid, "I've already done that, of my own accord, but it didn't do any good."

"Fool!" exclaimed Mayerl, "do you suppose your God is as great a master as Mayerl's?" . . .

Armed with Mayerl's authority, the Chassid went away and did as Mayerl had commanded him—and everything turned out all right. His cattle also recovered. . . .

As we have said, Mayerl was wont to speak about himself in the third person instead of the first person. Like this: Mayerl wants, Mayerl doesn't want, Mayerl here, Mayerl there. He was really quite right in this, for the pronoun "I" is only an auxiliary word to help our imperfect human speech out of its difficulties. In point of fact a person really has no "I". He is nothing, absolutely nothing, or as the cabbalistic book "Tikunim" puts it, the Hebrew word "ayin", which means "NOTHING", and the word "aniy", which means "I", are composed of the same letters, only differently assorted. There are other saints who do not use the word "I" but say "we" instead. This of course is not because they are conceited and hence might prefer to use the royal plural. The reason is that the human personality is not in any way separate but is a complex of many indivisible souls, and there can be no question of any "individuality". We are in no way fenced off from one another, because the whole of God's world is one mass, one body.

So if you want to make sure whether a person who is a stranger to you is a saint, you ask him: "Excuse me, are you Mr. X., or Mrs. Y.?" If he or she says: "Yes, that's me," you can be sure the person is not a saint.

Most of all Mayerl preferred to pray for the really bad sinners, to obtain God's forgiveness for them. And indeed God always pardoned them immediately he interceded for them. But once— it only happened once, of course, only one single time—when Mayerl interceded for a particularly hardened and shameful sinner, and God this time simply would not forgive, then Mayerl—just think of it!—actually stamped his foot at God. And the man was immediately pardoned.

If you are a father or mother, you will understand this. Remember how delighted you were when your little nipper first stamped his foot at you. Only the first time, of course, and it had to be the last time. Well, it was just the same sort of joy that this little Mayerl gave our Father Which is in heaven. Only Mayerl was not a little chap at the time. He was already a big fellow, and very big at that.

On Friday evening Mayerl decided that he would bless the Sabbath with a goblet of mead. You find that hard to believe,

I'm sure! Is it not expressly written in the "Shulchan Aruch" that the Sabbath is to be blessed only with wine and with no other drink? In Przemysl too they were very much taken aback at the time. But Mayerl took no notice and went his own way. He filled the golden cup with mead and had it placed on his holy palm. Then he opened all five fingers round the cup "like the five green leaflets round a rose bloom", and as soon as he had finished his blessing and drunk the cup of mead he explained his action to the people of Przemysl.

"The Hebrew for mead," said Mayerl, "is 'dvash', which is written DBS, for in Hebrew the consonants are normally written without any vowels, and the consonants 'b' and 'v' appear as one and the same letter. DBS means mead, and these are also the initial letters of the words *Daj Boze Szezeście!* (Give God the glory!), as our Polish brothers say." And the Chassidim were content with this explanation. So let us also be content and Give God the Glory!

Among Mayerl's Chassidim was a *lech*, that is, an honoured person of Christian origin. (For us, the word "goy" has more the meaning of peasant.) There is nothing surprising about a Christian being a Chassid. Other *Tsaddikim* have had many true admirers among the Christians, both among the people and the nobility. But none of them ever had such a fervent admirer as this *lech* of Mayerl's.

He became a *lech* the very first day he met Mayerl.

He was a Polish shoe-merchant who first came to Mayerl with a small and very ordinary request: he wanted Mayerl to ask God to give him a son. He was already an old man and had no heir.

"Your petition shall be heard," said Mayerl, "for God receives prayers from every mouth, and hence from you Christians too. Indeed we extol Him for this every day. But you must distribute forty pairs of boots to the poor!"

The man did as Mayerl said.

In due course the promised son was born to him that same year, and the good *lech* became a true Chassid of Mayerl's.

Naturally he did not renounce his faith. But he spent all his free time close to Mayerl and never ceased to distribute boots to the poor his whole life long. Everybody knew of him throughout the Chassidic world, and not only in Przemysl.

Mayerl was a great saint but he had his weakness. He was not as discreet as he should have been. A real *enfant terrible* he was, this Mayerl. As soon as he heard anything from heaven he immediately prattled about it to the people. This greatly vexed the other saints.

The saint who was most annoyed with him on this account was Reb Urele, known as the holy Seraph of Strelisk. He was so furious that he made up his mind to deprive Mayerl of all his magic power. To do this, however, he required the consent of the holy Reb Naftali of Ropshitz. So he dispatched a special mission to Ropshitz, composed of two dependable Chassidic diplomats.

The expedition arrived at Ropshitz on a Thursday and was given a magnificent reception. Reb Naftali welcomed Reb Urele's envoys most warmly. He conferred with them at length and was extremely friendly, and invited them to be his guests on the holy Sabbath. But Reb Naftali never inquired of them the actual reason why Reb Urele of Strelisk had sent them to Ropshitz.

(Clearly he was perfectly well aware why they had come. Nothing could be hidden from the sight of a saint, a gift of the spirit in a saint so mightily blessed as Reb Naftali.)

On the Friday Reb Naftali was so busy preparing for the Sabbath that it was not possible to trouble him with anything. Then of course the envoys did not dare to disturb the peace of the Sabbath.

On the Sunday they asked for a hearing. However Reb Naftali told them such interesting things that for some while the good diplomats forgot what the actual purpose of their visit was.

After this interview there was only one hope left to them— to be allowed to acquaint Reb Naftali with the purpose of their mission when they came to bid him farewell.

At the moment of parting Reb Naftali was courtesy itself.

But he would not permit them to say a word. He kept on talking to them until they reached the front of the house. Only when he had set them comfortably in their carriage did he say:

"Last night Reb Arn Leib—the late father of Mayerl of Przemysl—came to me and said: 'I have left behind me in the world a little flame, a *glovnele* '—that's how he put it—'Can it really be that they want to put out that little flame?! Just you listen to me, keep your hands away from him, don't you dare touch him!' "

No sooner had Reb Naftali spoken when the dust on the highroad flew up in a mighty column. Before the men from Strelisk could recover from their amazement, a chariot drove up, and riding in the chariot was none other than Mayerl. He drove in a standing position, holding the reins in his hand like an ancient Greek warrior, while his huge whiskers fluttered in the wind like battle pennants.

"My father," he cried, "called me a *glovnele*, a little flame, but I tell you he left behind him *a feuer flam, a great blazing fire!*"

He yelled out these words, then hurtled on his way again.

The holy Reb Urele of Strelisk was angry with Mayerl for some time after that. In the end however he was forced to forgive him everything.

It came about in this wise. Reb Urele had a Chassid who had been destined to live in even worse misery than the other Chassidim of Strelisk. Reb Urele refused to allow anything to move him to pray for the wretched fellow and so ease his misery by intercession with God. For Reb Urele of Strelisk prayed only for the spiritual wellbeing of his beloved Chassidim and never for their material welfare! Not even in the case of this unfortunate man would he deviate from this principle.

So the Chassid's wife urged her husband to make a pilgrimage to Przemysl and ask Reb Mayerl to intercede with God, since it was impossible to prevail upon Reb Urele of Strelisk to do so.

For a long while the Chassid resisted the impulse to make the journey. However his poverty weighed upon him more and more, and day by day his wife's words became more compelling.

Finally he made up his mind to go.

"What have you been doing for a livelihood up to now?"Reb Mayerl asked him.

"The miller, the grocer and the butcher have been allowing me credit."

"Do you think they will be patient enough to supply you on credit once more?"

"I think they might let one more Sabbath go by, although it's some weeks now that I've been in debt."

"So listen to what I have to say. I cannot help you because you are not one of my Chassidim; you belong to Strelisk. But I can give you advice. Go and buy everything you need for this Sabbath on credit. Keep half of it yourself, do up the rest in a bundle and take it to Strelisk. It shall surely rain the whole week long and there will be a lot of mud on the road. But on Thursday it will freeze, and snow will fall in the night, so it will be good weather for harnessing the horse to the sleigh, and you'll make good pace. When you get there, half open the door of Reb Urele's room, throw in the bundle, quickly close the door again, get back on your sleigh and drive off again without delay. Make sure nobody sees you and don't tell a soul. Don't worry about anything else. You will never go short after that."

The Chassid went his way and did exactly as Mayerl had commanded him. Everything turned out well. The shopkeepers agreed to wait another week, and it really did rain the whole week until Thursday came and brought the frost, just as Reb Mayerl had foretold.

It was very hard that week at Strelisk. Not a single Chassid showed up at the village the whole time. Who would want to plough through such mud? In short, nobody came, nobody brought anything. In point of fact it really would not have mattered very much, for they were used to fasting on weekdays at Strelisk.

But the holy Sabbath was drawing near. Freida, Reb Urele's wife, had no idea what to do.

Thursday evening came and there was still absolutely nothing to be found anywhere.

"Run along," Reb Urele directed his despairing wife. "Heat up the oven and boil some water to make the dough."

So great was his faith in the Almighty that he was convinced the Lord would help him at the last moment.

His wife went and heated up the oven, put on the water and got everything ready, but no miracle occurred. Nobody came, nobody brought anything.

Sadly she looked on as the fire slowly went out in the oven and the water cooled down.

Then she sat down on the bench, put her face in the palms of her hands, and wept.

Suddenly she heard somebody open the door and immediately close it again. She got up at once and went to see who it was.

In the half light she stumbled over something. Stooping down she saw a well-packed bundle. When she looked inside she burst into tears of joy, for there was everything they needed for the holy Sabbath. Everything!

Who knows but that God Himself had sent a kindly angel to present them with these riches.

Then the woman remembered how the prophet Elijah had hidden himself from the soldiers of the idolatress Jezebel and how God had taken care of His servant and sent him ravens to feed him with meat.

And what did the holy Reb Urele do in that moment?—The holy Reb Urele forgot his famous principles, forgot his resolve never to utter a single word before the face of the Most High for the material benefit of his beloved Chassidim, forgot everything in the sheer joy of seeing such unexpected riches brought to his house by an unknown stranger. And the holy Reb Urele cried out from the depth of his pure heart:

"May God be pleased to reward this man a thousand times!" . . .

This was exactly what the holy Mayerl of Przemysl had anticipated. The ingenious fellow had planned this very sequence of events. He had wanted to make the holy Reb Urele of Strelisk forget himself in his astonishment and on this one occasion at least deviate from his principle and pray for a poor fellow's earthly happiness, even if only with a single exclamation. This was the reason why the holy Mayerl had prompted the Chassid to do all these things and devised the whole plan so neatly, as related above. The holy Mayerl was undoubtedly a match for the holy Urele that time!

From that moment things began to show a continuous improvement for the poor Chassid. He soon paid his debts and suffered no further deprivation.

He was found out immediately, for the sleigh track which led across the fresh snow from his cottage to the house of the saint of Strelisk gave him away. Moreover it goes without saying that it did not remain a secret that Mayerl of Przemysl was at the back of it all.

"There you are," said Freida to her holy husband. "You're so angry with Mayerl, and all the time he's such a nice fellow and takes such good care of us."

That was the end of the war waged by Strelisk against the people of Przemysl.

Once again the true words of the Talmud were fulfilled: "*Scholars multiply peace upon the earth.*"

Mayerl and the holy Reb Yisroel of Ruzhen were very close friends. One day before the festival of Pentecost, Mayerl sent a messenger to the saint of Ruzhen to ask him what he should do at the forthcoming festival when *kreplach* had to be eaten.

First of all, however, I should explain to my readers, and especially to my women readers, what these Jewish *kreplach* are. Well then: *kreplach* are unleavened dumplings or three-cornered "purses" filled with finely cut meat. We eat them only on four days in the year, one of these important days being Pentecost. Only at Pentecost we do not fill the *kreplach* with meat and cook them in soup as on other occasions; instead we fill them with curd and cook each one separately. If you have never eaten *kreplach*, you have missed a treat.

It was this very question of how these *kreplach* should be

eaten at the forthcoming festival of Pentecost that gave Mayerl a great deal of thought. The inquiry he addressed to the saint of Ruzhen ran as follows:

"What ought Mayerl to do about the *kreplach*? Shall he eat only one?—that would be too little for Mayerl. But he can't eat two since it's harmful to eat anything in *pairs*. Is it not written in the Talmud that all *pairs* are subject to Ashmodai, the chief of the unclean spirits? Mayerl cannot eat three either, of course, or people will call him a glutton. So what is Mayerl to do?"

The people of Przemysl had already started preparing for the festival. They were adorning the rooms with green branches and skilfully cutting out pretty paper trinkets, *shviislach* and *reyzelach*, which they stuck on the windows. But Mayerl was on tenterhooks. Would the messenger return in time and bring advice from the saint of Ruzhen? Praise be to the Most High—he did come in time!

The saint of Ruzhen settled this knotty problem in a manner that was indeed worthy of Solomon. He sent word to Mayerl that he should eat only one *krepel* at Pentecost, but such a big one that it should be equal in volume to two *kreplach*. . . .

It is impossible to give a complete explanation of the profound meaning of this learned response. First of all we should need to know the mystical significance of the various foods, including the *krepel*. But this can only be known by the saints. We might perhaps be allowed to drop a hint to the effect that the festival of Pentecost is a day when God joins Himself through the medium of the revealed Law into one indivisible, mystical unity with Israel. In other words, two *kreplach* which in substance are only one.

One question of course still remains unsolved: why did Mayerl use a messenger? This question, incidentally, applies equally to the message referred to earlier which was sent to the holy Malkele of Belz. After all, *Tsaddikim* have no need of messengers when they wish to exchange ideas. It is well known that all the saints are uninterruptedly linked to one another in their thoughts, they know exactly what any other saint is doing at any given time, what he is thinking about, what he is praying to God about; indeed even the dreams he has are immediately known to his fellows. The greatest distance is no obstacle in this matter. So why the messengers?

That is also a great mystery of course. . . .

The friendship between the saint of Ruzhen and Mayerl remained unbroken until Mayerl's departure from this world. It was the eve of the new moon in the month of Sivan. That evening at Sadagor the two candles on the table of the saint of Ruzhen went out of their own accord.

"A great light has gone out," said the saint of Ruzhen.

A great light had gone out.

You, then, who wish to live, come with me into another Gate, for there you shall read:

. . . how Rabbi Pinchas founded the synagogue at Prague, and how Saul Wohl was elected king by the Polish nobility—how a traveller was filled with sadness at the sight of Mount Asamon —how Rabbi Pinchas, the wonder-worker, was a great man of wisdom, but as for his ass!—and how each of you should be gay —how the holy Reb Naftali made witty rhymes, or how the saint made even the Heavens laugh—how the holy Reb Naftali punished a nosy-parker and how he had a clever son—on the German language, and how our Yiddish is far more beautiful— how Leizer-gabai made a deal with God—how the saint's cough could not induce Leizer to move away and why Reb Naftali could not interrupt what he was doing.

The Third Gate

our teacher and our master

Model of mankind and heart of our mirth,
Saint—and very foundation stone of our earth

THE HOLY REB NAFTALI OF ROPSHITZ

may the light of his great merits protect us!

THE THIRD GATE

I have no doubt that you know the Pinchas synagogue in Prague. It gazes with such wisdom at the Parliament building, in silent amazement and expectation. Reb Pinchas, who founded it, was an ancestor of our holy Reb Naftali of Ropshitz. A Rabbi of Prague, this Pinchas was a great personality. He was also related to Saul Wohl, grandson of Meir of Padua, the learned Italian Rabbi. (The latter was also an ancestor of Karl Marx.) Saul Wohl was a great and wise man. He was so famous throughout Poland—this was a good three hundred and fifty years ago—that the Polish nobility elected him to be their King on the proposal of Prince Radziwil, who was a friend of his. He received all the honours due to the King of Poland and wrote his principles of justice and humanity in the court chronicle. The following morning he renounced the throne. He ruled for only one night. Reb Pinchas, the Prague ancestor of the holy Reb Naftali of Ropshitz, is buried at Cracow. Incarnate in him was the soul of Rabbi Pinchas ben Yair who was buried in Palestine one thousand, five hundred years earlier. He lies in a beautiful valley under the hillside where the idyllic little town of Safed perches, as though glued to the spot. On the opposite side of the little valley the magnificent mountain of Asamon dreams its ancient dream. I have no words to describe how sad is this dream, and how deep was the sorrow which filled my heart when I first set eyes on this mountain during my journey to the Holy Land. Surely the only reason why the mountain of Asamon appears so sad is that for centuries it has been gazing out over the grave of so sublime a saint as Pinchas ben Yair. Rabbi Pinchas ben Yair, you should know, was a great worker of miracles. The Talmud relates astounding things about him. It also tells us of the miraculous wisdom of his ass. It says:

"If our forefathers were angels, we are only human beings. If however, our forefathers were human beings, then we are only asses. And if that is the case, then we are far from bearing comparison with the ass of Rabbi Pinchas ben Yair."

The soul of Ismael, the ancestor of the Arab people, was incarnate in the ass of Rabbi Pinchas ben Yair. This accounts for the ass being so wise, for Ismael was the son of our father Abraham.

However I believe that I was originally going to tell you about the holy Reb Naftali of Ropshitz. Please do not hold it against me that I have wandered so far off the subject. You have already found out what discursive story-tellers we Chassidim are. But to tell you the truth, I have no desire to get back to Ropshitz. Not that it is any less of a charming place than our Belz, but because there are so few Chassidim there. Only one in three among the blessed three thousand souls there is a Chassid. If the holy Reb Naftali were not there, Ropshitz would be a very sad place. But as for the holy Reb Naftali, he could make the very Heavens laugh.

One day he was on his way to visit the holy Preacher at Koznitz. As he drew near the town—it was already late evening —he saw a light in the distance. So he branched off in the direction of the light and found that it came from a cottage. He went inside. A wedding banquet was in progress, but the bride was refusing to eat the Golden Soup from the same plate as the bridegroom! Many a beautiful eye has shed bitter tears over the nuptial Golden Soup. Not that the Golden Soup—which is made from chicken—was all that bad. Indeed, the exact opposite was the case. But how could a bride and bridegroom fail to be upset in such a predicament? The two young things might never have seen each other in their lives before, and now all of a sudden here they were, having to eat the Golden Soup together out of the same dish! In short, the bride was absolutely insistent that she would not eat the Golden Soup. But why? Because, she said, there was no *bädchen*. In this she was perfectly right. A *bädchen*, or as you would call him, a comedian or compère, must never be missing at any proper wedding. To entertain the bride and bridegroom is one of the most important duties of every god-fearing man, and what a *bädchen* can do with his witty rhymes composed on the spur of the moment is something none of you could possibly do. The holy Reb Naftali understood the difficult situation these good people were in and felt no small pity for them. So he gaily raised his voice and intoned:

> "*A bädchen you want, and nothing more, did you say?*
> "*Here am I—old Naftali of Kopitchinitse!*"

In point of fact, he did not come from Kopitchinitse at all. He came from Ropshitz. But it suited his rhyme just as well and he did not want to let on that he was the famous saint of Ropshitz, lest the simple village folk should get alarmed. Without more ado he rolled up his sleeves and began scattering rhymes out of them such as not even the most experienced of professional *bädchen* would have been able to produce. As each individual guest was named, he straightway had a clever rhyme ready, and every time, every single time, it hit the mark exactly. In short, it was indescribably funny. Tears of laughter flowed from the bride's eyes, and for a whole month afterwards, whenever the bride and bridegroom remembered this evening, they would collapse in side-splitting laughter. As midnight approached Reb Naftali was still producing rhyme after rhyme, and the wedding guests were still laughing and laughing, till the windows rattled.

Now at that very moment the holy Preacher of Koznitz was getting up, as was his habit, to say his midnight prayers. As usual, he smeared his holy brow with ashes and sat down on the ground at the threshold of his room.

And then what? The words stuck in his throat. That was not a good sign at all. When our Temple still stood on Zion and eternal fire burned on the altar, any one who came to sacrifice to the Lord was able to see for himself whether or not his sacrifice had been received with favour. If he was a just man, a royal lion would appear in fiery shape in the flames of the altar, whither it had descended from the heavens, and would devour the sacrifice; but if he was an ungodly man, the shape of an unclean dog would appear in the flames. Now that we have no Temple and no eternal fire on the altar, and now that our prayer is the only passionate offering we can make, we can still know if it is received with favour or not. If it is found acceptable, then the words flow from our lips as easily and quickly as they are poured forth from our hearts. But if it is rejected, we stutter and stammer and catch our breath. The saint of Koznitz realized that night that his tears were unwanted. At other times all the spheres used to help him to weep. The heavens thirsted for his holy tears like the fallow land for the spring rain. For on the day when our Temple was burnt down in Jerusalem—says the Talmud—all the gates of heaven were closed and have never opened since. Only the Gate of Tears—that has never shut up. But that day, so it seemed, even he, Reb Yisroel of Koznitz, had been completely forgotten in heaven and his tears were despised. Needless to say, his holy intellect immediately grasped the reason. They had no time for his tears in heaven that day. The jokes being made by the holy Reb Naftali of Ropshitz in the seclusion of that forest were at that very moment sending all the celestial spheres into convulsions. Even the most secret chambers of the Lord were filled with joy and gaiety. . . .

Reb Naftali is the central figure in many a humorous story. He was an unusual fellow, as you have no doubt realized. However he was no Jewish Til Eulenspiegel, like Hershel, the jester of Ostropolye. Reb Naftali was a saint. He dwelt more in the heavens than on the earth. However, in so far as he did live on the earth, he refused to become sour-faced and make people's lives miserable by going about looking woeful. Like every real saint, Reb Naftali wanted us to be gay and not sorrowful.

It is true of course that ever since the criminal hand of Titus burnt our Jerusalem sanctuary and the Romans scattered us among the nations—in this bitter *golus* (exile)—our troubles have been growing from hour to hour, as Moses prophesied. "In truth even the heaven is not so blue and love is not so sweet as when our sanctuary stood on Zion," says the Talmud. Nevertheless, ever since our Jerusalem was burnt, a new Jerusalem has been under construction. This new Jerusalem is being built in heaven by the angels of the Lord, it is being built with our purest prayers and deserving deeds and with the good inspiration we have when we study the Law. It is being built enthusiastically by day and night. The angels are as busy as bees at it. When they have completed their work, they will bring it on their fiery wings and place it on Mount Zion. Then the Messiah will come, and God will sit on His glorious throne and judge the nations.

We Chassidim need have no fear. The judgment cannot turn out badly for us. So why trouble ourselves? In truth there is no cause for sorrow.

The holy Reb Naftali entered heaven a second time. There he saw an angel carrying magnificent vessels of fine gold.

"Where did you get those vessels, and where are you going with them?" Reb Naftali asked him.

"These are sacrificial vessels," replied the messenger of God. "They have been fashioned by the prayers of your lips and the tears of your eyes, and I am taking them to the new temple."

The holy Reb Naftali had a son who although he had plenty of brains preferred playing to studying. Reb Naftali rebuked him for this:

"Do you know that the holy Baal-Shem said that man should model himself on the Tempter? Just as the Tempter is never idle but ever fulfils the mission entrusted to him by the Creator—to entice man into sin at all times—so a man should carry out his mission unceasingly, namely, to serve his Creator uninterruptedly and learn to do good."

"That's all very well," retorted the son, "but the Tempter has an easy task. It's not difficult for him to fulfil the will of the Creator at all times because he, the Tempter, does not have any other tempter inside him. But I do have the Tempter inside me."

On another occasion Reb Naftali said to his son:

"I'll give you a ducat if you can tell me where God is."

"Dad," said the child, "I'll give you a thousand ducats if you can tell me where God isn't. . . ."

75

Reb Naftali liked witty people, but he was not over-fond of busy-bodies. Here is a story of how he got his own back on such a person.

A young man insisted on knowing why Reb Naftali always wore trousers of white cloth.

"I can't tell you that," said the saint, "it's a secret."

When the nosy fellow heard the word "secret", his curiosity increased and he pestered the saint all the more.

"It's a secret I can only confide to somebody who has first fasted for six days."

The young fellow was so anxious to know that he really succeeded in enduring a six-day fast. Then he turned up again.

"So now I'll tell you, but promise me you won't betray the secret to anybody so long as you live."

The fellow solemnly swore not to.

Reb Naftali then led him off into a room, and from that room to a second room, and from the second to a third. Then he went back again to make sure that all the doors were well closed so that no unauthorized person should hear the secret. The young fellow was on tenterhooks.

Reb Naftali grew serious. Then he bent down to the student of mysteries and whispered in his ear:

"Know then that I wear white cloth trousers because they're the cheapest."

"So that's all it is!" exclaimed the disappointed nosy-parker. "Is that what I had to fast six days for? Why make such a secret of it?"

Reb Naftali smiled a mischievous smile.

"Because if people got to know of it, they'd want this sort of trousers too, and in no time they'd be more expensive. I shouldn't get them so cheap any more. . . . Now don't forget your promise, and don't tell any one, so long as you live!"

These two anecdotes—about where God is and where He is not, and curiosity punished—may perhaps seem somehow familiar to you. Maybe some of you will ask how they could have found their way to Ropshitz from the time of the Renaissance or even from antiquity. In point of fact however there is nothing very surprising about that. If souls can migrate, why should anecdotes not migrate too?

On one occasion somebody remarked to Reb Naftali that throughout their lives men sweat and toil from morning to evening and receive absolutely nothing in return for all their efforts.

"Shall I at least be happy after death?" he inquired.

"You foolish fellow," Reb Naftali replied, "if it is not given to you to get any pleasure out of this world even though you strive so hard after it, how do you suppose you will get any happiness in the next world, which you make not the least effort to strive after?" . . .

The Seer of Lublin once observed that God does not ask us to be clever in any way, but only requires us to serve Him in simpleness of heart. For it is written: "Be *simple* before the Lord thy God!"

"That's quite true," said the holy Reb Naftali, "but to be simple before *God*—that needs a great deal of cleverness."

The holy Reb Naftali was not exactly kindly in the way he summed up the three languages, Russian, Hungarian and German:

"Russian," he said, "is the personification of *retsiche*, or violence, Hungarian of *niyef*, or sensuality, while German personifies the worst quality of all, namely, unbelief—*apikorses*.

"It is true," he would continue, "that German resembles our Yiddish, but only in the same way as a monkey resembles a man. However, many a lie is so similar to the truth that it is almost impossible to distinguish between them." Or he would turn to you with the question: "Are we Chassidim in any way to blame if *they*—the *Yekes*, or Germans—have taken our beautiful Yiddish and turned it into their *Datch*, or German?!"

"The things they have done to it! May God punish them!"

"Our honest Jewish *youch*, it would seem, was not to their taste. They eat 'Suppe' instead. The ruffians, they took it out of the mouths of the French, spoon and all! Presumably our *mume* was not noble enough for them, the good-hearted old soul. So they borrowed her too from the French and called her 'Tante'! Even our *shelkes* (braces) did not suit them—except that their trousers are liable to come down without them, if you will pardon my saying so. True enough, they do not wear belts in any case and they hardly wear a *pasik* either. Do you know what a *Yeke* wears instead of *shelkes*?—'Hosenträger'! As though the tailor's apprentice who is sent by his master to take a pair of trousers to a customer were a pair of braces! Your *Yeke* does not wear *hentchkes* on his hands, not even when he goes to a ball! Do you know what he wears on his hands? A piece of footwear, if you please—he wears shoes on his hands: 'Handschuhe'. . . . That's what these German *batyars* are like—louts!

"Why, your true Germans discourteously turn up their noses even at our grandfather, our venerable *zeide*, and our wise *babe*, although their noses are in any case undersized, like the nose of premature babies that haven't turned out properly. There in the west they must have their 'Grossvater' and 'Grossmutter'. Idiots! The fact is that it is usually just the opposite—grandfathers and grandmothers are mostly quite small people and not 'gross' at all. But talk to the Germans about this! I ask you, just you try!

"And what about the few riches we do have? When the poor German gets up in the morning and asks his wife what they are going to have for dinner, he gets the same answer every day: 'Erdäpfel'. Very occasionally for a change he will be told: 'Kartoffeln'. What does he feel like, all day after that, poor man, when every morning he hears one and the same thing?!"

"How do we go about it?—Well, of course, we also eat potatoes and only potatoes the whole time, but at least we have something different every day: on Sunday, *kartoflyes*, on Monday, *zemakes*, on Tuesday, *erdepl*, on Wednesday, *bulbes*, on Thursday, *barbuyes*, on Friday, *krumpirn* perhaps, and on the holy Sabbath we make *kigel-bramboratchek*.

"So there! We shall remain true to our beautiful Yiddish until the coming of the Messiah." But this is only said in passing.

Each Rabbi has his assistants. We call them *gaboim*.

The holy Reb Naftali also had a *gabai*; his name was Leizer, if I'm not mistaken. This Leizer-gabai was a fellow of real sterling worth, except that he sometimes used to have some curious ideas of his own. But Reb Naftali was deeply fond of Leizer, more especially perhaps on account of this fault of his. Now this Leizer-gabai is the author of a joke which has long since spread far beyond the confines of the Chassidic Empire.

One day the holy Reb Naftali noticed that Leizer-gabai was somewhat downcast, so he asked him:

"What's up, Leizer?"

"I've got a quarrel with God."

"A quarrel with God? What about?"

"I said to God: 'God, our Rabbi says that a thousand years in Thy sight are but a moment. So, God, if a thousand years are like a moment in Thy sight, I, Leizer-gabai, tell Thee that a thousand ducats in Thy sight are like one ducat. God in heaven, would it harm Thee in any way if Thou wert to give me, Leizer, one of those ducats of Thine?'"

"And what did God say?"

"God said: 'Leizer-gabai, just wait a moment!'"

Some of the things we do must not be "interrupted", or disturbed by talk. *Mafsik sein*, the Jews call it. To begin with, we may not *utter* an everyday word during the main parts of the prayer service. We are not allowed to speak before a meal, from the moment when we wash our hands until we have said grace and swallowed our first mouthful; and finally we may not speak when we are where "there is neither day nor night"— to use the high-flown phrase. I am not talking about an Archaion but about the place where even the Emperor goes on foot, namely, the lavatory.

The holy Reb Naftali was getting ready for his afternoon meal. Leizer-gabai brought bread and coffee. Reb Naftali put on his belt, rinsed and dried his hands. As he did so, he looked at the table and noticed that there was no coffee spoon. Leizer had forgotten to lay one·

At that moment of course Reb Naftali could not "interrupt" by talking. So what did he do? Well, he did what any other Chassid would have done under the circumstances: he coughed.

A proper gabai understands this sort of cough. But as for Leizer, he didn't, of course! He squatted down on the bench near the oven, just as though he were a carved statue, and there was no making him understand what Reb Naftali's cough meant. The old fox!

So the holy Reb Naftali was obliged to hold his tongue and swallow a mouthful.

"Why didn't you lay a coffee-spoon here? Didn't you hear me cough?" he asked, when he had finished the mouthful.

"I didn't know that a cough meant a coffee-spoon."

By the time Leizer had waddled back from the kitchen with a coffee-spoon, the coffee was cold. Reb Naftali got annoyed. Of course he was not annoyed—a saint never gets annoyed. But it looked as though he was.

"Oh well," grunted Leizer, "next time I'll know what to do."

One day when Reb Naftali was in that place where there is neither day nor night, Leizer also wanted to go there. Finding the door locked, he sat down on a bench and waited patiently for the door to open.

But the door did not open. Under such circumstances moments are really like thousands of years. When he could stand it no longer, he stood up and banged on the door with all the weight of his determination. It was not politely done. But this time Leizer did not care a tinker's damn.

At that particular moment the holy Reb Naftali could not "interrupt". In order to drive his assailant away, he once again did what any other Chassid would have done in such delicate circumstances: he coughed.

Leizer went—and fetched a coffee-spoon. . . . That's the sort of rascal he was. . . .

Every year, on the eleventh day of the month of Iyar, we celebrate the death of the holy Reb Naftali of Ropshitz. We sing his beautiful songs, tell each other these wonderful stories and drink brandy. Only ninety-six per cent of course! At the same time we shake hands with one another and wish everybody *lechayim!*, which means "cheers!".

Reb Naftali is the author of "The Fleeting Hind" (Ayala Sheluha) and "The Seed of Holiness" (Zera Kodesh). These are sublime works and profound mysteries.

You, then, who wish to live, enter with me into another Gate, for there you shall read:

. . . of the holiness of our *bimah,* or how the holy Reb Sholem beheld mystic fire—how the wife of a coachman is a peerless lady, and how tailoring is a difficult trade—of the glorious circumcision of Urele and the singing of our forefathers—how the holy Urele received instruction and how he taught a nobleman—why we are burdened by hereditary sin—then there follows how the holy Reb Yibi taught him to eat and how he declined to eat any more—how Urele found a teacher, the holy Reb Solomon of Karlin—how the holy Reb Solomon was a Messiah and why he was torn from us—and how great a teacher and sage he was—how the holy Reb Urele returned to his wife—with what yearning he would pray—how he was nimble-witted, or his two godly cows—what he would not pray that the Chassidim should be granted, and why Vuvtchey was not one of his flock—what strange things old Eisik saw—and how even a surly bear felt somewhat put to shame—how the holy Reb Jude Hersch was a good-for-nothing and how the doves flew to him only that he might slaughter them—why tobacco wept at the creation of the world and what sort of vision Avram Simche saw—how there are no more saints left in the world like him, and how the Chassidim journeyed to Stretena.

81

The Fourth Gate

Blazing lion of the heavenly Academy,
God's Fiery Seraph,
Who shall expound his mystery?
And who shall tell his nobility,
And his wisdom's depth,
And the light of his virtue and sanctity?

Our teacher and our master

THE HOLY REB URELE OF STRELISK

may the Light of his merits protect us for ages and always!

The Torah is the holiest of all things for us—the Five Books of Moses in Hebrew, exquisitely and faultlessly written, in black china-ink, on white parchment calf leather, by the hand of a highly skilled scribe. It is a scroll several yards long whose two ends are wound on two wooden sticks. We call it the Tree of Life.

The parchment scroll of the Torah is most precious. So also is the velvet mantle in which we clothe it; beautifully embroidered, it is adorned with the ancient symbol of the six-pointed shield of David. On the tips of the Tree of Life we place silver crowns with little bells; on the neck of the scroll, wrapped in its mantle, we hang a little silver hand with the index finger extended, and on the scroll itself a silver shield. The Torah is kept in the House of Prayer, in a sacred ark behind a magnificent curtain.

On the holy Sabbath and festivals, when the Torah is carried through the synagogue during the services, we rise from our seats before it with greater respect then other peoples before their kings. We touch and kiss its mantle. If—God forbid—by an unhappy chance the Torah should fall to the ground, we should fast seven times to cleanse away the disgrace. When for any reason the scroll can no longer be used for reading aloud, we bury it in the cemetery with due honour.

God has entered into the Torah and its holy letters, and in this way has given Himself to us. Before the world was, the Torah was, the mysterious Law of God. It was written *in white fire on black fire*, says the Talmud. And in the holy Zohar it is written: "God and the Torah and Israel are one and the same."

The Torah is read out to the people every Sabbath and festival. In the course of the year we read it right through and begin again at the beginning. This has been going on for thousands of years. It is not easy to read aloud from the Torah, for it has no vowels and no diacritical marks to distinguish the letters. You cannot recognize the Hebrew ch from k, v from b, s from t, and so on. Every word has its own melody and has to be intoned when read out. The next word has an entirely different melody. A skilled reader must know all this by heart if he is not to cut a sorry figure. A devout audience is very critical and excitable.

Each little letter of the Torah hides a profound mystery. The more sublime mysteries are contained in the vowels while those that are still more sublime are to be found in the annotations. But the most sublime mysteries of all lie submerged in the undefined sea of whiteness which surrounds the letters on all sides. No one is able to unravel this mystery, none there are that can fathom it. So infinite is the mystery of the whiteness of the parchment that the entire world we live in is incapable of comprehending it. No vessel is fit to receive it. Only in the world to come will it be understood. Then shall be read not what is written in the Torah, but what is not written: the white parchment.

There are thousands upon thousands of readers who are adept at reading swiftly and impeccably from the Torah. But none indeed can be compared with the holy Reb Urele of Strelisk!

The holy Reb Sholem of Belz once came to Strelisk for the festival of Pentecost. It was on this festival that God gave us the ten commandments. Every year at Pentecost we read the appropriate chapter in the Torah. Reb Sholem had been invited to come and see how his teacher read.

All at once the parchment disappeared before Sholem's sight and he beheld the Torah as it had been before the creation of the world: *a white flame on a black flame!*

Naturally only a disciple like the holy Reb Sholem can behold the sacred Torah, and even then only when it is read by a saint like the holy Urele.

Urele's mother was a great *Tsaddik*—a perfect saint. Her name was Rivkele. She was an orphan. She was brought up by her old grandfather and grandmother in a village not far from the town of Janov. Both died when she was still young. A *poritz*, or nobleman, had her grandfather whipped, and her grandmother died of grief. Rivkele went into service. She was not yet twelve years old. She was employed at an inn and was quiet and hard-working. The innkeeper and his wife never tired of singing her praises.

Many coachmen came to the inn. Rough and coarse, they played cards the whole time, and had no thought for God. They did not wash their hands before eating, and Rivkele never saw them praying. Because of this she took no notice of their remarks about her beauty. One of the coachmen however was quite different. Every morning he would tie on his little phylacteries and pray devoutly. He washed his hands before meals, and afterwards gave thanks to the Lord who "feedeth the whole world with His goodness, with grace, with loving kindness and tender mercy; who giveth food to all flesh, and who hath given us, as an heritage, food for all His creatures, and who hath given us the good earth, a desirable, good and ample land, and His Law, and the sacred commandments and holy Jerusalem, His city". He would never touch cards. His name was Pinyele, or Pinchas. The innkeeper's wife soon noticed that the girl was taken with this Pinyele and told her husband. They agreed it would be a good thing if they were to marry their orphan to the coachman. From that moment Pinchas and Rivkele were betrothed.

By chance the holy Rebe Reb Ber, Preacher of Meziritz (the Great Maggid)—may the Light of his merits protect us!— happened to be passing through the village. Pinyele asked his advice about the marriage.

The saint replied: "Your bride is a girl without stain. She will bear you a son who shall be a true blessing of God."

Rivkele, it would seem, was not happy in her marriage. Pinchas was too simple a soul for so profound a nature. However she soon reconciled herself to her lot. After all she had married with the consent of the holy Rebe Reb Ber! Her happiness was complete when finally a son was born to them.

His father gave him the name of Urele from Israel.

The story goes that on one occasion during her pregnancy Rivkele went to Meziritz. As she crossed the threshold of the

87

saint's room, the holy Rebe Reb Ber rose respectfully from his seat. His pupils were much amazed that a saint should get up for an ordinary woman.

Whereupon the holy Rebe Reb Ber said to them:"Know then that the child this devout woman carries under her heart shall one day be a light to lighten all Israel."

Little Urele was a strange child. One day he was playing near the house when, suddenly, for no reason at all, he burst into a terrible fit of crying, as only children can.

"Pinyele, run and see what's wrong!" called Rivkele to her husband from the kitchen.

"It's nothing, Daddy, there's nothing wrong," said Urele. "All at once I felt so sorry for the dear Lord. How sad it must be for him, not having all His children with Him!" . . .

A coachman goes travelling for days on end and earns a mere pittance. As for Pinyele, he wanted to spend all his time with his Urele, so he left his coach to look after itself and moved to Janov. He became a tailor overnight. But in Janov every seventh Jew was a tailor, and parading about in fine garments meant little to the people there. The festive *bekish* (caftan) was passed down from father to son to the third and fourth generation, and not even the richest inhabitants bothered if their weekday clothes were reduced to rags. There was very little work and still less money.

Urele's parents were poor. They could not even afford to pay a teacher to instruct their son in the word of God, though he was nearly three years old.

Fortunately, in the neighbouring village there lived a wealthy Jewish farmer who had a private teacher for his somewhat older children. This farmer agreed to let Urele study the word of God side by side with his sons.

Indeed it was high time. Urele was about to have his third birthday. His hair was cut—we do not cut our children's hair until they are three—his head was shaved and only his side-whiskers were left. The little lad was bathed and dressed in a

Sabbath caftan. Then they put him on a table and placed on his head not his father's Sabbath *shtreimel*, as is the usual practice on such occasions, but the broad, black velvet hat worn by men who have had a famous Rabbi among their ancestors. The child's face could hardly be seen. Moreover he had no famous ancestor. Round his neck they hung a beautiful golden chain, so heavy he could hardly stand up. The innkeeper's wife had inherited it from her dear great-grandmother—peace to her memory!—and used to lend it to good children only on their third birthday. In this rig-out little Urele had to preach from the table. There were no dainties for him, poor lad. Still it was indeed an unforgettable birthday, Urele's, for when he preached it was not like other three-year-olds "preaching" on their birthday: little Urele, the wise Urele—he really preached. Like a great and learned man! Thus did Urele start as a disciple.

From that day on Urele would walk through the meadows and woods day by day to the farthest villages. He walked alone. No one accompanied him. This must have been ordained by omniscient God, for it was in no small measure due to these daily wanderings that the child's soul developed so early, to be as beautiful as the flowers in the meadows where he walked.

Urele went his way deep in thought.

The *poritz* in this district was a good and well-educated man, who liked reading, and knew all the wisdom of the Christians, which they call philosophy.

One day the *poritz* caught sight of Urele coming back from his lessons, walking as in a dream.

"Urele! Urele!" he called.

Not a murmur from Urele who had seen and heard nothing.

"What are you so lost in thought about?" asked the good *poritz* when he had finally succeeded in attracting his attention.

Urele made a polite apology and launched forth into speech. It was remarkable. Everything, every little thing that the *poritz* had ever read was mentioned by Urele, and a great deal more besides, which the *poritz's* philosophers had never even dreamed about.

By the time Urele was thirteen years old he knew all the thirty-six tractates of the Talmud and the entire four Orders of the Shulchan Aruch. At fifteen he understood all the secrets of the Cabbala. Disciples would come from far and wide to ask Urele to expound to them the mysteries of God. And the good-hearted Urele was never able to refuse them.

He knew the works of Maimonides word for word by heart, including the commentaries.

Years later Urele related the following circumstances regarding his birth:

"My father, of blessed memory, started life as a coachman and later became a tailor. He lived in a village and was very poor. There were no Jews in the village. When I was born, there were not available the prescribed ten men in whose presence I could be circumcised and received into the covenant of our forefather Abraham. Father's wretched condition defied description. He did not even have enough to pay ten men to make the journey from the neighbouring town, which was the usual practice with village Jews at such times and in such circumstances. And even had he been able, how could he have given lunch to so many people?

"On the eighth day after my birth, the day fixed for the circumcision of a new-born child, my father stepped out of the cottage and sat down in despair on a boundary stone. He trusted in Almighty God that He would send him help, that perchance some travelling Jews would pass that way who would deliver him from his difficulties and help him fulfil his religious duty according to custom and ordinance. Hour after hour went by, and it seemed that on this particular day no travelling Jews were going to show up.

"When the whole morning had passed, Father broke into sobs.

"And lo, in that very moment, a cart was heard in the distance.

"Father looked up and saw that the travellers were Jews like himself.

"All at once the cart arrived.

" 'Hey there, why the tears?' they cried.

" 'It's my son,' said my father. 'He was born just eight days ago. And now he has to be received into the covenant of Abraham. . . .'

"He broke off. Tears held back the words.

" 'What luck!' laughed the strangers. 'There are exactly ten of us and one of us is a Rabbi. There's a *mohel* (one who circumcises) here too, and even a musician who can play to us after the ceremony, so we can have some proper dancing. A real expert. We've got plenty of food too—we've just come from a wedding and they rewarded us well. We've also got some spirits to drink.'

"In short it was a festive occasion such as eye had not seen and ear had not heard in that village since the world began. When everything was over, the guests got back into their cart and drove off. Nobody has ever seen them since."

Would you like to know who the strangers were?

Well: King David was the musician who played for the ceremony. Moses was the Rabbi who preached them the Word of God. And Father Abraham himself performed the circumcision. The godfather was the prophet Elijah. I expect you can guess who the others were.

We shall see them all again when the Messiah comes. In the meantime we shall sing them our old Chassidic song. Come on, all of you, sing it with me!

> *Abraham, Abraham, our old father,*
> *our old father,*
> *Why do you not come,*
> *Why do you not pray*
> *To the Lord for us?*
> *To build our tabernacle,*
> *To bring up our children in the Law*
> *and the fear of God,*
> *To bring us to our land,*
> *To our land!*
> *Isaac, Isaac, our old father!*

Sing slower and don't shout so much! Or do you perhaps think he doesn't hear us up there?

> *Moses, our faithful shepherd! Moses, our*
> *   faithful shepherd!*
> *Why do you not come,*
> *Why do you not pray*
> *To the Lord for us?*
> *To bring up our children in the Law and*
> *   the fear of God,*
> *To bring us to our land,*
> *To our land!*

According to the Cabbala the souls of all people were contained in the soul of Adam. It is for this reason that the weight of hereditary sin clings to us, the descendants of Adam, for we have all sinned with Adam.

But the holy Reb Urele said that when Adam was about to commit the first sin, several souls who did not wish to sin, fled from within him and hence have never tasted the forbidden fruit, and are not burdened by hereditary sin.

He, the holy Reb Urele of Strelisk, was one of these unsullied souls.

Urele's wife, Freida by name, was patient, faithful and humble, a true Chassidic Jewess. Urele and Freida moved to Lvov where Freida, like Urele's mother before her, went into service to earn a livelihood.

Later on, when money was somewhat short, Freida opened a little bargain shop. She did not make much money—only just enough to feed herself and her husband, who spent days on end in the House of Study. Urele did not stay long at Lvov. One day he seized his stick and set out into the world. He longed to find a saint who would show him the way to God.

He wandered a long way before he found his saint. He visited many saints, he came to know many ways to God, everywhere he acquired something useful, but it was only after long journeying that he found his saint.

First he went to the holy Rebe Reb Melech at Lizensk (Elimelech). Then he went to Ostroh where the holy Reb Yibi taught him to eat—which took Urele one evening.

This came about as follows: Large dishes were placed before Reb Yibi, full to the brim with different foods. After blessing God, Reb Yibi launched into the food with astonishing appetite. As though by magic, pounds of meat and ladlefuls of thick Chassidic mash disappeared into his holy mouth. No other mortal could have kept pace with him. None the less he was not equal to the entire contents of the dishes. A little food remained on the bottom of one of the dishes. The holy Reb Yibi—may the Light of his merits protect us—bent over the dish and with tears in his eyes begged the spirit in that confounded food to forgive him but today he could not manage any more. Maybe, they say, he even did so a second time. Then he said grace with unusual fervour and spent the whole night on his knees and in the study of the Law. His real name was Jacob Joseph. We call him Reb Yibi because this was the name he gave to the book he wrote.

Early next day Urele set off again.

Not even the holy Reb Yibi was destined to be his teacher, for he did not meet the inner need of his soul. Urele was aware that only a man who filled him with the same awe as we feel before God Himself would be his teacher. Thus saith the Talmud: "Let thy fear of thy teacher be as thy fear before the Lord!"

From Ostroh Urele travelled on until he came to Koritz. But no sooner had the holy Reb Pinchas of Koritz caught sight of him than he said:

"Go in peace! I am not your teacher."

So Urele did not stop at Koritz but set out without delay on a further pilgrimage. He visited the holy Reb Motele at Neschiz but did not stay long. It was the holy Reb Motele of Neschiz, you know, who was able to conjure up a full moon out of his candlestick. I have seen this wondrous candlestick with my own eyes. It was a rare experience. The candlestick is of pure silver throughout!

Not till he reached Anipol where he visited the holy Rebe Reb Sussya did Urele pause awhile. Even here, however, he had no peace, although he greatly enjoyed being with the holy Rebe Reb Sussya. Finally, after journeying for a long time, he arrived at Karlin. Reb Shloymele of Karlin was resting near the road, seated on a corner-stone in front of his house. Seeing the new-comer, he got up and shook hands, greeting him with words of welcome.

"Sholem aleychem!"—"Peace be with you!"

From that moment Urele was his—his disciple.

For in that moment he was seized by that holy fear such as we feel only before the face of the Most High.

Urele spent several years at Karlin. Only once, over the festival days, did he visit his Freida at Lvov. It was only after his teacher had met a martyr's death that he returned to live with her.

The holy Reb Shloymele did not devote much time to his disciples. The greater part of the day he spent in meditation in his room. Nevertheless Urele learnt a great deal from him, a very great deal.

Before I say anything more about the disciple I must tell you something about his teacher.

The holy Reb Shloymele of Karlin was a disciple of the holy Rebe Reb Ber, the disciple of the Baal-Shem. We also call Reb Shloymele of Karlin Baal-Shem, but only *Little Baal-Shem*, of course. All the same you can see from this what a sublime saint he was. He used to pray with such fervour, with such concentration of all his strength, both spiritual and physical, that after the service blood would exude from him, out of sheer exhaustion. For Heaven had laid on the holy Reb Shloymele the task of praying with such ardour that he would compensate God for the prayers of all those who do not pray hard enough, and even of those—may the merciful God watch over us!—who do not pray at all.

He once said to his disciples: "Everyone must realize that he

94

is the only one of his kind in the world and that there has never been and will never be another person like him. So we must all make the best use we can of our moral qualities and improve our personalities as much as possible. Only thus will the world approach perfection."

On another occasion he said: "A man once saw a precious object very high up. Wanting to fetch it down he asked a number of people to make a 'tower', so that the topmost person could reach for the object. Supposing one of them—the lowest, for instance, had said: 'What's the point of my being here? After all I'll never reach up so high in any case!' and, so saying, had jumped aside, his action would have been extremely foolish and would have endangered the lives of the others. We are all equally necessary—the highest and lowest. If so much as one person fails, the whole will not reach the desired goal."

On yet another occasion the holy Reb Shloymele said this: "God does not wish us to live in a state of continuous rapture like the angels. On the contrary He wants us every now and again to lapse a bit, for after we have repented of our error we rise through our very repentance to a higher level than we were on before our fall. And with our upward movement we carry the entire world with us. God therefore requires of us that in our love for our neighbour we should sink to the level of other people."

Reb Shloymele did not enjoin fasting on those who repented of their sins. He declared that he would allow people to fast only under the following conditions:

Firstly, if their sin was in truth a most grievous one.

Secondly, if the penitent was strong and perfectly healthy.

Thirdly, if he would undertake to fast in the winter when the days are shorter.

Fourthly, if he would take a substantial meal before sunrise.

"And all this," said Reb Shloymele, "only if I see that the penitent would be caused real sorrow if I did not require him to fast." . . .

One day a man invited Reb Shloymele to visit him the following day. "I cannot promise you that," replied the holy Reb Shloymele. "This evening we shall confess our faith in the one God, and when we come to the word 'one' it is our duty to offer ourselves to God. Tomorrow, at morning prayer, our souls will pass through the higher worlds; supposing they like it there and do not return to this world? Once again we shall confess our faith in the one God and offer Him our lives. After the main prayer of the day we shall again fall on our face before the Lord and offer Him ourselves. What if God were really to accept our offering and keep our souls for Himself? How can I promise today that I shall be your guest tomorrow?"

The holy Reb Shloymele foretold correctly. It was his profound desire that he should die while at prayer, the death of a martyr. Not immediately, but at a somewhat later date. Thus what he had prayed for all his life was fulfilled.

On the 22nd day of the month of Tamuz in the year 5552 (1792), he was saying morning prayer with the Chassidim as usual. But when he reached the verse: "Everything in heaven and earth is under Thy rule!"—a voice went up such as had never been heard before, for at that moment Cossacks swept into the House of Prayer and stabbed the saint at the *bimah*. This happened in the presence of the holy Reb Urele, his beloved disciple.

Reb Shloymele of Karlin was a Messiah. Not the Messiah of the House of David whose coming we so much yearn for, knowing neither the day nor the hour, but the Messiah of the House of Joseph who was to come before the Son of David and be executed in accordance with the old prophecy. But the holy Reb Urele said that his sublime teacher had to be murdered because he bore within him the soul of Abel, who perished in a similar manner: by the murderous hand of Cain, his brother. Reb Urele returned to his wife at Lvov.

Shortly afterwards a famous *cabbalist* came to Lvov, the holy Reb Hirsch of Ziditzov. Reb Urele went to visit him.

"I will tell you a great mystery," said Reb Hirsch to him,

"which I think about every day to the greater glory of God, whenever I make the confession of faith, *Hear O Israel, the Lord is one.* You will not find the mystery I have in mind in the writings of the holy ARI. It came to me from Heaven."

Thus saying, he whispered into his ear the cabbalistic formula of his secret musing. Then he asked inquisitively:

"And what secret mystery do you read into this sentence?"

"I've no idea," said Urele simply. "I just shut my eyes, lose myself in the Infinite and call out: *Hear, O Israel, the Lord is one!*"

The holy Reb Urele shouted these words with such a voice of thunder that the whole room shook and plaster fell from the ceiling. When Reb Hirsch saw how the room shook and plaster fell from the ceiling, he shook his head in amazement and said in a low voice:

"I can't do it like that, to be sure." . . .

Reb Hirsch of Ziditzov wrote some remarkable cabbalistic books: "Ateret Zebi" (The Crown of Beauty), "Peri Kodesh Hillulim" (The First Holy Fruits), "Bet Elohim" (The House of God), "Sur Mera" (Keep Away from Evil) and many more. He was a pupil of the Seer of Lublin and the soul of *that child* was within him—the wonder child who in the mystic book "Zohar" so often expounds the deepest mysteries to the wise. It is not in vain that the consonants in the word "Zohar" form the initial letters of the words: Reb Hirsch Ziditzov, in reverse order, of course.—But what is all this compared to the godliness of our holy Urele?

Reb Urele did not study the Cabbala in the manner used by unauthorized persons of little soul. Only fools, he would say, studied it to learn the mystic names of the angels and misuse them for acts of magic. When Reb Urele met an angel in the course of his study he would close his eyes and not even look upon him, not caring to learn his name. From the angels of the Lord he learnt only humility and the fear of God.

At that time there lived at Lvov the wealthy Reb Leib

Mimeles who was related by marriage to the holy Seer of Lublin. Reb Leib Mimeles was very fond of the learned Urele.

One day he asked him:

"What do you live from?"

"Cho zvai kee," replied Urele laconically.

Anybody would have understood from these words that Urele had two cows, for a cow in Yiddish is "kee".

This was how Mimeles understood it, and because he wished to help the godly man he gave orders at home that in future they should get their milk exclusively from Reb Urele.

In due course men came to the cellar which was Urele's home. Not a cow was to be seen.

"How could you tell me yesterday that you have two cows!?" the rich man reproached him the following day.

"Oh forgive me," said Urele, apologizing, "I didn't mean it like that. It wasn't the *Yiddish* word 'kee' I had in mind but the two *Hebrew* 'ki' in the verse in the Holy Scriptures: '*For* our hearts rejoice in the Lord, *for* we trust in His holy name.' "— The Hebrew "ki" means: *for*. . . .

At Lvov a son was born to Urele who called the child Shloymele after his holy teacher. Reb Leib Mimeles was godfather at the circumcision ceremony.

From that moment the rich godfather heaped presents on Urele's family. Urele was obliged to flee from Lvov—to escape from so much generosity. He had no desire to get rich. To serve God, if necessary in the greatest poverty, from the cradle to the grave, is more beautiful than all the treasures of this world.

So one day Urele and his family climbed into a cart and moved to the little, poverty-stricken town of Strelisk so that in future he might be spared the gifts of the rich Maecenas. Hence Urele's noble title: Reb Urele of Strelisk.

Fame was equally repulsive as riches to Urele. He would say: "It were better for a man to jump into the heat of a foundry than to become famous."

The Chassidim at Strelisk were every whit as poor as their saint, the holy Reb Urele. The reason for this—as indeed you already know—was that Urele would not pray for earthly riches for his Chassidim in spite of the fact that all the other *Tsaddikim* were wont to do so. Reb Urele would pray only for the spiritual welfare of his faithful.

He was once reproached for this odd habit by another saint who came to visit him. What did Reb Urele do? He called a Chassid who happened to be passing that way and told him:

"Know that this moment when I am sitting with this *Tsaddik* is an hour of special grace. Whatever desire you may express will be fulfilled. Even if you ask to become the richest man in the world, it shall happen as you shall will it." The Chassid was not long in making up his mind.

"I want the Lord to help me to pray the prayer 'Blessed be *He who spake, and the world existed. . . .*' with as much fervour as when you pray it!"

"You see," said Urele to his guest, "you see what sort of riches my Chassidim desire."

Freida, Urele's wife, also felt sorry for the poverty-stricken Chassidic households—though she lived in similar penury herself.

"Pray for them, that things may go better with them!" she urged her husband.

"Very good," sighed Reb Urele, "tomorrow they shall have whatever they shall wish."

The next day at morning prayer, as the Chassidim came to the words in the prayer: "*Riches and glory come from Thee, O Lord!*", the holy Reb Urele went up to them and said:

"If any of you want any money, dip into my pocket quickly and take out a handful of ducats!"

Not one of them put his hand in.

However, there was one wealthy man among the Chassidim at Strelisk. His name was Vuvtchey.

"Oh, Vuvtchey, Vuvtchey, I am very fond of you," Reb Urele told him one day, "but I should be much more fond of you if only you were as poor as all of us."

Vuvtchey was horrified. He was excessively spoilt. On one occasion when his shoelace broke, he was so put out by this little matter that he was unable to concentrate his thoughts on prayer. Supposing his big toe began to show, as happened with the others—where would all his piety be then?!

The holy Reb Urele of Strelisk is called a Seraph by the Chassidim. We know from the Holy Scriptures who the seraphim are. The prophets Isaiah and Ezekiel have given us an exact description. According to them the seraphim are angelic beings with six wings and four faces. Their bodies are like burning coals of fire.

Many people think that it is because of these coals of fire that we call the saint of Strelisk a Seraph. Indeed he prayed so burningly, so fierily, that he would fully deserve the title of the fiery Seraphim.

He used to say that the biblical hero Samson drew strength from heaven to succour all the weak and ailing that shall be in all the generations until the end of the world, and that King David with his songs drew inspiration from heaven and gave it to mankind.

He, the holy Reb Urele of Strelisk, with his praying drew from heaven the inspiration of David and the strength of Samson.

But this is not the reason why we call Urele a Seraph. The real reason is a more curious one.

I will tell you about it.

In a village not far from Strelisk lived an aged Chassid named Eisik. Eisik was not a Chassid of the saint of Strelisk but of the holy Seer of Lublin, to whom he travelled every year for the great festivals. Out of politeness he always called at Strelisk on these occasions.

One day, on his way to Lublin, he stopped at Strelisk and spent the night in the House of Study with the other pilgrims. Everybody was asleep—on the benches, on the floor, as is usual—everybody was sound asleep. Only the old man could not go to sleep.

Towards midnight the saint of Strelisk went into the House of Study. It was his habit to go and make sure that the visitors did not lack for anything.

Eisik lay on the floor among the sleepers, not making a sound. He also appeared to be fast asleep.

But he was not.

It was indeed a remarkable sight that met his eyes.

Reb Urele walked through the House of Study, among the sleepers, like Aaron of old among the living and dead. So lightly and quietly did he walk that it was as though his holy legs never even touched the ground.

He walked hither and thither, and Eisik, stretched out on the floor, watched him out of the corner of his eye.

Not for a single moment could Eisik tear his gaze from the saint's face, so fascinated was he by the mysterious glow that played upon it.

Then Reb Urele turned with his back towards him and went through the House of Study in the opposite direction.

When Eisik saw the saint turn his back he was unhappy because he would not see his holy face any more. But wait, what was happening?! Although Reb Urele had his back to him, Eisik could still see the face of the saint absolutely clearly—in fact every bit as clearly as when he was facing him.

It was in vain that Eisik rubbed his eyes. What he saw, he saw. In whichever direction Reb Urele walked—his holy face continued to be visible. Eisik told no one of what he had been vouchsafed to see that night, but he made up his mind that he would tell everything to the holy Seer when he arrived at Lublin.

It is a long way from Strelisk to Lublin, and old Eisik had a poor memory. Before he reached Lublin he had forgotten everything.

After the festival he went to say goodbye to the holy Seer.

"When you get to Strelisk," said the saint of Lublin, "tell the saint of Strelisk that I know about his having two faces!"

"That's just what I wanted to tell you!" cried Eisik in surprise.

"Just you tell him what I've said! Don't forget!" he warned.

If Eisik had hastened to Lublin, he hastened now to Strelisk all the more.

"That's not quite correct," observed Reb Urele, when he had heard the Seer's message. "It's not two faces I have, but four."

So now you know why we call the saint of Strelisk a Seraph: Because it's only the angels of the Lord, known as Seraphim, that have four faces, as the prophet Ezekiel has described them to us.

Let us not suppose, however, that Eisik was the only mortal to whom it was granted to behold the angelic face of Urele. That face was seen by a wild beast, too.

One winter's night, Reb Urele was travelling through the forest in a sleigh with some Chassidim. Suddenly the horses stopped and positively refused to go any farther. In the middle of the road stood an enormous bear, growling horribly.

The Chassidim turned blue with fright. But what did Urele do? He smiled so sweetly, as only he could smile, climbed out of the sleigh, walked up to the bear as if it had been the most ordinary thing in the world, and spoke to it.

The animal looked up in surprise at the holy face of the saint, gave another short growl, then hung its head and slouched off, like a dog with its tail between its legs.

Jude Hersch of Stretena was Urele's favourite disciple. The two were bound together by a love as wondrous as the love of David and Jonathan, nay even more wonderful perhaps.

After the death of Freida, Urele married Blime, daughter of Reb Kopel, who was a pupil of the holy Baal-Shem. As a result of this marriage Reb Mendele of Kosov became Urele's brother-in-law.

"There's only one thing I envy my brother-in-law: his disciple, Jude Hersch of Stretena," said Reb Mendele of Kosov. "I've never known a teacher think so unceasingly of his disciple, nor have I seen a disciple so hang upon his teacher, as Reb Urele and Jude Hersch. Like Moses and Joshua they are. Moses and

Joshua, says the Talmud, were like the sun and moon—the moon which reflects the light of the sun."

The holy Reb Urele spoke thus of his disciple:

"When the Messiah comes—may it be soon, during our lifetime!—all the saints will go to meet him, with the holy Baal-Shem at their head. I shall go with my Jude Hersch, and believe me, I shall have no reason to be ashamed of him."

Reb Urele sent Jude Hersch on missionary journeys to Hungary. He used to say that nobody would ever appreciate all the good work he did in that country. Nor would it be revealed to the world until the coming of the Messiah.

On one of these journeys Jude Hersch went to Kalev near Debrecin. Here the *Tsaddik*, the holy Reb Yitzhak Eisik Toub, asked him to expound one of the true sayings of Reb Urele.

"Impossible," returned Jude Hersch. "The words of my teacher are like manna. As the manna came from heaven—so it is with his holy words. Even as the Talmud tells us that he who partook of the manna left none of it outside his body but utterly consumed the heavenly bread, so that every little crumb of it passed straight into his blood—so do the true sayings of our master feed our souls. They enlighten our whole being. It is impossible to give them out at all for they have become the very blood of our body."

"Then tell me at least of his deeds and virtues, so that I can imagine them clearly."

Jude Hersch bared his breast and said:

"Look into my heart! There you shall see all that my teacher is."

By profession Jude Hersch was a butcher—but no ordinary butcher. Animals had no fear of his knife; on the contrary they longed for it.

From far and wide the doves flew to Stretena, laid their heads of their own accord under his sharpened knife, and cooed and begged him to dispatch them with his loving, holy hand. It was because of this that Urele put off making Jude Hersch a Rabbi for such a long time. He knew that there were thousands of poor souls incarnate in the animals, waiting to be set free by Jude Hersch's butcher's knife.

Besides, how could Reb Urele allow Jude Hersch to become a Rabbi? Why, once when he merely allowed him to sing the semi-holy Sabbath hymn which is sung after food, his yearning as he sang had caused him to faint. They had spent two whole hours bringing him round. Whatever would happen if he were a Rabbi and had to pray the most sacred prayers at the *bimah*?! He would certainly pass out once and for all. That's the sort of *batlen* he was, a *ne'er-do-well*. . . .

Before I go on to tell you something more about this saintly good-for-nothing, there are one or two things I should explain to you:

Know, then, that when God created the world, all creatures rejoiced. The reason for their rejoicing was that once the Chassidim were here to enjoy them, they (the Chassidim) would praise God for it. The loaf made a joyous crunching noise because it knew that once we came to eat it, we would praise the Lord, the King of the universe, "*that He causeth the bread to come up from the earth*". The wine rejoiced that we should bless "*the fruit of the vine*", the trees that we should give thanks for "*the fruit of the tree*", the vegetables and grass that we should bless "*the fruit of the earth*". Goats and heifers, lambs and sheep danced and capered, the hens clucked, and the ducks quacked and chased the fish. The delightful creatures just could not wait for the moment when the Chassidim should fry their flesh and praise God for it. Likewise also water and brandy laughed for joy. Were they not all already destined, even at that time, to hear us say over them: "*Blessed art Thou, O Lord our God, King of the universe, by Whose word all things exist?*"—Even the sweet-smelling spices knew that once we had caught their scent we should bless the Lord "*that He had created odorous plants*".

And thus it was that everything rejoiced, everything exulted, everything laughed for joy—and only *tobacco* wept.

"Lord of the universe!" it moaned, wet through with tears.

"Lord of the universe, the Chassidim shall bless Thee and exalt Thy name for everything. Only for me Thou hast not ordained any blessing!"

"Weep not, my child!" our Heavenly Father comforted the plant. "I will recompense thee plentifully. Know that by no other means in the world shall people do so much good to each other as through thee."

In very truth! By no other means in the world do we acquire such merit, so easily and effortlessly, as with tobacco. It never causes us the least harm, it costs us next to nothing; and nobody to whom we show charity through tobacco is offended thereby, and no one blushes that he has been obliged to accept such charity. And with tobacco we are all equal—rich and poor, evil and good, niggardly and generous.

A neighbour comes in for a gossip and we have nothing to offer him. Not a slice of bread, not a pinch of tea, and no vodka. And yet God desires us to perform an act of hospitality as perfectly as our father Abraham who could slaughter a calf for his guests while his wife Sarah cooked cakes of fine meal.

How can this be?—Well, in this wise:

Our neighbour pulls out his pipe, hunts for his tobacco pouch in the pocket of his caftan, knocks out his pipe, stuffs it with tobacco and looks around.

We see our neighbour looking around and guess what he wants.

What do we do? We get up, take the shovel, scratch away at the ash in the stove, and carry a glowing coal to our guest on the shovel.

Our neighbour will not let us serve him of course. He merely waits until we rejoin him. But once we are there, with the coal on the shovel, he takes the handle from our hand and lights up on his own.

Our neighbour smokes away to his heart's content, and we chat happily together. Then when the social call is over, he goes away in peace.

Has our hospitality cost us anything?

No.

Has it harmed us in any way?

Not in the least.

None the less we have performed an act of hospitality and acquired imperishable merit thereby. Our neighbour is happy, and so are we.

Thanks to tobacco we acquire similar merits almost every day and on all manner of occasions.

No, tobacco has no reason to complain.

Once, during morning prayer at Strelisk, Jude Hersch wanted to take snuff. He took out his *pushke*, his tobacco case, I mean, opened it, shut it again, and put it down in front of him—because it was empty. There was not even a single pinch of snuff in it.

Avrum Simche of Galiga was a very smart fellow. He noticed Jude Hersch opening and shutting his *pushke*, and guessed what was up.

What did he do?—He went and tipped a good half of the tobacco from his own *pushke* into Jude Hersch's *pushke*.

Reb Urele was at that moment praying at the *bimah*.

Jude Hersch was concerned that Avrum Simche's deed should not remain unrewarded for a single moment.

What did he do?—He pulled out his *fatchele*—his handkerchief, I mean—went up to Avrum Simche and opened out his *fatchele* before his eyes.

The sight that Avrum Simche of Galiga beheld through Jude Hersch's handkerchief was a wonder of wonders. Avrum Simche looked through it, and lo! It was not Reb Urele standing at the *bimah* at prayer. . . . Above the *bimah* was a pillar of fire, and this pillar reached to the sky. And on the pillar souls were climbing up to heaven—hundreds and hundreds of souls, the souls of the wretched who had died without merit. From far away they had flown down to Strelisk, poor little naked things, and the holy Urele had washed them with his tears, dressed them in white raiment, and led them on to eternal bliss.

The vision lasted only a moment. Jude Hersch took his handkerchief from Avrum Simche's face—and the pillar of fire was no longer to be seen; there was not a trace of the souls, but only the holy Reb Urele praying at the *bimah*, and all around the ordinary Chassidim.—May they all have long life and health! And may the merciful God help us to attain perfection while we are still alive and in this incarnation, AMEN!

The Seer of Lublin had been urging the saint of Strelisk a long time before the latter finally agreed to Jude Hersch becoming a Rabbi at Stretena and ceasing to be a butcher. All the souls incarnated in the cattle and poultry had already been redeemed by his butcher's knife.

One day some Chassidim were journeying to Strelisk. We cannot of course travel on the Sabbath and so these Chassidim were obliged to keep the Sabbath at Stretena. They felt sad that they would not be hearing the holy Reb Urele expounding the word of God on that day. However, what they heard from Reb Jude Hersch was so profound and glorious that after all they were very pleased to have spent the Sabbath at Stretena.

When they reached Strelisk on the Sunday, their first thought of course was to inquire what their holy Reb Urele had said the day before when he expounded the Law.

Wonders of wonders!—What they heard was precisely the same as they had heard the day before at Stretena from the lips of Reb Jude Hersch!

The Chassidim asked the holy Reb Urele what was the reason for this remarkable coincidence.

"This is how it is," the holy Seraph told them. "When I listened to them expounding the word of God in heaven on Saturday, Jude Hersch was with me and he also heard everything. He then spoke of this at Stretena while I did so here at Strelisk."

And he added with a smile:

"That Jude Hersch will finish up by stealing the very whites of my eyes from me!"

Needless to say, Reb Urele was not often in the habit of telling the Chassidim about things that happened in heaven. But once—it was the 21st day of the month of Elul—he said:

"At the gate of heaven sits a permanent court, deciding

whether or not souls are to be received into paradise. Up to that time one of the judges had been a saint who had died in ancient times and had long since forgotten the temptations of this world and human weakness. In consequence he was a very strict judge and hardly wanted to allow anybody into paradise. Then he was recalled from that court and became a member of a still higher court up in heaven. His place on the lower court fell vacant. . . ."

Three days after this Reb Urele passed away.

It was the duty of his son, Reb Shloymele, to recite the mourner's prayer, *kaddish*, over the sepulchre, that his father's soul might ascend to heaven.

However, he said no more than the first sentence of the prayer: "Magnified and sanctified be this great name in the world!"

There he left off praying and said:

"An angel like my father needs no more for the raising up of his soul."

When Reb Hirsch of Ziditzov heard about these words of Shloymele, he said:

"There are few children who are so well aware of what a father is, as Reb Shloymele."

Reb Shloymele survived his holy father by only four months. When before his death the Chassidim begged him not to leave them, he replied:

"How can I go on living when I had such a wonderful father?!"

The people of Strelisk were orphaned.

They wanted to find another saint to take the place of their Urele. But they wandered through the world in vain. They found no place that pleased them.

Finally they remembered Reb Jude Hersch of Stretena. The Chassidim of Strelisk became the Chassidim of Stretena. I shall never forget the magic of the prayer chanted by the old Chassidim of Stretena. I shall recall its sound till my dying day.

Neither he who selects pearls, nor he who weighs gold, can be compared to the Chassidim of Stretena, expressing the holy words of prayer. Slowly, ever so slowly, and softly, the sweet words flow on, permeated with such humility and love, and such yearning, that they cannot be described or compared to anything on earth.

The praying of the Chassidim at Strelisk was stormy and fiery like the passionate sound of gipsy violins, while that of the Chassidim at Stretena was a long drawn out, tender song, softened by the mute of profound humility and resignation. He who has not heard it has yet to learn true piety.

FROM THE WISDOM OF REB URELE OF STRELISK

—Windows are symbols of mystery.—

—Some people are exceptionally thin and frail, and other people think that it is easy for such people to overcome the devil and serve God. This is a mistake. There is a devil whose name is "Scragginess", and it is more difficult to overcome this devil, and drive him out, than to overcome all the others.—

—How can a person be proud and conceited?! After all, nothing that we have is from ourselves! It all comes from God. Even our piety is a gift from God.—

—Before the coming of the Messiah the Rabbi's office will be filled for a certain time by downright scoundrels, men who will be so skilled in deceiving the Chassidim that the latter will hold them to be perfect saints and will believe in them blindly. But in His great loving-kindness the Lord will reward the Chassidim equally for this their faith as if they had believed in true saints, and will deliver them from learning the evil ways of their spiritual leaders. Even as David prayed in the Psalms: "May he protect the steps of his Chassidim (the godly), may he keep them from the evil-doers!"—

—The celestial Torah has 600,000 letters, and 600,000 souls are scattered around among the people of Israel. Each soul is identical with one letter of the Law. If but one single letter were missing from the Torah, the entire scroll would be invalidated. Likewise if but one of us were not in his place among all the others, we should be nothing.

But why are the Hebrew letters of the Torah not joined? So

that we should follow their example and separate ourselves one from the other from time to time and give ourselves up to meditation in solitude.

—When I was a little boy and the teacher had just taught me to read, he once showed me two little letters, like square dots in the prayer book, and said: "Urele, you see these two letters side by side? That's the monogram of God's name, and wherever you see these two quadrangular dots side by side, you must pronounce the name of God at that spot, even if it is not written in full." I continued reading with my teacher until we came to a colon. It also consisted of two square dots, only instead of being side by side they were one above the other. I imagined that this must also be the monogram of God's name and so I pronounced the name of God at this spot. But my teacher told me:

"No, no, Urele, that does not mean the name of God. *Only where there are two sitting nicely side by side, where the one looks on the other as an equal—only there is the name of God; where one is under the other and the other is raised above his fellow—there the word of God is not. . . .*"

—Even in the fratricide Cain there were sparks of good. The saints who are the incarnation of these sparks from Cain are the very greatest saints.—

—"Urele is not afraid of being judged for not being such a great saint as Moses or Abraham," Reb Urele said of himself. "But Urele is very afraid of being judged for not being as good an Urele as Urele ought to be."—

And now all you who wish to live, enter with me into another Gate, for there you shall read:

—how Rebe Reb Yoynosn of Prague was *sweet à la Moravian,* or how he was something of a Chassid—how the holy brothers wandered through the world and how Sussya was a man of happy temperament—some stories of birds, ants and mother earth, and about Sussya's wings and his ecstatic behaviour—and how he studied at Mezeritz—how the saint of Frankfurt maintained that those Polish Jews were very pushing—upon which there follows an account of how the holy Rebe Reb Melech of Lizensk (Elimelech) fought against the Emperor at Vienna—and why our young men so hated enlisting and cursed the army —and how the holy Rebe Reb Melech upset the soup—how the Emperor Joseph secretly consulted a famous sorcerer at his castle in Vienna, and how the holy Rebe Reb Melech of Lizensk showed him his hands—how the Devil tried to browbeat the saint and multiplied the Chassidim—then follows an account of how the court at Lizensk passed its famous judgment on God, and of the strange things that befell Melech in the forest —how he never preached in one week in the year and what sweet delights he has left us—

The Fifth Gate

Two golden trombones in the angelic choir,
Most saintly pair from one sire.
Holy in body, two hearts of precious merit,
In life so pure,
So humble in spirit.

Our teacher and our master

THE HOLY REBE REB MESHULEM SUSSYA OF ANIPOL

may his merits protect us for all eternity,

And his holy brother
Our teacher and our master

THE HOLY REBE REB MELECH OF LIZENSK (ELIMELECH)

may his merits protect us all!

THE FIFTH GATE

When speaking to the Chassidic saints we use the title "Rebe", but in speaking about them we use the shorter title "Reb". "Reb" of course signifies a somewhat lower degree of worthiness. However, there are some saints whose greatness neither of the two titles can approach. In consequence we give them both titles together: "Rebe" and "Reb". To be sure, there are not many such saints—only eight altogether. Foremost among them is the holy Rebe Reb Ber, or the Preacher of Mezeritz (the Great Maggid), and then some of his pupils: the Moravian saint, Rebe Reb Shmelke of Mikulov and his brother, Rebe Reb Pinchas of Frankfort; the two brothers, Rebe Reb Melech, or more correctly Elimelech, of Lizensk, and Rebe Reb Sussya of Anipol. Then there are Rebe Reb Shimen of Jaroslav and Rebe Reb Borechl of Medziboz. It is rather a curious custom—as though in ordinary life we were to address a doctor as "professor doctor", only "Rebe Reb" is much more saintly and magnificent. But let us not forget the eighth of these saints, or to be more precise, the first! This is Rebe Reb Jonathan Eibeschutz of Old Prague. We call him Rebe Reb in spite of his having lived long before the holy Baal-Shem and hence before the beginning of the Chassidic era. But we are quite right in this for he was a precursor of Chassidism. There are several precursors of Chassidism, for instance—not counting the holy ARI of Palestine—the Great Rabbi Loev of Prague, Moshe Chayyim Luzzatto of Italy, Rabbi Jonathan Eybeschüte of Prague, that is, our holy Rebe Reb Yoynosn. Rebe Reb Yoynosn became a Rabbi in Prague in 1711 when he was only twenty-one. Before that he had lived in Moravia. He deserves his Chassidic title if for no other reason than for the unlimited respect he enjoyed with his disciples at Prague. In those days they felt almost the same respect for him in Prague as we Chassidim do nowadays. He equally deserves it on account of his modesty and the forbearance he showed towards his adversaries.

Subsequently, when he was called to Hamburg, he became known in Germany as the Rabbi who was *sweet à la Moravian*. Indeed, how sweet are the writings of the holy Rebe Reb Yoynosn! When we read his "Yearot Devash" (Honeycomb), or his "Ahavat Jonatan" (The Love of Jonathan), there are moments when we have the impression we are reading the works of a real Chassidic saint. So when we call him Rebe Reb, we know what we are doing. Nevertheless he was not a true Chassid; he forbade the use of coffee, tea and even smoking. Well, we might be able to manage without coffee. But just imagine us Chassidim without tea, or even tobacco! It simply is not possible. You must know that to a true Chassid smoking is a very sacred act, in fact it is almost equivalent to a sacrifice. As the holy Talmud tells us: "Let everything you do be solely to give pleasure to Heaven!" This of course applies to smoking too—more than to anything else, in fact. After all smoke really does go up to Heaven.

But let us not get too far away from our subject! We are supposed to be talking about those two holy brothers of ours, and meanwhile we are wandering half way round the world, almost like they did years ago. The brothers Rebe Reb Sussya and Rebe Reb Melech, you see, wanted to share with God the torments which He bears through all our vices and wickedness, in this our bitter Exile. And so they set out on their journey through the world, after the example of the ancient ascetics.

In fearful hardship and unending privation they wandered through district after district, country after country. They avoided those villages over which they did not see the glory of God shining, and entered not into houses above which the mystic name of the Lord did not appear to their holy sight. And all the while they were lighthearted and gay as true Chassidim should be.

Especially the elder brother, Rebe Reb Sussya. "How can one be sad?!" the holy Rebe Reb Sussya would ask in amazement.

"The past—we're certainly not going to start grieving about that; after all it's behind us. The future—none of us knows what's ahead of us, so what's the point of worrying?! And the present?—Why, that's only a very brief moment and then it's gone. Is it really worth while getting upset about it?"

One day Sussya passed a bird-seller's where he saw an enormous cage with any number of singing birds in it. What did Sussya do? He said to himself: David, King of Israel, says in his Psalms: "God taketh pity on all creatures." Saying these words he went and opened the cage. In a trice the little prisoners had flown out of the window into the freedom of God's world.— That, then, was what Sussya did. What about the bird-seller? Well, he seized hold of a stick and started belabouring Sussya as he deserved. Do you suppose Sussya cried at all? Not a bit of it! He broke his sides with laughing!

At another place the ascetic Sussya wished to put his body at the mercy of the ants, so he lay down on an anthill. But the ants did not touch his holy body. Not a single one would bite him. "Lord of the world," moaned Sussya. "What a useless creature I am! Not even the ants want me. . . ."

Sussya was likewise sorry for mother earth and comforted her after this fashion:

"Dear earth, I know that you are worthier than I am, and yet I tread on you. But don't worry! Before you realize it, I shall lie underneath you, and you shall tread on me."

We know, then, how fervently the holy Rebe Reb Sussya loved all kinds of suffering and how gladly he would undergo it. Now, however, you shall learn how God made suffering more intense for His Sussya and in His mercy bestowed it upon him whenever occasion offered.

You have probably heard the story which the Christians relate about their God when He was here on earth with one of His saints. (The Christians also have their saints and tell instructive stories about them.) One day this saint wanted to have some respite from being beaten and asked his Lord to take his place. For this he received more blows. A similar fate once befell our holy brothers during their wanderings. Except that it was somewhat different, having as it were a somewhat different *tip*, or point, as you would say.

One day our two brothers came to a tavern and lay down on the oven to have some peace; the poor fellows were worn out. But they had no peace, because the tavern was full of musicians who danced and shouted and brawled to the point of being disgusting. Suddenly these drunkards remembered that Jew on the oven and decided he ought to be beaten up a bit, the lazy lout. Off they went and grabbed hold of the holy Rebe Reb Sussya, starting with him because he was on the very edge of the oven. They set Sussya on his feet and ordered him to dance for them. The holy Rebe Reb Sussya obeyed, and danced before the musicians like the princess Salome before King Herod. He danced and turned and skipped while they laughed and roared. When he swooned they kept him going with a whip. Nor did they desist until they had the holy Rebe Reb Sussya lying motionless on the floor.

But even musicians are not without a heart. When they saw that the Jew boy could no longer move they threw him back on the oven to get his breath back. After a while the holy Rebe Reb Sussya recovered consciousness. Seeing this, the holy Rebe Reb Melech bent over him and whispered in his ear: "Sussya, my brother, come and lie in my place for a bit and I'll lie in yours." But Sussya would not budge. He would not hear of it. At this the holy Rebe Reb Melech started sobbing and said: "Do you think that you alone have a right to all the suffering of the world? You always want to drink it all yourself and you won't leave a single bitter drop for other people. You don't even want to allow me any, your own brother. Have I not also a little right to some suffering for the glory of God?"—And the holy Rebe Reb Melech whimpered and whined.

Finally the holy Rebe Reb Sussya took pity on his dear brother and gave him his place on the edge of the oven while he himself took his brother's.

"Now let's get going on the other one,"—cried the musicians who by this time had got bored again. So they climbed up on the oven and threw down "the other one".

This other one of course was again our holy Rebe Reb Sussya. He was "in luck". For the drunkards did not notice their mistake. Out came the whip and the holy Rebe Reb Sussya started his dancing a second time. He felt like laughing at the way he had double-crossed his brother, but he knew that to mock the unfortunate is a sin. So he controlled himself and did not laugh at Melech, his brother, having to stay on the oven and look on helplessly while he, Sussya, suffered so nicely for the glory of God. For the second time the holy Rebe Reb Sussya danced his famous dance of the whips. He danced and danced until he again fell to the floor, and the musicians realized that this time their Jew would not regain consciousness so easily.

> However, here below, earth's fate
> May toss and twist and rage,
> The Sussyas' fate was e'er the trait
> Of our hard pilgrimage.

That is how some great poet described it—Vrchlický by name.[1]

As we have mentioned, Sussya was a disciple of the holy Rebe Reb Ber, the Preacher of Mezeritz. But he was a most remarkable pupil, this Sussya! In all the years he spent at Mezeritz he never heard a single exposition of the word of God from the lips of his famous teacher.

The holy Rebe Reb Ber would open the Book and begin to read: "And the Lord said . . ." and that was enough for dear Sussya. He was seized by such ecstasy as soon as he heard those four words that he was unable to listen further. This happened each time. Whenever he heard the words, "The Lord hath spoken . . ." he was carried away in rapture. He would begin to shout at the top of his voice: "The Lord hath spoken. . . ! The

[1] There is a pleasant touch of deliberate understatement here, for Vrchlický, one of Bohemia's greatest poets, is a well-known name, for every Czech. The lines quoted here are in the nature of a jingle. (Translator's note.)

Lord hath spoken. . . !" and would not stop, so that his famous fellow-disciples were obliged to put him out into the courtyard to have some peace and quiet. Sussya offered no resistance. He had no idea at all what was going on. His whole body shook. In the courtyard he would continue his shouting: "The Lord hath spoken, the Lord hath spoken!" and throw himself about like an epileptic. It was always a long time before he quietened down. When he was finally able to return—the master's exposition would already be over long since. Thus it was that Sussya never heard a single exposition by the holy Rebe Reb Ber.

We call this sort of ecstasy *hislahaves*.

In a mystic book called "Tikunim" it is written that Love and Fear are the two wings on which we can soar up to God.

Sussya however had only one wing, although a large and powerful one, needless to say. The second wing never grew properly. Try to fly with one wing! You will not be able to. You'll see.

All through his life Sussya served God solely through Love. But on one occasion he badly wanted to have both wings and serve the Most High with Fear as well, like the angels of God. So he prayed to God to grant him the favour of His fear.

And the Lord heard Sussya's prayer and filled his heart with fear. But do not imagine that as soon as he had two wings Sussya would fly up into the heights like a bird. Quite the contrary! Seized with holy fear before the Lord of all the universe, he crept under his bed like a cowering dog and shivered all over with fear.

"Enough, Lord, enough!" he cried out from under the bed, like Jonah from the depths of the sea. "Take away Thy holy fear from me! I am not able to serve Thee as Thine angels do. I would rather serve Thee again only as ordinary Sussya."

And the merciful God heard Sussya's prayer yet again. The wing was cut off and Sussya crept out from under the bed, and from that time on he served the Lord God only as "ordinary" Sussya, with nothing but pure love.

German Jews have always rather looked down on our Polish

kinsmen. God knows why. They really cannot think all that highly of their learning and still less can they boast of their piety. But at Frankfurt-am-Main there was one man who did indeed have reason to look down upon "the Poles". However, this man did not despise them—on the contrary he was more likely to ridicule his own fellow-countrymen. His name was Rabbi Nathan Adler.

I fear it is probable that you have never yet heard his name. On the other hand you have probably heard the name of his most famous disciple, Rabbi Moyshe Schreiber, the author of that famous book "Chatam Sofer", who was also a native of Frankfurt. Later on he became very famous as the chief Rabbi at Bratislava (Pressburg), more especially on account of the curse he called down on the philosopher Mendelssohn and his translation of the Holy Scriptures into German. In fact he must really have won for himself undying merit through this, for his descendants are clearly so learned by nature that they can straightforwardly inherit the office of head Rabbi in Bratislava, without any difficulty, down to this very day.

Now Rabbi Nathan Adler of Frankfurt was a truly miraculous personality. But we shall not write about him at any great length since he was not a king in our Chassidic Empire. Let us then content ourselves with saying this little bit about him, quite incidentally: Rabbi Nathan Adler knew all the extraordinarily difficult Talmudic discourses by heart, and all his lectures to his pupils were given exclusively from memory. One day this Rabbi Nathan Adler—peace be over him!—made this pronouncement at Frankfurt:

"These Polish Jews are really terrible, the way they push themselves in. Just think: Whenever my soul rises to Heaven, I can always see from far away that Sussya standing in front of the heavenly gate. God alone knows how that man always succeeds in finding his way there, but whenever I come he's always there before I am. There's no doubt these Polish Jews are exceedingly pushing!" he would repeat.

For these words Rabbi Nathan Adler certainly merits my telling you something more about him.

The good people of Frankfurt, you must understand, were not particularly fond of their Rabbi, Nathan Adler. They even went so far as to excommunicate him—but it was only a *minor* excommunication, of course. In consequence, and quite unexpectedly, Nathan Adler had to escape from Frankfurt. For some time he came to be a Rabbi in our country, at Boskowitz in Moravia, where he performed many wonders. As a result of this he had once again to flee to Frankfurt. But in Frankfurt they again excommunicated him, and this time it was a severe excommunication, to boot. And all this merely because he was fond of us Chassidim! What a pity it is that he never completely became one of us! We should have made it hot for those gentlemen at Frankfurt! When he died, the funeral oration over his coffin was given by the holy Rebe Reb Pinchas whom I shall shortly be telling you about.

It is a very strange thing that Rabbi Nathan Adler did not pronounce our holy Hebrew tongue in the same way as we and our forefathers have pronounced it from time immemorial. He spoke it like a *Frenk* in spite of the fact that he was not a *Frenk*.[1] For instance, he did not say "hu-oylom" (world) as we do but pronounced it "ha-olam", just like the *Frenks*. But it is not seemly to relate unpleasant things in recalling the dead, and Rabbi Nathan Adler—peace to his memory!—must surely have been well aware of what he was doing and why he did it, even if our brains are incapable of understanding it.

And now let us take a look at that holy brother of our good Sussya, the holy Rebe Reb Melech.

While the holy Rebe Reb Melech was holding sway at Lizensk the Emperor Joseph II was reigning in Vienna. Relations between the two rulers were strained. *Kire*, that is the Emperor, wanted young Jews to do military service; the holy Rebe Reb Melech, on the other hand, did not so wish. It would not have been difficult for the holy Rebe Reb Melech to break the will of the *Kire* at Vienna. He had no army, no bailiffs and

---

[1] *Frenks* is the name we give to the Jews of oriental, Mediterranean and Balkan countries. Most of them are descendants of exiles from Spain.

no policemen, but he was gifted with the gift of a divine spirit
and the power of holiness, in both of which the Emperor was
lacking. These are qualities against which all earthly powers are
totally unavailing. However, on the side of the Emperor were
almost all the other Rabbis, under the leadership of that most
learned Prague Rabbi, Noda Bi-Yehuda (Ezekiel Landau).
Needless to say even a saint like the holy Rebe Reb Melech was
quite powerless against such superior odds.

Are you wondering why young Jews did not want to do
military service and why our holy Rebe Reb Melech supported
them in this?—

Know, then, that it was certainly not because they did not enjoy the gay life of a soldier. Yakl Prezent, alias Edlman, for instance, had always been as enthusiastic about military service for
the Emperor as neighbour Ivan, alias Potapenko. But Yakl Prezent was aware that in the army he would be compelled to dese-
crate the holy Sabbath, to eat forbidden foods, and even perhaps
be unable to pray. Still less would he be able to study the Law of
God by day and night. Ivan Potapenko had no such worries.
This was the only reason why the holy Rebe Reb Melech made
such mighty efforts to see that Jewish recruits should court
death and sacrifice their young lives rather than join the army
and serve the Emperor. He knew that in this way the Emperor's
plans would be foiled, that the *Kire*, I mean the Emperor, would
have to give way in the end, and Yakl Prezent—known as
Edlman—would be free of the army for all time.

The other Rabbis, on the other hand, maintained that "dine
de-malchusse—dine", that the law of the country is binding and
that defensive war is allowed by the Talmud, nay, that it is our
sacred duty, and that the gracious *Kire* will certainly never em-
bark on an aggressive war, wherever and whatever the issue
may be. In short, the holy Rebe Reb Melech was outvoted by
his learned colleagues and ever since then our good Yakl Prezent
—alias Edlman—has willy-nilly had to do his military service
even if his heart has been torn as a result of his being compelled
to infringe the holy commandments of God. In return he will be
a general when the Messiah comes.

A saint like the holy Rebe Reb Melech, however, does not give in so easily. The *Kire* at Vienna was obliged to carry on a lengthy struggle with him on this issue.

One day the holy Reb Mendele of Rimanov—may the light of his merits protect us!—came to visit Lizensk. When one saint visits another, they partake of soup out of the same dish like brothers. On that holy Sabbath there were many honoured guests at the lunch table at Lizensk—all good Chassidim they were. Every one was admiring the polite way the revered saints were eating their soup. The holy Rebe Reb Melech would wait until his guest had taken a spoonful of soup, and while he was raising the full spoon to his holy mouth, very carefully so that not a single drop should spill, he, that is our holy Rebe Reb Melech, would once again very slightly dip his spoon into the soup, and then his holy guest would again wait until Rebe Reb Melech had taken a spoonful of soup, and so it went on the whole time. Ah well—saints! You could not take your eyes off them. We ordinary Chassidim most certainly do not eat our soup so harmoniously. But our saints—they eat gravely and in silence. Seven spoonfuls of soup had now been consumed by the holy Reb Mendele of Rimanov and seven spoonfuls had been consumed by the holy Rebe Reb Melech. It was now the holy Reb Mendele's turn, and he was due to take his eighth spoonful. He was just about to dip his spoon into the dish when suddenly, quite out of the blue, the holy Rebe Reb Melech seized hold of the cloth, snatched at it and jerked it, and overturned the dish. The entire soup was upset on the table. If it had been the Purim Festival, you would have supposed that the holy Rebe Reb Melech was having a joke. But the holy Rebe Reb Melech was not a joking man, and the day was not Purim.

The holy Reb Mendele of Rimanov turned pale and in his fright the spoon fell from his hand.

"Whatever are you doing," he shouted at the holy Rebe Reb Melech, "do you want to get us locked up?"

"Sh! sh!" interjected the holy Rebe Reb Melech trying to calm his guest, "Don't let us lose our trust in the Almighty!"

At this both the holy Reb Mendele of Rimanov and the Chassidim became sore afraid. What they saw they understood not, and what they heard they likewise understood not.

They would probably never have understood it until the day of their death if it had not chanced that Aaron Shiya happened to be at Vienna on business that day. Less than a week passed when a postilion arrived with a letter from Aaron Shiya to Lizensk. Aaron Shiya wrote to say that he was well, God be praised, and that with God's help his business was prospering. He described how expensive everything was in Vienna, and how much eggs were, and how much feathers were, and how wonderful it was in Vienna and that he, Aaron Shiya, had actually been at the Emperor's castle but that he, Aaron Shiya, would not give in exchange for the castle at Vienna so much as a broken bench leg from Rebe Reb Melech's room at Lizensk—may God grant him long life and health! Next he mentioned that he was looking forward to the possibility of being home at Lizensk for the next holy Sabbath, and then he went on to write a number of other remarkable and important matters, for it was a very long and comprehensive letter, as always with Aaron Shiya's letters. At the end of his letter Aaron Shiya had hurriedly added the following brief postscript:

"I had nearly forgotten the most important news of all. I have learnt from a reliable source that at noon, yesterday, on the holy Sabbath, the Emperor wanted to sign a Letter Patent to the effect that all our sons must go into the army, from which may the merciful God be pleased to save us. The Emperor was about to sign this Letter Patent and had already dipped his pen into the golden inkstand. But just as he was holding his pen in the ink, the golden inkstand, suddenly, totally unexpectedly, upset and the Letter Patent was drowned in ink. This the Emperor declared must be an evil sign and so he refused to sign that Letter Patent. So we shall not be going into the army after all, thank God! This then is all the news, from your unworthy Aaron Shiya."

So that was how it was!—At the very moment when the holy Rebe Reb Melech was sitting round the Sabbath soup with the holy Reb Mendele at Lizensk, the Emperor was sitting with his

ministers at his writing desk in Vienna. And that is why the holy
Rebe Reb Melech—knowing everything in his holy spirit—
deliberately upset the soup at Lizensk, thereby overturning the
imperial inkstand in Vienna at the very same moment. The
Emperor of course had no idea who and what had brought this
about, but he was aware that some mysterious hand was
frustrating all his designs. Only he did not know whose hand.

The good Aaron Shiya had written that with God's help he
would be coming home to Lizensk on the following Sabbath.
But weeks and months passed, like the waters of the Danube,
and Aaron Shiya stayed on in Vienna.

On another occasion the holy Rebe Reb Melech was sitting
at table with the Chassidim at Lizensk. They were sitting and
meditating when the saint suddenly bowed his holy head and
hid his face in his hands, as though he were actually hiding from
somebody. His whole face was hidden by his two hands. Not
even his beard or side-whiskers could be seen, but only his
hands. Whom was he hiding from? There was no one in the room
but themselves, all good Chassidim. It was quite a long while
before the holy Rebe Reb Melech uncovered his face.

At that moment there was a powerful magician visiting the
Emperor at his Vienna castle. This magician was urging the
Emperor to allow him to make use of his magic powers.
The Emperor Joseph had no particular liking for magic. How-
ever since the sorcerer was so pressing he finally gave in:

"All right, so be it!" he said. "Since you are so insistent,
show me what it is that is frustrating all my plans!"

This the Emperor said merely in order to get rid of the
sorcerer. But the magician set to work in earnest, and it was not
long before the Emperor began to see stars. Suddenly he saw. . . .
What did he see?—*Two unknown hands far away in the distance.*
All this was ferreted out by our Aaron Shiya who had friends
everywhere among the clerks, ministers and servants.

As already explained, we do not as a rule write the vowels in
our Hebrew script. If we were to embellish the text of our holy
Torah with vowels, we should not be able to read aloud from it

in the synagogue. The vowel signs are found in prayer books, for instance, which are not for the exclusive use of the learned but are also for children and *amharatzim*, I mean for the uneducated. Those who know the Hebrew language do not need the vowel signs. They can read without them. When written, the vowels appear as follows:

If, for example, we want to show that an "a" is to be read at any given place, we write a little horizontal dash: "—" under the preceding consonant. A short "e" is denoted by three dots under a consonant, like this: "∴". If there are only two ordinary dots under a vowel side by side: ". .", we read it: "ei", and so on.

Do not suppose, however, that these insignificant dots and dashes, the majority of which we do not write at all, are unimportant trifles! Quite the contrary. They hold within them the key to great mysteries, as we have already explained. A person who overlooks these vowels when praying, or who makes mistakes in reading them, will be haunted after death by all the dots and dashes which he has read so carelessly, and will be accused by them before God. So take the same care, when praying, both with the vowel signs and the consonant signs, and you will be saved a great deal of trouble.

The holy book "Tikunim" gives us the following instructions regarding the importance of the dots and dashes used for the vowels: "They seem to be small and insignificant. But the stars in the heavens also seem from afar to be small and insignificant, and yet in reality they are vast worlds."

In the holy books of our Cabbala the ninefold mysteries of the vowel signs are explained in full. The little horizontal dash, "a", under a consonant is the *threshold* before the gate of the Wisdom of God. Those two dots side by side, "ei", are the *origin* and the *aim*, the lofty throne of the Lord from Whom all souls come forth and to Whom they return again (and before Whom the angels tremble in both their wings). The three dots in the form of the *three points of a heart*, "e", are Love. And so on with all these precious signs. But this does not really belong here. I put it in merely to keep the story going.

The holy Rebe Reb Melech did not write any books. But one

day a literary gentleman came to visit him. Like others of his kind, this worthy fellow was incapable of talking of anything else than his own works. When he imagined that he had thoroughly entertained the saint in this way, he asked him, but only out of politeness of course:

"And what about you. Have you got any work in hand?"

"I have," replied the holy Rebe Reb Melech.

"And what is your work to be called?"

"It will be called 'Nekudes Halev' in Hebrew, or 'Die Pinte-lech funm Hartz' in Yiddish. That is: 'The Dots of the Heart.' I have already finished two dots (the ones we write as "ei"), so the first part is complete. Its title is 'Eimes Halev', 'The Fear of the Heart'. Now I've only got to add one dot to it and I shall have— *Emes Halev, The Integrity of the Heart* (for we write 'e' with three dots '∴'). I hope that with God's help I shall finish the work before I die."

On another occasion the holy Rebe Reb Melech received a visit from a man who spent a great deal of time fasting, praying and studying the word of God, but always in secret so that no-body knew anything about it. This man imagined himself to be a saint. When he entered Rebe Reb Melech's room, the holy Rebe Reb Melech quoted a well-known verse from the Holy Scriptures without looking at the fellow.

"If a man were to conceal himself in a hiding-place—and I should not see him?!" Only the holy Rebe Reb Melech did not say the verse in this way. He did not say it with the stress that we normally give it when we read the Holy Scriptures. Instead he slightly delayed the pause, thereby giving the verse an entirely different meaning.

"If a man were to conceal himself in a hiding-place and (his) I—(I) should not see him."

This means that whatever secret merits a man may have, if at the same time he is conscious of his *I*, or if he even imagines he is a saint—then all his fasting and prayer is quite valueless. He is a conceited man and God does not look with favour upon such a man.

The visitor understood the allusion. He felt wretched that he had wasted his whole life merely for his *I* and that all his fasting had been pointless, and he begged Rebe Reb Melech to tell him how he could put matters right.

And the holy Rebe Reb Melech offered him a solution—but a solution such as only a saint, as richly endowed with spiritual piety as he was, could offer.

He commanded him thus:

"From this day forth you may not pray at all, you may not pronounce even the shortest of blessings, until you have completely forgotten your *I*, even if this means that you have to live a whole year without praying."

A true saint is not conscious of his *I*. His soul is permanently linked with the infinite and is continuously merging with it.

One day the holy Rebe Reb Melech came to visit a town, and when he went away he was accompanied by the entire community.

"Where are all these people going behind the carriage?" Rebe Reb Melech asked the coachman.

"They're going with you," the coachman told him.

"But why?"

"Well, they're probably anxious to win merit by paying homage to your learning."

"You don't say!" said the holy Rebe Reb Melech in amazement. Then suddenly he made up his mind:

"If that's how it is, I want to follow their example. I too want to acquire merit."

Thus saying he alighted from the carriage and started walking with the others behind the empty vehicle. . . .

Satan implored the holy Rebe Reb Melech to cease oppressing him. He threatened him that, if he did not stop, he, Satan, would make everybody a Chassid, and what would then remain for Rebe Reb Melech to do in this world? But the holy Rebe Reb Melech dismissed Satan's threat with a wave of the hand.

The devil then set to work.

The ranks of the Chassidim suddenly began to multiply noticeably. All sorts of people became Chassidim. Hundreds and hundreds of souls came in almost every day, until in the end Rebe Reb Melech became really worried. He grasped hold of his stick and went into the House of Study to throw out all who had no business to be there.

But on the threshold of the House of God he stopped short. After all, he thought, it's better to be devilish Chassidim than not to be Chassidim at all.

Moreover the devil soon grew tired of this unusual work, for as time went by the devilish Chassidim became true Chassidim.

Thus they became living proof of the holy truth of the Talmud: "Even he who learns the Law only for material motives ends up by becoming a true idealist. For in the end the light of God that is hidden in the Law will convert every man."

Through his love for his neighbour the holy Rebe Reb Melech once sat in judgment over God Himself. It happened in this wise:

One of the inhabitants of Lizensk was a certain Moyshe Wolf. This man's daughter was dead-set on getting married, but she was unable to amass the necessary four hundred thalers which the Emperor at that time required of his Jewish subjects in return for permission to marry. Moyshe Wolf, not knowing what to do, turned to the holy Rebe Reb Melech. He was quite certain that his misfortune was the work of the Almighty, and something told him that his only hope of redress lay with the court of the holy Rebe Reb Melech.

So he came and said:

"I come to bring a legal action in accordance with the Law."

To pronounce just judgment is infinite merit. A judge who executes just judgment becomes—"a co-worker with God in the construction of the world". Thus it is written in the Talmud. The holy Rebe Reb Melech therefore wasted no time in summoning the two judicial assessors of Lizensk, Reb Yakl Mayr and Reb Duvid Shiya. Then he commanded Moyshe Wolf to bring forward his suit and name the defendant.

Moyshe Wolf launched forth into a detailed explanation about his beloved daughter, about the learned son-in-law whom he had sought out for her, about those confounded four hundred thalers, and so on and so on.

"But why the court?" asked the judges in astonishment. "Whom are you bringing your action against?"

"I accuse," stammered Moyshe Wolf, "I accuse—God."

The assessors drew back in horror. Never before had they heard such insolence! Only the holy Rebe Reb Melech kept his peace.

Whereupon Moyshe Wolf, encouraged by the saint's silence, took courage and elaborated his suit in detail.

Yes, he, Moyshe Wolf, citizen of Lizensk, accused the Lord of all the universe. He accused the Most High of not fulfilling what He had promised by the hand of Moses and the prophets, of not protecting His people of Israel in their bitter exile, of allowing the Emperors and the mighty of this world to invent laws by which they enslaved us and caused him, Moyshe Wolf, to be unable to marry off his daughter.

The holy Rebe Reb Melech stood up and went to the cupboard where his great folio-volumes of the Talmud were kept. He took out one volume and opened it. It was the tractate known as the Chagiga. Then he returned with it to the assessors and pointed out to them what he had found on the very second page.

All three judges inclined their heads over the holy lines.

It stood written there that God had not created the world in order that it should remain desolate but in order that it should be peopled. And it stood written there that he who was so enslaved that he could not take a woman to be his wife should be freed from the hand of his master by the power of the court.

The famous Maimonides shares this opinion with the Talmud and it is also codified in the holy Shulchan Aruch, Volume II, Chapter 267, Section 2. All this the holy Rebe Reb Melech pointed out to his worthy assessors.

There was thus no doubt that both the charge brought forward by Moyshe Wolf, and the reasoning behind it, were not after all without some foundation.

131

"The duty of the court," said the holy Rebe Reb Melech, "is to examine all charges brought before it, whomever they are directed against, and all persons who do not wish to be declared unjust must submit to our judgment. Moyshe Wolf, citizen of Lizensk, do you insist on going through with your suit?"

Moyshe Wolf did insist.

"Well then!" continued the holy Rebe Reb Melech as President of the Lizensk court. "We have heard the case for the prosecution. As for the defendant, that is God, Lord of all the universe, we do not need to hear Him for all His words and all His objections are known to the court from the books of Moses and the prophets. In accordance with the holy Talmudic legal code we now call on the two parties, both the plaintiff and the defendant, to leave the court room while the court considers its findings."

The plaintiff bowed low before the noble court and went out from the court room to the porch. Not so the defendant. Being omnipresent, Almighty God *could* not leave the court room. This of course was very much of an aggravating circumstance for Him.

A rabbinical court is thorough. All the arguments, for and against, were carefully studied, while Moyshe Wolf impatiently kicked his heels in the porch.

Finally they called him in and the holy Rebe Reb Melech— may his Light protect us!—acquainted him with the illustrious decision of the Lizensk court, a court from which there is no appeal.

"Since the defendant, God—may He be praised!—in spite of the court regulations in force, did not leave the court room while the court was considering its findings, and because, further, the plaintiff is clearly in the right, in accordance with Section 2, Chapter 267 of the second part of the Shulchan Aruch, the court, after careful consideration of all extenuating circumstances, resolves unanimously and irrevocably that the defendant shall bear the full consequences of the sentence which the Law requires to be passed upon Him. The court recognizes as just all the claims of the plaintiff, that is Moyshe Wolf, citizen of Lizensk, against the defendant, that is God, Lord of all the universe, and charges the most illustrious accused to be pleased graciously to respect these most humble claims."

Moyshe Wolf no longer had to go in search of his four hundred thalers. Three days after the memorable judgment of the Lizensk court, the Emperor Joseph II repealed the inhuman laws against the Jews by his Edict of Toleration. The red dawn of freedom began to appear for all the oppressed, among whom were the sorely tested Jews.

The holy Rebe Reb Melech had also been a young man once. In his youth he often used to walk from the town to a nearby village. His way took him through a forest. One spring day he stayed in the village rather later than usual, and it was already night when he returned through the forest. Melech was unafraid. He knew no fear save before Almighty God. The forest murmured sadly and mysteriously. Melech continued on his way stumbling from time to time over tree stumps. The forest seemed never to end, but Melech had no fear. None the less a strange feeling overcomes a person who walks alone at night through a deep forest. At last Melech saw a light in the distance. As he drew closer, the light grew. A human dwelling!—Had he lost his way? He had never noticed anybody living in the forest before. A few more steps and Melech pushed aside a branch and found himself in a glade. And lo! in the middle of the glade was a cottage, beautifully painted like a toadstool. By now Melech was able to see without difficulty. The moon was shining as sweetly as the cottage window. Melech walked in—and stood on the threshold as though bewitched. At first he thought he must be dreaming. Never in his life had he seen such beauty. In the middle of the room stood a young girl. She was almost naked and yet seemed quite unashamed. Her golden hair reached down to the ground. Dear God, how long it was! She was evidently still a maiden, since her hair was not cut like that of married Jewish women.

"Yes," she said, "I am single and live entirely alone here. I have often watched you going through the forest—always so alone, like me. I have often wondered when you would come and see me. But you have always continued on your way without heeding me at all. Be not shy, I am clean, I have bathed at a spring in the forest, and I have long since had a soft bed ready. No, I am not learned, but this much at least I know: the sin will be only a slight one, but the enjoyment will be abundant, oh so abundant. Come!"

Her voice sounded as sweet as the silver bells on the parchment scroll of the Law of God, on festival days in the synagogue, but at the same time it was as powerful as the throb of blood in Melech's temples. Only gradually did Melech grasp the meaning of the words that flowed from her red lips, like little wavelets on a brook.

He stood still, not knowing what was happening to him. Can God take pleasure in such a union, when there is no Rabbi's blessing, no wedding ring, and no wedding canopy?!

"Come! I have bathed at the spring, I have made ready the softest of beds, the enjoyment will be abundant."

The girl's hair quivered like the forest grass fanned by a spring breeze. On the tips of her breasts something seemed to grow red, like two strawberries under their leafy green.

"No!" shouted Melech. It was the shout of a drowning man.

"No-o!" came the deep echo from the forest.

Then Melech found himself alone, so alone, on the green forest sward. The girl had disappeared and the cottage seemed to have fallen together. Only a cluster of glow-worms was to be seen, dancing their mysterious dance in the thick grass.

Mere temptation it had been, a delicious prelude devised by Satan, like everything else that leads us astray in this world, to make us sin, and forget God.

The holy Rebe Reb Melech did not forget Him. May the Light of his merits protect us!

We have a precious reminder of the holy Rebe Reb Melech —the sermons in which he expounded the Five Books of Moses every Sabbath, throughout the long years of his blessed life. They were faithfully taken down by the Chassidim and published under the title "Noam Elimelech", that is, "The Delights of Elimelech".

When the transcripts were submitted for Rebe Reb Melech's approval, he cried:

"What's this? Have I preached all this?!"

During his sermons he was wont to be in a state of such profound ecstasy that he was not conscious of the meaning of his words.—

The Torah is divided into fifty-four sections for the fifty-two weeks of the year. On each Sabbath the reader at the synagogue reads one section, and sometimes two sections. The holy Rebe Reb Melech preached sermons on all the sections of the Torah except one. Throughout all the years there was one week in the year when he never preached—the week in which we always read the last but one section of the second book of Moses. And it was in this very week—on the 21st day of the month of Adar (1786)—that the holy Rebe Reb Melech passed away.

FROM "THE DELIGHTS OF ELIMELECH"

—At all times and at every moment, but especially in moments which a man spends in solitude and inactivity, or when he lies on his bed unable to sleep, he should imagine a large and terrible fire blazing before him, reaching up to the sky. And he, a human being, should imagine himself overcoming his natural instinct for self-preservation and hurling himself into the flames for the glory of God. The merciful God looks upon purposeful determination as being equal to deeds. A man must never be idle but must continually fulfil God's holiest commandment: "I shall be sanctified in the hearts of the sons of Israel."— Sanctified through their self-sacrifice at least in thought.—A man must have the same thought in mind at meal-times and during sexual intercourse. Whenever he experiences bodily delight, he must say with heart and mouth that he would feel a far greater sweetness, a much more lovely delight, than this sensual one, if he were allowed to offer his life for God. He must prove to himself that to die for the glory of God would be

sweeter to him than any other delight. He must tell himself that
to die for the glory of God is more beautiful than any physical
experience, and that even if he were to be dragged away from his
food, or from sexual intercourse, and tortured in the most
horrible way, a martyr's death would be more welcome to him
than any physical enjoyment. But let everyone see to it that his
thoughts are sincere and genuine, for the all-knowing God
cannot be deceived.—

—Because of His boundless love for living creatures, God has
performed an infinite miracle in that He has created them from
nothing, thereby violating the age-old laws of logic and nature.
However, there is a still greater miracle: that God in His love
for some creatures *destroys* other creatures. For if in creating the
world God acted merely against the laws of nature, without
thereby violating *His essential nature*, namely His love, in this
other thing, namely *the destruction* of His creatures, He acts
against the natural character of His own godly person, that is,
against love. It is for this reason that the miraculous departure of
the Israelites from Egypt was a greater wonder than the creation
of the world. In order to save Israel God destroyed others of His
creatures, the Egyptians, by a direct act of interference in the
world order, in disharmony with His own creative love. He
thereby acted against the character of His own person and nature
and not only against the mere laws of Nature which He created.
It is for this reason that the Holy Scriptures remind us more
often of the wondrous departure from Egypt than of the
creation of the world.—

—The souls of women come to this earth from higher worlds
than the souls of men. The Law therefore sets women free from
those commandments whose fulfilment is limited to a particular
period, to a particular time of day or season. For the world in
which the souls of women have their origin is raised above the
conception of time.—

—It seems to us that the saints live side by side with us on this
earth. But in reality this is not so! They are like the sun which
gives us warmth but stays permanently in the heavens.—

—If a man does not want the light of his soul to be absorbed in the infinite light of God after his death and sink into it without trace, it is up to him to obtain as much merit as possible during his earthly life, for all merit is a source of Light, as the Scriptures say—Light which never goes out. And if a man adds merit to the little spark of his soul, then his soul becomes so powerful a Light that not even the Infinite will swallow it up and it will never be absorbed.—

—When we see something beautiful, or when we taste something good, let us be aware that that *pleasant taste* and that beauty are—*God* Himself.

Wherefore you who wish to live, enter with me into another Gate, for there you shall read:

—how the brothers quarrelled when they became famous, how they finally crossed the threshold and heard a parable—how devout they were and how they honoured Sussya—how we have to be courageous and how even people can be angels—next how the people of Mikulov gave Shmelke a great welcome—and how they made a fool of him—how a devout young man does well to act as an unbeliever in one matter at least, or how Rebe Reb Shmelke gave away every little thing he had and called back a beggar—about Rebe Reb Shmelke's vigil, or the prophet Elias's candle—and how even our sleep is a form of service to the Creator—how a saint sailed among the ice-floes and had no fear of the Danube—and how he sang a song—whereupon there follows an account of how the Emperor kept his eye on him and fulfilled his request—how the holy Rebe Reb Shmelke was able to bring to life people who had died many centuries before —whereupon a ghastly story is related—how his brother cared not for this world, or an account of all he wrote at Frankfurt.

The Sixth Gate

Two pillars of the Law of God,
two wondrous candles of heavenly light.
Mystic twain of the eternal azure
from one father,
noble in birth,
humble in spirit
and pure in heart.

Our teacher and our master

THE HOLY REBE REB SHMELKE OF MIKULOV

and our teacher and our master

THE HOLY REBE REB PINCHAS OF FRANKFURT

faithful and holy brothers, inseparable in life and death.

Hear all that they suffered—
how they fought for us sinners—brave as lions,
that we may live devoutly for ever—
and fulfil the will of God—and perish not.

May they protect us for evermore by the Light of their merits!

THE SIXTH GATE

Many a place in Bohemia and Moravia has been hallowed by the steps of saints and thinkers—men who were so learned, so steeped in the Talmud and the Cabbala, that it is almost impossible for us to imagine them nowadays. Yet today, for the most part, the only testimony on this earth to the one-time glory of these eminent people is a mere few lines, a short mention in a history book. Sometimes only a decaying granite stone in some deserted country cemetery will tell us, through its barely legible Hebrew inscription, of the distinguished savant "hidden" underneath, and these few words carved in stone must suffice to tell us of his life, his work and tribulations.

But some of these long since departed are still vividly remembered. The sound of their words is still to be heard, if not in our country, then at least somewhere to the east, far from the borders of the Lands of the Czech Crown. The names of some Czech and Moravian towns—and not merely the most important—are known to Jewish children in Eastern Europe as places where distinguished Rabbis once worked in centuries long past.

One such place was Mikulov in Moravia. Many a learned man has contributed to the fame of the great Jewish community that used once to live here. Rabbi Loev himself was Rabbi at Mikulov before he came to Prague. But we are more especially interested in Rabbi Shmelke Levi Horovitz. To this day those who chance to visit Mikulov are shown with piety and pride the tombstone, the House of Prayer, and the room where Rabbi Shmelke used to study the Cabbala.

At no time did the mystic wave of Chassidism sweep beyond the borders of the Slav countries of Eastern Europe to the west. In the territory that once belonged to the Magyars, where Reb Moyshe Teitelbaum worked at Ihel (Uihely) and Reb Yitzhak Eisik Taub at Kalev, the spread of Chassidism was for the most part merely on paper. Only the Horovitz brothers, Pinchas and Shmelke, descendants of our Prague Rabbi, Pinchas, succeeded in penetrating any farther to the west.

I am going to tell you what I have heard and read about these saintly brothers in the old Hebrew books.

The younger brother, Pinchas, became chief Rabbi at Frankfurt-am-Main, the older, Shmelke, at our town of Nikolsburg, or Mikulov. How this came about is worth noting.

The two rabbinical chairs fell vacant at the same time and as a result the two famous brothers received the offers of the two towns simultaneously.

"You go to Frankfurt!" Shmelke advised the younger Pinchas. "You are more important than I am, and Frankfurt is a bigger town than Nikolsburg."

"No, no!" said Pinchas. "You shall go to Frankfurt! You are more important and you are older, too. I'll go to Nikolsburg. In either case it's too great an honour for me."

The two brothers argued for a long time as to which of them should go where. For each thought more highly of the other than of himself. Finally they decided to travel to their teacher, the holy Rebe Reb Ber of Mezeritz, and do whatever he decided. They had wanted to go and see him in any case to ask him to expound a particular passage that was not clear to them in the mystic book, the "Zohar".

When they reached Mezeritz, a further argument broke out between them on the very threshold of the saint's house.

"You go first, since you're more important than I am!" said Shmelke to Pinchas.

"No!" retorted Pinchas angrily. "You must go first. You are the more important."

As they were quarrelling thus, the holy Rebe Reb Ber suddenly thrust his head through the window and shouted:

"Let the one who's going to be Rabbi at Nikolsburg go in first. He is the more distinguished."

Shmelke quickly stepped in first. It was not that he considered himself the better man, but he wanted his brother to become

Rabbi at the larger town, Frankfurt. There was nothing Pinchas could do. If he had gone in first, Shmelke would have become Rabbi at Frankfurt. But it would have looked as though he, Pinchas, considered himself to be the better man. That was a thought he could not bear. In short it was decided. The younger brother Pinchas, was made Rabbi at the famous town of Frankfurt, the older Shmelke, at little Mikulov—which also of course meant that he became head Rabbi for the province of Moravia.

The holy Rebe Reb Ber then received the brothers duly "reconciled". He congratulated them on their new positions and proceeded to tell them a delightful story about a prince who ruled an immense empire with the help of his nobles. When he had finished, he sent the brothers on their way in peace.

They returned to the inn. Here they suddenly remembered that they had wanted to inquire of the holy Rebe Reb Ber as to the meaning of that puzzling passage in the Zohar. They were much annoyed at having forgotten to ask. Suddenly they recalled the story the saint had told them about the prince. As they pondered upon it, lo and behold! the passage in the Zohar became instantly clear to them. The story of the prince had been a parable which had explained everything.

On an earlier occasion they went to Mezeritz to ask the holy Rebe Reb Ber to expound the Talmudic commandment which bids us to praise God for all that is evil as full-heartedly as we praise Him for all that is good.

The saint told them:

"Go to the House of Study and seek out my pupil Sussya. Ask him about it! He'll be able to tell you best." So the brothers went to look for Sussya.

Dear God, what a sorry fellow he was! On his body, dreadfully emaciated from hunger and want, hung the few rags that served him for clothes. His whole appearance showed that his life was nothing but privation and tribulation.

"How can it be that we are to praise God as much for all that is evil as we do for all that is good?" asked the brothers.

"I really can't explain that to you," said the pitiful Sussya, lost in thought. "To tell you the truth, you see, nothing *evil* has ever befallen me yet. . . ."

There is no evil in the world. In reality, everything is good. *All that matters* is whether we accept our lot with love, humility and resignation, like our good Rebe Reb Sussya.

It was Sussya who led the two brothers on the Chassidic road to salvation. They had originally been disciples of one of the greatest opponents of the Chassidim, Rabbi Elijah "Goen" (Gaon) of Vilna, and at first our Chassidic customs were quite contrary to their ideas. They could not understand the holy Rebe Reb Ber's way of life. The holy Rebe Reb Ber, you must understand, painstakingly concealed his deeds from the eyes of the world; in consequence he seemed to the uninitiated to be an absolutely ordinary person. Sussya opened the brothers' eyes. Through him they learnt that even the Lord's angels can live on this earth as ordinary people.

The brothers quickly penetrated to the most secret depths of Chassidism. It was not long before their fervent piety spread to the other pupils of Rebe Reb Ber.

Whereupon the holy Rebe Reb Ber said:

"Up to now my house has been full of candles, but the candles have not been lit. Now two little sparks have fallen on them— and all the candles are lit."

When he finally left Mezeritz, Rebe Reb Shmelke said:

"At first I fasted a great deal, wanting to teach my body how to bear the light of the soul. But at Mezeritz, where I experienced so many wonderful things, my soul learnt to bear with the darkness of the body."

The people of Mikulov had prepared a tumultuous welcome for the new Rabbi. The speeches were all ready.

First, however, the holy Rebe Reb Shmelke asked to be left alone for a moment. When they had gone, he started welcoming himself with speeches in praise of his learning and piety. He spoke in a loud voice and the men in the next room heard everything.

"It's like this——" he told them afterwards by way of explanation, "when you come to do me honour, I shall hear so many eulogies from your lips that I might get proud if I were to believe them—and God preserve me from that! So first of all I say the praises over to myself. This is the best way for me to see how ridiculous and untrue all these comedies of welcome are."

Rebe Reb Shmelke was received in Mikulov with great enthusiasm and pomp, it cannot be denied, but life there was never a bed of roses for him. The people of Mikulov had caught the scent of western enlightenment and were not inclined to be friendly disposed towards the mystical strivings of a Chassidic Rabbi from the East. His relationship with the people was clouded by one habit of his in particular. Unlike the other Rabbis he would not speak Yiddish, still less German. As a rule he used only pure Hebrew, and at that time the educated people of Mikulov were almost entirely ignorant of the language of the prophets. Often enough the discord was such as to make necessary the intervention of the holy Rebe Reb Melech of Lizensk, who was an expert at finding a way to speak to any man, even to the worst of sinners. In fact Rebe Reb Melech was always able, if not to bring about a permanent settlement of the various arguments that arose at Mikulov, at least to achieve some temporary reconciliation.

One day some Mikulov swells were baiting Rebe Reb Shmelke.

"You must allow, Rabbi, that we have one great advantage over you Poles."

"Oh, how is that?" asked the holy Rebe Reb Shmelke, somewhat astonished.

"We are always absolutely clean and you won't find a single dirty mark on our clothes. But with your fellow-countrymen, even if they are learned Rabbis, the dirt literally drips from them. Yet it is written in the Talmud that a learned man commits a mortal sin if he allows a dirty mark to stay on his clothes."

"You're right!" replied Rebe Reb Shmelke readily. "That is

indeed written in the Talmud. It is also written that cleanliness is the first of the steps leading to a holy spirit. For us Polish Jews it is never impossible to acquire a holy spirit. That's what the Devil's afraid of, and that's why he makes it so difficult for us from the very outset. He does his best to stop us reaching even the lowest, first step: cleanliness. With you there's no danger of your ever acquiring the gift of a holy spirit, so the Devil can calmly let you live in bodily cleanliness and rely upon you. He knows you don't care a fig for piety. So just be nice and clean!"

At every step we are in duty bound to trust in God's help and encourage both ourselves and our neighbours to have faith in the Most High. How many times a day do we cry out in our troubles, "God help me!"? There's no counting how often. Yes, we must at all times hope and comfort our neighbours, even though we know what sinners we all are and that we do not deserve God's help. But the grace of God knows no bounds. Only unbelievers do not know this. How much they are to be pitied for this! How sad must their lives be! No, it is not even life! It is death—death without hope, without the light of Faith. God save us from so wretched a life! However, in one thing— so the holy Reb Samson of Ostropol tells us—even we are obliged, in fact we are all obliged, to be absolute *unbelievers*! Yes, unbelievers, without a thought for God's help. In one instance it would be a sin to say: "God help me!" namely, when a poor man comes to us and asks for alms. We may not simply rebuff him with a few empty words of consolation and call upon God to help him. Far from it. In this instance we are not allowed to say anything, we must "open up our hand for our poor, unfortunate brother, and give and give", as it is written by the hand of Moses. In this instance, then, we really must be "unbelievers". Hence the injunction of the holy Reb Samson of Ostropol: Be unbelievers!

It goes without saying that our Rebe Reb Shmelke also put this principle into practice. And how thoroughly he did so! In those days the Rabbis at Mikulov received considerable incomes. But there was never much money at the house of the holy Rebe

Reb Shmelke. Every single beggar who knocked at the door was rewarded so liberally that Rebe Reb Shmelke and his family had hardly a bean left. All the money he received during the day was given away to the poor ere sunset. By the time the stars came out, not even a single brass farthing was allowed to be left in his house. The holy Baal-Shem had set him a glowing example in such behaviour. If by any chance there was no money to hand, the holy Rebe Reb Shmelke would even give away the furniture fittings, if need be. Whatever it was possible to give, in fact.

To one beggar he presented a precious ring.

"What have you gone and done this time?!" moaned Mrs. Shaindl-Bine, Rebe Reb Shmelke's ever harassed wife. "Why, that ring cost four hundred Rhenish ducats!"

Mrs. Shaindl-Bine was also infinitely saintly, to be sure. May the Light of her merits protect us! Given to good works and full of charity. She would have shared her very heart with the poor. But four hundred Rhenish ducats were four hundred Rhenish ducats. You can't just throw them away.

The holy Rebe Reb Shmelke paused a moment. To his wife's delight he gave orders for the beggar to be called back at once.

"Listen," he told him, "I've just learnt that the value of that ring is four hundred Rhenish ducats. Be careful! When you come to sell it, don't let anybody swindle you. . . ."

Rebe Reb Shmelke had another peculiar habit. In one respect he was like the Comte de Lautréamont: he hardly ever slept. The whole time he did nothing but study and meditate. If now and again he did decide to have a short rest, he would not lie down on a bed but slept sitting so as not to lose too much time.

Rebe Reb Pinchas tried to imitate his brother and do without sleep. But he did not succeed. Like a good brother, Rebe Reb Shmelke explained to him what was the reason for his failure:

"It's because my soul comes from the world of the eternal Sabbath whereas your soul comes from the world of the eternal new moon."

Miriam, their sister, related this story about Rebe Reb Shmelke:

"One night, after being awake for several days, he bowed his head and fell asleep. When he awoke after a short while, he noticed that his candle had gone out. Being afraid lest he might have to interrupt his study for a while, he went out of the little attic room, to the roof of the house, still half asleep, with the extinguished candle in his hand. Lo! As he reached the roof, an unknown hand gave him a light. Rebe Reb Shmelke lighted his candle, and without giving a thought to the donor of the light and the other unusual circumstances, returned to his book.

"A moment later, however, it occurred to him that something unusual had happened. Who was it who had offered him a light? Nobody could reach from the ground to the roof, and there was no ladder.

"Then the holy Rebe Reb Shmelke prayed to God, and it was revealed to him that the interruption of his studies had been felt in Heaven as a grievous loss, so the prophet Elijah had been sent down to bring him a light.

"When the holy Rebe Reb Shmelke heard this, he wept. Afterwards he fasted many days because he, who was so unworthy, had caused the prophet so much inconvenience on his behalf."

But healthy sleep is a gift of God. One day Rebe Reb Shmelke was obliged to recognize this. He had invited the holy Rebe Reb Melech of Lizensk to Mikulov. Melech himself made the master's bed, smoothed out his pillows and begged him for once to have a good night's sleep. Rebe Reb Shmelke could not say no to such an honoured guest. He slept all night and when he awoke in the morning he felt more fresh and fit than he had ever felt before.

After taking his bath as usual, he went to pray in the House of Prayer. . . ! Never before had the old synagogue at Mikulov heard such beautiful prayers!

At the end of the service he observed:

"Now I know that God can be served by sleep as well."

Nobody can fathom the mysteries of the thoughts of the holy
Tsaddikim in the hour when they stand in prayer before the
face of the Most High. Here, in his own words, is an account
given by an eyewitness, Reb Moyshe Teitelbaum, concerning
the holy Rebe Reb Shmelke:
"He was praying at the *bimah* on a festival day and pondering
on the loftiest of mysteries. All the while he kept singing long
and continually fresh melodies of wondrous beauty, such as no
human ear has ever heard or ever will hear. It was evident that
he was himself not aware what he was singing—while his
spirit stayed in the heights, his voice drew miraculous songs
from his lips, inexpressibly sweet to all who heard them."

The Emperor at that time was busy preparing a new ordinance.
Had it come into force this new measure would have meant the
end of the holy community at Mikulov. So the holy Rebe Reb
Shmelke set out for Vienna to intercede with the Emperor. He
was accompanied by one disciple only, Moyshe Yide Leib,
who later became Rabbi at Sassov.
It was spring. The ice had just started breaking on the Danube,
and no ferryman would undertake to cross the swollen river.
Nothing daunted, Rebe Reb Shmelke would not give up his
intention of seeing the Emperor. The very existence of the entire
community was at stake. Who would have hesitated to risk his
life?! So they decided to cross the river themselves. But nobody
would lend them a boat. However, there was a fellow there, who
looked like a baker, carrying a kneading-trough. "I'll lend you
my kneading-trough," said this man, "you can launch out on
the Danube in it if you want." He said this only to tease them,
but there was no teasing the holy Rebe Reb Shmelke. "All
right!" he said. He put the kneading-trough in the water, and he
and Reb Moyshe Leib got into it. Naturally they could not sit
down; there is not enough room in a kneading-trough. So they
navigated standing up. The holy Rebe Reb Shmelke started up
the old song which Moses sang with the Israelites, when they

fled from Egypt through the Red Sea, and which he will again sing with us after the resurrection from the dead. Reb Moyshe Leib of Sassov joined in with his teacher.

> *"I sing to God—He has risen up,*
> *Smitten horse and rider into the sea.*
> *God—is song and defiance.*
> *Hear, God of my fathers, I worship Him. . . ."*

Behold, no sooner had the first words of this holy song rung out over the waves of the Danube than the kneading-trough disengaged itself from the bank, respectfully avoided by the ice-floes which seemed to have been touched by the magic of the song.

> *"At the breath of Thy nostrils the waters heap up, O God,*
> *The waves tower like castles, the torrent stiffens in the*
> *bowels of the sea."*

The little kneading-trough sailed on with our saints, sailed on among the ice, and as it approached the other side, the sensation-loving Viennese gathered on the bank to gaze at the unfamiliar spectacle and cheer it on bravely. But we take no notice of them, the rascals.

> *"May the abysses of the sea swallow them up,*
> *May they sink like a stone in the depths!*
> *Destroy all Thine enemies with Thy pride,*
> *Let Thy wrath blaze forth and consume them like straw!"*

Even the Emperor, disturbed by the shouting, got down from his throne to observe the remarkable sight with his ministers from a window in the palace.

> *"May they be seized by horror and dread*
> *Ere Thy people reach the other shore, O God,*
> *Thy people who belong to none save to Thee!*
> *May the Lord reign for ever and ever, ever and ever. . . ."*

The song ended. The kneading-trough hove to safely, and lo! there was the Lord Emperor welcoming our sailors. The holy

community of Mikulov was saved! This Emperor was an unusual fellow. We have had occasion to mention him already.
His name was Joseph, and as chance would have it he was
reigning at the time on behalf of his mother, Mrs. Maria
Theresa.

One day, the holy Reb Chayyim of Sanz (Nový Sandec) related how the holy Rebe Reb Shmelke once raised a man from
the dead. The Talmudists among those present shook their
heads over this story.

The holy Reb Chayyim waxed indignant:

"If anybody told me that the holy Rebe Reb Shmelke of
Nikolsburg had gone through a cemetery several hundred
years old and brought to life as many as a hundred of the dead
people lying there, I should believe him and I shouldn't go
shaking my head."

And the Seer of Lublin said:

"I've been studying at Nikolsburg for eighteen years and I
can't remember a single moment when the holy Rebe Reb
Shmelke was not lost in thought of God."

The holy Rebe Reb Shmelke departed from this world on
the second day of the month of Iyar, 5538 (1778). Incarnate in
him was the soul of the prophet Samuel.

His successor at Mikulov was his disciple, Reb Mordecai
Bannett, author of several Talmudic dissertations, the most
famous of which is his exposition on the writings of his mediaeval
namesake, Mordecai. Reb Mordecai Bannett was an astonishing man, both during his lifetime and after his death. Time and
again the holy community of Mikulov lay in ashes, but one
house in it was always consistently unaffected, being avoided by
the flames.

At that time this house belonged to a good Christian to whom
the holy Reb Mordecai Bannett had given his blessing on
account of some kindness. This blessing survived for centuries
and protected the house from the horrors of fire. May it also
protect us and the roofs over our heads from all evil (—may it

never come!—) so that we may live in peace to see the Messiah come soon and even in our lifetime, with all the faithful of Israel, AMEN!

Rebe Reb Shmelke did not write much. Only his expositions on the Five Books of Moses have come down to us, annotated by his disciple, the holy Reb Yisruel of Koznitz, in his terse style and called "Divre Shemuel" (The Words of Samuel.)

His brother Pinchas of Frankfurt, on the other hand, was a distinguished literary figure who wrote seven books in all, the most famous being his "Haflaa". In his old age Rebe Reb Pinchas went blind with cataract. He had himself operated on one eye only, saying that it was unnecessary to look at this world and that one eye was enough for him to serve God with.

He died in the year 5562 (1802)—may the Light of his merits protect us!

There is something very important I had nearly forgotten. The holy Rebe Reb Shmelke was also able to read the future:

In the holy community of Mikulov there lived at that time a man who had once been wealthy but who had lost all his property. This man kept on importuning the holy Rebe Reb Shmelke to write him out some sort of certificate which would make it clear that he was not just any old beggar but a worthy citizen. Armed with this piece of paper he intended to start wandering from place to place, in the sure knowledge that no fellow-believer, confronted with such a sacred document, would ever drive him away from his threshold, poor man. But Rebe Reb Shmelke would not give him the certificate he asked for, saying that he would rather support him all his life than do something which would most probably result in a great deal of evil. Realizing that he was unlikely to have any success with the holy Rebe Reb Shmelke of Mikulov by honest methods, the man, without properly considering the matter, decided on a scheme that was certainly far from praiseworthy. He applied to a certain person of exalted rank with the humble request that he should most graciously prevail upon the saint to do what he wanted. The nobleman, who remembered the suppliant from the time when he had been well off, duly granted his request. Much against his will, the holy Rebe Reb Shmelke was thus obliged to fulfil his ill-considered wish, whereupon the man collected the certificate and started out on his wanderings without further delay. As it turned out, luck was indeed on his side. In a few years he had begged so much money that he was quite sure that the people of Mikulov would welcome him as the richest man among them as soon as he returned to his Moravian fatherland.

All went well until one day he happened to meet a journey-man on the road. (That honourable beggar's guild.) This gentle-man, seeing the document signed by the holy Rebe Reb Shmelke, insisted that our compatriot should give it to him and in return he would give him his purse as a souvenir—full, of course, as it should be. As you might expect, the worthy citizen of Mikulov granted the journeyman's request—out of friendly solidarity, so to speak. (By that time, of course, the holy Rebe Reb Shmelke of Mikulov was no longer among the living: this too requires to be mentioned.) The two men then took respect-ful leave of each other and went their separate ways.

The journeyman, poor fellow, had not travelled far after this when he fell seriously ill. None of the quacks who examined him was able to help him. On the third day he died, and the kindly people buried him. As they were putting him in his winding-sheet they found the holy Rebe Reb Shmelke's certi-ficate in his pocket. Without wasting a moment, they dispatched the document to Mikulov so that the people there should know that they had buried their worthy citizen. (Or so they supposed.) When the paper reached Mikulov, there was no reason for the people to suppose anything else than that their fellow citizen had indeed met his death. Meanwhile, of course, ignorant of what had happened, the fellow continued his wandering through the world a healthy man, confident that he would be able to keep his children by begging, even without the document. But his efforts were in vain; no one gave him anything and in due course the poor man spent all the money he had acquired by begging. Finally, after seven years of hunger and deprivation, he returned home as he had set out, without a bean.

Now let us hear what had been happening at Mikulov in the

mean time. When the false report about his death reached the community, his faithful wife was exceedingly sorrowful, for she imagined herself to be a widow. Whereupon she wasted no time and hastened to get married again to a second husband and bear him three children—without having taken leave of the first. Three *mamzerim*! How terrible that is, I will tell you. Through no fault of their own, such children are destined to suffer a cruel existence all their life. Let him who is a *mamzer* never enter the married state; let him be cursed and despised until the end of his days! Thus saith our divine Law. In such Spartan fashion do we protect the pure flame of our family life.

In short, to bring this sad tale to an end: when our good pilgrim returned home and all of a sudden saw these urchins—his heart burst with grief and he died in that very moment. All this had been brought on by that fateful certificate. It had all been foreseen by the holy Rebe Reb Shmelke in his holy spirit seven years before it happened—what other reason could there have been at that time why he should have refused so resolutely to give the poor fellow the testimonial he asked for?—The holy Rebe Reb Shmelke!—May his merits protect us and our descendants from all evil for evermore, AMEN!

The other day I heard that some of those writer chaps— the modern ones, whose books we Chassidim refuse to have anything to do with—have got this story all jumbled up and made novels out of it. They have not, however, had the courtesy to acknowledge where they got it from: *our Chassidic Empire!* (Ah well, I suppose they must have forgotten.)

FROM THE WISDOM OF THE
HOLY REBE REB SHMELKE

The holy Reb Avrom Chayyim of Zlotchov, author of "Orah la-Chayyim" (The Road to Life), once asked the holy Rebe Reb Shmelke how we could possibly love our neighbour as ourselves at times when our "neighbour" did us harm.

"The answer to that question is to be found in the final words of this commandment of God: . . . *as thyself*," the holy Rebe

Reb Shmelke told him. "All souls together form one indivisible whole—one body of the spiritual nature of love and wisdom, which in the Cabbala is called 'The Soul of Adam'—and each human soul is only a member, one of the spiritual limbs or organs, of this spiritual whole. If you hit your own hand or kick your own leg, will you then punish your hand or leg? And if you do something stupid with your head, you would be mad to box your own ears on that account. If then somebody does you harm, remember that all souls are linked and that you and your neighbour are really part of one supra-personal *I*, in the same way as your hand, leg and head are all part of one body. If you remember this, can you then be angry with *yourself*?"

And how can we love those who sin against God?

"All souls are sparks of divinity. If a spark of the eternal God falls into the mud and mire, shall we not be sorry? Shall we not help it to free itself again and shine with all its lustre? Of course we shall, it is a part of God Himself!"

For our generation:

"I have compared thee, O my love, to a company of horses in Pharaoh's chariots."—This is a simile used by the divine Bridegroom in Solomon's Song of Songs to address his Bride, the holy Community of Israel. At the same time these words have a special significance for our generation. In the normal course of affairs, one sees living beings pulling lifeless things behind them, and not lifeless things pulling living beings behind them. This *did* happen, however, when the Israelites crossed the Red Sea. The chariots—that is, lifeless things—pulled Pharaoh's horses and riders after them into the sea, that is, living beings.—This of course was not natural. What is natural is that a living being should pull a lifeless thing, as it used to be in days gone by—for in days gone by people considered spiritual uplift to be more important than material well-being. In other words, in the past, the Spirit, that is life, used to pull matter after it. Spiritual things came before material things. But in our generation the exact opposite is the case. People today look upon material experience as more important than the needs of the soul. In other words, dead matter pulls living beings after it—as it did when Pharaoh's chariots dragged the horses and riders after them into the abysses of the sea. . . .

And now something for Kierkegaard:

The significance of Abraham's testing lies not in the fact that his obedience to the Lord's command made him prepared to offer up his only son for love of God, but in the way he behaved when God ordered him to set his son free and let him live. In other words, its significance lies in the fact that God declined the offering the moment after He had demanded it. If Abraham had rejoiced because the life of his beloved son was saved, or if he had grieved because he had not been allowed to show his love for God by actually carrying out his sacrifice—in either of these cases he would have failed the test.

But Abraham rejoiced—as can be seen from a careful reading of the Scriptures—that, in carrying out God's new command, to spare his son, he was allowed to bring to God a still greater sacrifice than the actual offering up of Isaac would have been. In being prepared to offer his son to God, he showed that for him the command to sacrifice was something even higher than his love for his child. But when God gave His second command, Abraham gave up the performance of this sacrifice, in other words, he sacrificed even that sacrifice which had previously become so dear to him, for this was the only way he could show his infinite love to the Creator. He rejoiced in the new sacrifice whose significance lay essentially in the fact that he had renounced the offering up of his son. This is the climax of his testing.

And for Einstein:

Each physical body conceals within itself something that is the exact opposite of its visible qualities. For the elements of which all things are composed are forces that are mutually antagonistic. Nevertheless the Creator has so ordained things that these elements are brought into unity through the fact that each one effectively neutralizes itself in so far as it is in relation to the

Infinite. In the Infinite they disappear, passing into Nothingness. This Nothingness is thus the cause that brings about unity among elements that are otherwise mutually antagonistic. (And in this Nothingness the prophet submerges himself to seek for a miracle.)

But you who wish to live, enter with me into another Gate, for there you shall read:

—how Moyshe Teitelbaum journeyed to Lublin, how the holy Seer read his heart and dispelled his doubts—how a key caused him concern during prayer, or how the holy Seer followed his spirit and then scolded him—upon which there follows how the holy Yismach Moyshe stood up for the poor, how he offered his own face to some roughs and thereby fulfilled the prophecy of Jeremiah—how we bury our dead and what we take care to do for their happiness—whereupon we learn how the holy Yismach Moyshe sent disciples to Lizensk, or how every soul likes to receive presents—how longingly and unceasingly the holy Yismach Moyshe expected the Messiah—how even in heaven they had their difficulties with him, and how to this day he is still preaching to the angels—upon which there follows how the holy Ohev Yisroel was reincarnated ten times, aye, and how he was a high priest in Jerusalem—what the Chassidim from Lublin saw at Kalev and what they heard from the holy Seer—why the saint of Kalev dressed himself in paper and why he carried a whip—and how he prayed in Tartar—and how a shepherd sang a song.

The Seventh Gate

Three tall tamarisks in the broad plain
Raise their topmost branches to heaven's domain.

Our teachers and our masters

THE HOLY YISMACH MOYSHE OF IHEL

and

THE HOLY OHEV YISROEL OF APTA

may their merits guard us and protect us,

and

THE SAINT OF KALEV

the last is always the dearest.

THE SEVENTH GATE

Men of learning are called by the Chassidim *ashlei ravreve*, which means: powerful tamarisks. So firmly rooted are they in wisdom and Faith and holy deeds! Like tamarisks in the land of Palestine.

But in point of fact the holy Yismach Moyshe was not a tamarisk! He was a sweet date-palm. His name, you see, was Moyshe Teitelbaum and the actual meaning of "taitlboum" is: *date-palm*. However, when we speak about a famous author, we usually call him not by his own name but by the name of his most important book, or sometimes by the name of the place where he worked here on earth. Rabbi Moyshe Teitelbaum of Ihel (Uihely) wrote a book to which he gave the title "Yismach Moyshe" (May Moyshe Rejoice). Thus we do not say, "Reb Moyshe Teitelbaum did this or that," "Reb Moyshe Teitelbaum said this or that," but, "the holy Yismach Moyshe did it", "the holy Yismach Moyshe said it". The author and his book are one and the same. The name of a saint's work or his place of work is used instead of his name. Think about it and you will agree that this is the case.

The holy Yismach Moyshe was a highly learned person even as a young man. He was not content with mere erudition. He knew the truth of the words in the Talmud, that "he who is concerned only about learning and nothing else, is as it were without God". So the holy Yismach Moyshe sought his way to God.

Chassidism made a strong appeal to him. There was only one thing that he did not understand: how was it that the Chassidim could be so light-headedly gay all the time? Is it not written in the Talmud that nobody is permitted to be over-cheerful in this world, that our mouths are never to be brim-full of laughter until the Tabernacle has been rebuilt on Mount Zion.

So the holy Yismach Moyshe decided he would travel to

Lublin to see the Seer there. Before he set out on his journey, the holy Yismach Moyshe prayed thus in his heart:

"Lord of the universe! Thou knowest the most secret thoughts of man and Thou knowest that I endeavour to serve Thee with all my heart and all my soul. Thou knowest also that I suffer when my thought is weighed down with doubts. Yet our savants, of blessed memory, tell us in the Talmud: "He who comes to purify himself receives help." Naturally the Talmud does not say: "receives help from *God*", but "receives help". This means that it is not only Thou, O God, that helpest man to purify himself, but that Thou helpest him through Thy saints, our teachers. Grant then, O Lord, that the saint of Lublin may help me to know the Truth so that all my doubts may be banished for ever!"

Thus did the holy Yismach Moyshe pray in his heart before setting out on the road to Lublin.

When he arrived, the saint of Lublin looked him in the eyes and said:

"Why are you so sad?—It is true that we must always grieve for the destruction of Jerusalem and the burning of the Temple, but the greeting once given by a certain wise man is also true: Let joy be on thy face, sorrow in thy heart! My old teacher, Rebe Reb Shmelke of Nikolsburg," continued the holy Seer, "used to illustrate this with a beautiful parable: There was once a king who was deposed from his throne and driven out of his empire. For a long time he wandered through the world, having nowhere to lay his head. However, this unfortunate king had one friend from the days of his youth, and in the end he took refuge with him. This man was a poor man but he gladly opened his doors to the royal outlaw and gave him hospitality in his wretched cottage. He did his utmost to see to his friend's needs and sweeten his bitter lot. Within his soul he grieved over the fate of the ill-starred king but outwardly he appeared gay and cheered the king in every possible way. This king who was driven out by his people is the King of kings, the gracious God, may He be praised! We are his old friends. Outwardly we never stop rejoicing, for we want him to be gay with us. But within us our hearts bleed with secret sorrow over God's Exile."

"Perhaps it is not right of me," continued the holy Seer, "to reveal the deepest mysteries of the soul's sorrow before you. But the Talmud says: 'He who comes to purify himself receives help.' This means that it is not God alone who helps people but that it is also up to us teachers to be helpful to God in purifying human souls."

Such was the intimate knowledge possessed by the Seer of Lublin of each man's thoughts, down to the meanest detail, that he was indeed an adept at banishing all doubts.

On another occasion the holy Yismach Moyshe went to Lublin for the Sabbath. He prayed with the Seer and the Chassidim in the House of Prayer. When they came to the prayer, "The soul of every living creature blesses Thy name, O Lord . . .", a prayer that we are obliged to pray especially earnestly, since it is during this prayer that we change our Sabbath-night soul for our day soul, it suddenly occurred to the holy Yismach Moyshe that he had forgotten the key to the cupboard in his room at the inn where he had some money. It was money which he had begged on the way for the Chassidic poor. Supposing somebody were to notice the key in the lock, open the cupboard and pilfer the money?

It was in vain that he kept telling himself that nobody at Lublin would be such a villain as to steal on the holy Sabbath. The whole time he saw before him the key sticking out of the cupboard door, and was quite unable to concentrate on prayer.

In the end he realized that these thoughts were a snare laid by the devil; this was the devil's way of tempting him away from his devotions. So the holy Yismach Moyshe took a stern grip on himself and started praying fervently. He thought no more of the key.

After the service, as the Chassidim were sitting at table with the saint of Lublin, the Seer suddenly turned to the holy Yismach Moyshe with the words:

"What's come over you, Reb Moyshe? Until we reached the prayer 'The soul of every living creature' I saw your soul going with us in our devotions. Then it got lost and I didn't see it again until we got to the doxology for the Creator of Light and Darkness. Can one allow oneself to be so put out—over forgetting a key. . . ?"

One day, as he was begging for charity for the poor, the holy Yismach Moyshe noticed some men playing cards at an inn. A choice gang indeed! Horse dealers, showmen from travelling fairs, rough types, illiterates, and all kinds of hucksters. But even such people should not pass unnoticed by us. It is our duty to love them and not despise them. If we can cause them to win for themselves such great merit as is acquired by the giving of alms, we must not let slip the opportunity. So the holy Yismach Moyshe went up to them and asked them for a contribution. Infuriated that anybody should dare to interrupt their game, the card-players leapt at the holy Yismach Moyshe and, instead of charity, rained blows upon him. The holy Yismach Moyshe waited patiently until they had spent their fury, then he said:

"That was for me. Now what are you going to give the poor?"

The saint's words sounded so meek and simple, and at the same time so powerful, that the ruffians were quite disarmed. They reached into their pockets and indeed were far from stingy. Their merit was immense, for the holy Yismach Moyshe forgave them the humiliation and pain they had inflicted on him and blessed them for all they had given.

Thus were fulfilled the words of the prophet Jeremiah (Lamentations 3. 30): "He giveth his cheek to him that smiteth him: he is filled full with reproach."

One of the ten acts through which we acquire everlasting and earthly bliss is the "burial of the dead" and we never delay in the performance of this duty. Except on Saturdays and festivals we bury our dead as soon as they have breathed their last breath—at all events before sunset. In the East we pay little attention to the Christian law which requires a waiting period of three days before burial takes place. True, even the Talmud tells the story of what happened to a certain young man who was buried in a grave hewn out of the rock: how the watchmen, whose task it was, according to the custom of that time, to mount guard for three days over the cave where a person was buried, heard the sound of knocking coming from inside the tomb, how they rolled away the stone and delivered the young man who had meanwhile regained consciousness. That youth then went on to live for many years and had twenty-one sons and daughters. But as to the possibility of such revivals inside a tomb taking place in our time, truthfully nothing of the sort has ever been known. The merciful God would surely not allow anything so awful to happen. So we bury our dead without delay. Moreover we always make sure that death has really taken place. We hold a goose feather to the deceased person's nostrils, and, if it shows not the least flicker of movement this is indubitable proof that the *dead man* is well and truly dead. . . . The sooner he is buried after this, the better for him. An unburied body suffers much greater torture than the pains caused to it in the grave by worms and putrefaction. And if you have taken every care throughout your life to see that no forbidden food or drink should ever touch your lips, then you need have no fear whatsoever of putrefaction in the grave. Saints never rot at all in their tombs. They lie as sweetly in the grave as if it were a cot, and they will continue to lie there until the resurrection. You can easily make sure that I am not lying by referring to the holy book "Reshit Chochmah" by Rabbi Elijah de Vidas. There you will find plenty of proof that the bodies of deceased saints are not subject to putrefaction.

We do not bury our dead in coffins, as you probably do. God forbid! We place the corpse on the floor of the grave, so that it lies directly on the bare lap of mother earth. As it is written: "to dust thou shalt return". The only thing we do, once the person has been lain in the grave, is to place two boards on either side of him. If he was a learned and eminent person during his lifetime, we add another board by way of covering, so that when we come to fill in the grave we shall not throw any clods on a man of learning, even after his death. Naturally we are not allowed to place anything of value in the grave with the corpse, or bury it with him. Even his prayer mantle, which serves as his shroud in the grave, must be so torn before burial takes place that no living person could wear it. On the eyes of the deceased we place two potsherds, one on each eye. These potsherds do not stay on the person's eyes for all time. The first falls as soon as his first grandchild is born, and the second when the second grandchild is born.

At first, when a person dies, his soul is as it were stunned—like when one goes straight from pitch darkness into violent light. It is a little while before it awakens out of this state. It does not free itself from the body all at once. The first seven days it spends alternately in the grave and in the home where the person died. This is the reason why on these seven days ten men go to the home of the deceased and join in the normal daily prayers with the mourning relatives. The unfortunate soul is very glad to return home and hear the sacred Hebrew words it knows so well. For seven days a lamp of remembrance is kept burning in the house, and next to the lamp are placed a glass of water and a towel. The soul washes in the glass and dries itself with the towel. After seven days it leaves the old home for good. During the first year, it flies from the grave to the sky and from the sky back to the grave, then again to the sky, and so on continuously. It is not until the first year is over that it settles permanently in the heavens, but even then it does not forsake the grave entirely. From time to time it likes to return, as for instance on the holy Sabbath, at festivals and at the new moon, or when friends and acquaintances come together there to pray. This is the purpose of the grave stone, so that the soul has somewhere to rest. The stone is white, to match the bones.

Why do I tell you all this?

Because the holy Yismach Moyshe once sent two of his disciples to Lizensk, to pray at the grave of the holy Rebe Reb Melech, for whoever pays but a single visit to the grave of the Rebe Reb Melech is certain not to die impenitent. For the journey there the holy Yismach Moyshe gave his disciples this advice:

"When you enter the Good Place (I mean the cemetery) at Lizensk, say: We promise that the alms we shall shortly give to the poor will count towards the salvation of the first soul to tell the holy Rebe Reb Melech, in heaven, that we have come to pray at his grave.

"When the souls of those who have recently died hear this, they will race off with all speed to bring the news to the soul of the saint. Each one will want to be first so as to secure for itself the merit of the alms, for in the other world charity brings infinite merit."

The holy Yismach Moyshe was one of those souls whom God from time to time sends down to this world to ennoble it and sanctify it. He used to say that this was the third time he had been on this earth.

The first time he was born a sheep—one of those tended by our forefather Jacob at his uncle Laban's. The holy Yismach Moyshe would show us the strange scars he had had on his holy body since birth—marks left by blows with sticks from the time when he was one of Jacob's sheep. For our forefather Jacob was a very strict shepherd.

"The second time," he would continue, "I was one of the Israelites whom Moses led out of Egyptian bondage. But in the wilderness I allowed myself to be enticed away by the haughty Korach, and so it came about that I found myself in his band of two hundred and fifty men who were subsequently swallowed up alive by the land, as it is written."

"But Rabbi," objected his disciples, "how could you have allowed yourself to be incited to rebellion against our beloved teacher Moses?!"

"Oh, if only you knew what wisdom Korach put into his arguments against Moses, and how sweetly convincing he could be!" replied the holy Yismach Moyshe.

Nobody knows when the Redeemer is coming. He may come any day, even this very day. Thus it is written in the Talmud and thus it is codified by the holy Maimonides in his thirteen Articles of Faith. We all believe this too, and hope for it. The holy Yismach Moyshe put this Article of Faith into practice more effectively than anyone else in all the wide world.

Every day of his life he continually looked for the Redeemer's coming, and at night, when he lay down to rest, he used to tell his servant to keep watch and wake him up as soon as he saw the Redeemer had arrived. Up to the very last day of his life on this earth he believed he would live to see the coming of the Redeemer.

Shortly before his death he cried out and said:

"Lord of the universe, all my life I have trusted that Thou wouldest grant me to see the coming of Thy Chosen one; and Thou, God—Thou hast *deceived* me, '*du host mich gefoppt*'! . . ."

Only the most beloved sons of the Lord can dare speak to Him with such daring. As it is written by the hand of Moses: "My first-born son—Israel."

The holy Yismach Moyshe died in the firm conviction that after death he would be able to achieve what he had not been vouchsafed to do during his lifetime: to hasten the coming of the Messiah.

A dead body is not entirely deprived of life until it is buried. It may perhaps not react to outward phenomena, but it has a vague consciousness of everything that is happening and being said around it. As the Rabbi was pronouncing the funeral oration over the body of the holy Yismach Moyshe, and mentioning the dear departed's conviction that he would send us the Messiah as soon as his spirit rose up to heaven, his dead body was violently shaken before the eyes of all present. Proof that he had not forgotten!

In heaven there was acute embarrassment. Many souls had still to be redeemed and many holy sparks freed and purified from the mire of matter, before the day of salvation could come. What attitude was to be taken towards the newcomer? What was to be done about his plan, to prevent him carrying it out? The first clods had fallen on the saint's body, and his spirit, freed of its earthly shackles, was on its way to heaven. The angels received it with great glory. Before it was able to say a word, however, they bestowed upon it the honour of being given a special task—to preach them a little sermon, as beautiful as the sermons the saint had preached while still on earth.

The holy Yismach Moyshe, who had been accustomed to preach all his life, could hardly refuse the angels' request. What did it matter if he continued his earthly activity a little while longer in heaven? So he embarked on his sermon.

He preached to the angels of the Lord and to all the saints in heaven—about the service of God, about humility and simplicity, about joy and love, just as he had once taught us on earth. He preached and preached—up there, in eternal bliss, time passes very swiftly—supporting his deductions with quotations from the Holy Scriptures, the Talmud and the Cabbala; he preached to the angels, preached and preached—and he is still preaching to them. He is still far from the end of his sermon.

So the Son of David has not yet come down among us. He sits there, in His royal chamber in heaven, bound in fetters, shedding tears of blood over our suffering, unable to help us. And the holy Yismach Moyshe is still preaching and preaching. . . .

We have said that the holy Reb Moyshe Teitelbaum was able to recall his earlier incarnations. In this he was no exception among the saints.

The holy Rebe Shiya Heshl of Apta, or the holy "Ohev Yisroel" (The Friend of Israel), as we call him after his life's work, used to relate that he was on the earth for the tenth time. Unlike Reb Moyshe Teitelbaum of Ihel, he always held a leading position. Thousands of years ago he was the high priest in the Temple of Jerusalem, at another time he was president of the Sanhedrin, the supreme court at Jerusalem. He had many interesting memories from those days. He was also a prince of the Jews in Mesopotamia, and so on.

The order of service for our most sublime festival, the strict feast of the holy Day of Atonement, tells us, in the prayer of Musef, how the high priest in the Temple at Jerusalem used to observe this festival. This prayer reads: "When the high priest entered into the most sacred place in the temple, he prayed. . . ."

When the holy Ohev Yisroel prayed at the *bimah* at Apta on the holy Day of Atonement, he used to sing:

"When *I* was high priest at Jerusalem, *I* prayed. . . ."

When the holy Ohev Yisroel died, the angels of the Lord brought him by night from Poland to the Holy Land. There the heavenly gravediggers buried him in the holy town of Tiberias, on the banks of the clear waters of the Sea of Galilee, next to his namesake, the prophet Hosea.

The Scriptures describe Moses as "the servant of God" both during his lifetime and after his death. This is strange. How can anybody serve God after his death? The holy Ohev Yisroel explained this as follows:

It is written in the Talmud that God commanded the dying Moses that his soul should make it known to his forefathers in paradise that the Lord had fulfilled His promise and had given the land of Canaan to their descendants. The soul of Moses did indeed do this, and thus, as the Lord's messenger, even after he had departed this life, Moses carried out the will of God, and is therefore rightly called "the servant of God" even after his death.

The Holy Scriptures often speak of the hand of God, the right hand of God, the ear of God, the eye of God, the mouth of God and the feet of God. But God is endlessly the same—measureless, timeless and without any likeness. How, then, can there be any talk of the eye of God, the ear of God, and so on?—The holy Ohev Yisroel explained this as follows:

In the same way as our body forms its likeness on the earth by the shadow it casts, so do we, by our activity, form the eternal God to our likeness: If we act well, we form thereby the *right hand* of the God-Man. If we resist evil, we form the *left hand* of the God-Man. If we do not look at ugly things, we form His eyes. If we do not allow our ears to hear lies, we form His ears and so on. God asks this of us and we have always to be conscious of it, so that we can always do right and not sin, AMEN.

The holy Seer once sent two disciples from Lublin on a long journey into Hungary. Not to Ihel! To Kalev near Debrecin. He told them that this time they were to keep the feast of Pesah with the Rabbi at Kalev, and not at home at Lublin. The Rabbi's name was Reb Yitzhak Eisik Taub.

The journey took a whole month. When the two disciples reached Kalev, it was already the eve of the festival. They were given a cordial welcome at the Rabbi's house. But how great was their disappointment! The Rebetzen, I mean the Rabbi's wife, was not dressed as a chaste daughter of Israel should be dressed. She was all dolled up like a Christian woman. The Rabbi himself was not wearing the long caftan of a Rabbi, but was dressed as an ordinary peasant. He even carried a whip in his hand.

The festival evening arrived. Everybody sat down to the sacred Passover feast, our *seder*. On the table were lighted candles in silver candlesticks, and three *matzot* had been covered with a snow-white cloth. Real Hungarian wine sparkled in the goblets. Bitter herbs, a bone charred in ashes, the Passover egg, parsley, grated apple and cinnamon—everything had been duly assembled, in accordance with ritual, and prepared for the household ceremony, as it behoves us.

The disciples, however, were highly embarrassed. The whole environment was so unusual, and their hosts' "Gentile" appearance hardly inspired them with conviction that the foods had been prepared in accordance with the strict ordinances for the Passover! Dare a Chassid so much as touch food in this house? Had it not been that their all-knowing teacher had sent them here, they would indeed not even have drunk the water.

Very soon the disciples became even more embarrassed. The Rabbi stood up and pronounced the opening words of the ceremony, in accordance with ancient custom:

"This is the bread of suffering which our fathers ate in the land of Egypt. Let him that is hungry enter and eat with us! Let him that is poor come and celebrate the Feast of Deliverance with us! This year we are still here, but next year we shall be in the Land of Israel. This year we are still slaves, but next year we shall certainly be a free people."

Scarcely had the Rabbi finished speaking when the disciples heard a carriage draw up outside, and in no time new guests stepped into the room. Not very devout people, it appeared, if indeed they were Jews at all. Had they not come by carriage after the stars were out—actually on the festival itself? Yet travelling on a festival is forbidden to us. None the less the Rabbi and his wife welcomed them like good old friends, with great joy, and even with deference. The two disciples turned pale, for they found themselves face to face with three gallant Hungarian officers in uniform, accompanied by a lady to boot. She was exceedingly beautiful. Like the Shulamite in the Song of Solomon. What exquisite clothes she wore! Her body, which was shapely like a palm, was draped in a snowy-white dress of delicate muslin, as in a little thin cloud. On her jet-black hair, which rippled in ample plaits down to her waist, she wore a glorious, golden diadem, on which there glittered pearls, rubies and diamonds like the loveliest stars of heaven. Perfumes that might have come from paradise were wafted to the disciples. You could easily have thought that some queen had come to spend this festival at Kalev. Naturally the disciples at once lowered their gaze. Not for anything in the world would they look on the face of a woman. All that they saw they took in, in the mere twinkling of an eye.

In this society the disciples were obliged to sit down to the *seder*, which had been interrupted a moment by the welcome given to the guests. The ceremony was indeed exceedingly odd.

Neither the Rabbi, nor the Rebetzen, nor the guests opened the Passover prayer-book, the "Haggadah". They all washed their hands, it is true. They all ate matzot and bitter herbs, and they all drank four glasses of wine, as required by the Law. But they did not pray. They spoke only in Hungarian, they joked and sang in Hungarian. The disciples of course did not understand a word. For they did not know *totrish*, that is, Hungarian. Which is hardly surprising, since they came from Lublin.

However, nobody took any notice of them. Quite undisturbed, they were able to read through the entire Haggadah and cap it with the story about the lamb which a father bought for twopence, and about how a cat bit the poor little lamb to death, how a dog devoured the cat, and the dog was beaten to death with a stick. How the stick was destroyed by fire which in turn was quenched by water. How the water was drunk by an ox which was then slaughtered by a butcher who in his turn was slaughtered by Death, and how Death will be finally abolished by God, may He be praised! So the good disciples read through the whole of the Haggadah and finished up with the lamb, just as we do every year. Finally the guests got up and bade farewell to the Rabbi. At this moment the lady turned to the disciples and, with a bewitching smile on her lips, addressed some inquiry to them: if they were pleased, or if they had enjoyed themselves, or something like that. It can only have been out of politeness. Such exalted ladies are accustomed to talk in this way.

The disciples were quite at a loss for an answer, so great was their confusion. Why, the very next moment they had completely forgotten what the lady actually said to them. It could hardly have been Hungarian, because if it had been they would not have understood her at all.

How glad they were when the festival days were over and they could return to Lublin! Never before had they spent a festival so miserably. What terrible sins had they committed to cause their holy teacher to humiliate them in this way and send them to this Tartarus?

"Foolish fellows!" exclaimed the holy Seer, as he welcomed them on their return with a sad smile. "If you had said 'yes' when you were asked *if you had understood*, you would have brought eternal Salvation to the world. Know that the three men whom it was granted to you to behold, were our forefathers Abraham, Isaac and Jacob, and the queen was the very Glory of the majesty of God. Upon your 'yes' the coming of the Messiah depended, the union of God and His Majesty, and the destruction of Death and corruption for all time. Ah, why did you miss this opportunity! . . ."

Such, then, were the guests whom the saint of Kalev was wont to entertain!

On the evening of that festival, when the disciples from Lublin were away at the house of the saint of Kalev, the holy Rebe Reb Shmelke, the latter's former teacher, who lived at Mikulov, exclaimed in surprise:

"How strange that I can't hear the Rabbi of Kalev today! He must be praying in Hungarian again."

The *Tsaddik* of Kalev, Reb Yitzhak Eisik Taub, was a most unusual saint, one of the greatest that have ever lived. None knew where he would come from or where he would go. His was a mysterious life. He used to dress in peasant's clothes—but made out of paper. His body was so weakened by his constant fasts that he could not wear normal clothes. He used always to carry a whip and beat himself with it.

One day as he was going through the fields, after the example of our forefather Isaac, he heard a shepherd singing a Hungarian song about a rose and a cock. The saint of Kalev stopped and listened. When the song ended, he went up to the shepherd and asked him to repeat it for him. For this he rewarded him with a ducat. Three times he had the shepherd repeat the song, and gave him three ducats. When asked a fourth time, the shepherd found he was unable to sing. From that moment he forgot the song for all time.

It was one of the songs the Levites used to sing long ago in the Temple of Jerusalem. In Israel it has long since been forgotten. The entire song is in Hungarian, though one verse is in Hebrew. Now all the Chassidim know the saint of Kalev's song. We sing it in Yiddish, but happy is he who is able to sing it in Hungarian. In Hungarian?—Not on your life. It is not Hungarian. No, it is not. The words of the song are compounded of the mystic names of the holy angels of the Lord. It only seems like Hungarian.

Who is the cock and who is the rose? Only the saints know this.

The saint of Kalev died on the seventh day of the month of

Adar, the day when we mourn the death of our teacher Moses. He lies in a dark vault and only his name adorns his tomb. Above him burns an undying flame.

> *Wait there, little rose, wait till it be*
> *that the Lord shall give me to thee!*
> *When shall it be,*
> *Oh, when shall it be?!* . . .

But you who wish to live, enter with me into another Gate, for there you shall read:

—how the beautiful Ruth was incarnate in the holy Shelo of Prague, and concerning the sweet delights of union in marriage —What the virtuous maiden Beyle was doing at home, and what strange things the saint saw in the cattle—How a lustrous glow shone out from a piece of paper, and why the unhappy bride was so full of tears—Next comes an account of all that a worthy cabman did—How Ironhead reproached the Seer— How a sinner was always in such good spirits and how the holy Seer was more fond of him than anyone else—Whereupon there follows how the Devil took umbrage and drummed on the window—How Beyle was a watchful guard, how the Seer met a fearful end, and how his prophecy was tragically fulfilled —What the holy Dyvre Chayyim related about the saint, and how his daughter was also the daughter of a learned man— How while listening to song the holy Dyvre Chayyim declined to enter the gate of paradise—How he attempted to say the Creed, and how it is fitting for us to remember the doctor from the land below the Carpathians—what the holy Seer used to teach—Therewith this epistle ends.

The Eighth Gate

Mystic shining Mirror and—wondrous wonder—
Saint—the Eye of all-seeing God—what splendour!

Our teacher and our master

THE HOLY REB JACOB YITZHAK OF LUBLIN

may his undying merits protect us!

THE EIGHTH GATE

In 1570, a man was born in whom was incarnate the soul of Ruth, the devout Moabitess who was an ancestress of the house of David in the Old Testament. This was Rabbi Isaiah ben Abraham of the tribe of Levi. As the family came from Horovice near Prague, they acquired the name of Horovitz. Hence the numerous Horovitzes, Hurwitzes and so on. How many of them there are, all over the world! But not everyone bearing this name is a descendant of this famous family on the male side. Only those are members of it who belong to the tribe of Levi, and then only if they have the right—in signing their names in Hebrew—to put the title "ish" before the name Horovitz, ish Horovitz, which is the equivalent of: Freiherr von Horovitz.

Rabbi Isaiah ben Abraham Levi ish Horovitz was a Rabbi at Prague. During the Thirty Years' War he moved to the Holy Land and died at the town of Tiberias in about 1630. He wrote a large cabbalistic book, "Shene Luhot Haberit" (The two tablets of the Covenant). We call the author of this book "Shelo", after the *initial* letters of the title, and add the attribute "Hakodesh", Shelo Hakodesh—*the holy Shelo*. He is one of those people whom we call "holy", even though they lived before the holy Baal-Shem and do not belong to Chassidism.

We have many a proof that Ruth the Moabitess was truly incarnate in the holy Shelo. Both were equally forthright, equally loyal, equally hard-working. The actual proof, however, that the devout Ruth was *destined* to be incarnate in him is this:

The Hebrew original of the biblical Book of Ruth has a striking characteristic. Almost every verse begins with the letter V. Only eight verses start with different letters, and the first letters of *five* of these eight verses compose the complete name *Isaiah*. The remaining three verses begin with the letters: B, A, L, and B.A.L. is an abbreviation for Ben Abraham Levi!—

The holy Shelo's grandfather was the famous Rabbi Joshua Sheftl who wrote a very beautiful cabbalistic book, "Shefa Tal" (The Abundance of the Dew). This work vividly describes the infinite delight that fills all the spheres at the moment of union between married persons in purity and sanctity.

I should not mention this book at all if Rabbi Sheftl were not from Prague. But he is indeed an illustrious Prague writer.

Our Reb Jacob Yitzhak Levi ish Horovitz of Lublin, the famous *choyze*, that is, seer, was a direct descendant of the holy Shelo. He was a disciple of the holy Rebe Reb Shmelke of Mikulov and the holy Rebe Reb Melech of Lizensk.

His ability as a seer was apparent while he was still a young lad. He used to say that when he was born he saw the entire world absolutely clearly from one end to the other. However, he very early became convinced that it was not advisable to look at all the evil things of this world. So he begged God to take away his clairvoyance. His prayer was only partially granted. Everything that happened up to four hundred miles away from him he continued to see as clearly as if it had happened a mere four feet away. The rest of the world he saw as it were through a net. If a father lost his son and wanted to know where he was and what he was doing at that moment, or if a wife were searching for a husband who had forsaken her, they only had to turn to the holy Seer of Lublin. He would fix his eyes on the book of Zohar and tell them everything in perfect detail, even if he had to seek for them beyond the sea. The very word "zohar" means a shining glare. A blinding light such as would blind the unworthy turns a saint into a clairvoyant.

On the Sabbath day before he was married, he astonished all his friends in the House of Prayer by describing exactly what his intended bride, Beyle, was doing at that very moment at home.

It was not only the present that was revealed to the holy Seer of Lublin in all its details. He could also read the future like a book.

When a butcher slaughters an animal, it is his duty to make a careful examination of each part. If he finds any irregularity or defect in the *entrails*, we are not allowed to eat it. It is *tref*, prohibited. The butcher loses a great deal in this way.

One day a butcher came to the holy Seer before the festival days. He was extremely worried: what if the beast he was taking to be slaughtered turned out subsequently to be *tref* and couldn't be eaten?

"Make me out a written list of your cattle!" came the saint's instructions. "Then add a description of the exterior of each one!"

The butcher did as he was told.

The saint of Lublin looked through the list and, after thinking a moment, said:

"This one and that one are sure to be *tref*, but this one and that one are certain to be good, *kosher*. I may not tell you anything about the others, for the irregularities that will be found in their entrails will be such as to embarrass the butcher. He will not know if they are *tref* or *kosher* and will take them to the local Rabbi for an expert opinion. But the Rabbi's opinion has the effect of a court sentence. So I mustn't anticipate it with a forecast made by clairvoyance."

When the animals were slaughtered, the Seer proved to be right in all three groups. He had not made a single mistake.

One day some Chassidim travelled to Lublin. When they reached the town, the cabman asked them to hand in his *kvitel* to the holy Seer. He could not go to him himself, he explained. The Chassidim agreed. They wrote down the name of the cabman and the name of his mother and placed the *kvitel* before the saint of Lublin.

"I see a lustrous glow above this man's name," cried the holy Seer, who was almost unable to tear his eyes off the *kvitel*. "A lustrous glow!"

The Chassidim were surprised in no small measure at the saint's words. The cabman was well known to them. They knew him to be a very ordinary man, far from outstanding in either piety or learning. But they also knew that the saint of Lublin never spoke empty words.

They walked through the town until they came to the market. From far off they heard the sound of gay music and singing, and soon they caught sight of the cabman. He was dancing and leaping like one possessed.

"I wanted to have a bit of fun," came his answer to their inquiry. "So I came to the market. There was to have been a *chasune* (a wedding; weddings always take place in the open air). But as the bride was an orphan she could not afford to buy the usual gift of a prayer mantle for the bridegroom. So the bridegroom's parents refused to give their consent to the marriage and stopped the wedding at the last moment. It was an act of Providence. The poor bride wept so much, it touched my heart. It's terribly sad when a girl can't get the young man she's been longing for so long. So I took out the money I'd earned from you on the journey and bought a nice *talis* (prayer mantle), a real Turkish one, and gave it to the bride for her bridegroom. So, after all, the two young people did get each other. Who wouldn't be pleased about that?"

Thus saying, he went whirling off again, shaking the very ground under his feet. He gave the Chassidim no further thought. As for them, they realized now why the Seer had said that a lustrous glow shone above the man's name. A lustrous glow indeed!

The whole of Lublin believed in the holy Seer—the whole of Lublin except for the chief Rabbi, who stubbornly refused to believe in him, even though he was a relative of his. We are right in calling him "Eizene Kop", "Iron Head". His real name was Azriel Horowitz.

The chief Rabbi reproached the saint of Lublin with deluding people; the Seer, he said, made himself out to be a saint whereas in fact he was nothing of the sort.

"But what can I do to stop them thinking me a saint?"

"Well, you can make a public declaration that you are not a saint, but an absolutely ordinary person like anybody else."

The Sabbath came, and hundreds of the godly pressed into the synagogue. The saint of Lublin mounted the *balmemr*, the raised platform from which the Word of God is read. A hush fell on the congregation who expected the saint to deliver his sermon.

But the saint of Lublin did not preach. He merely stated what he had always been convinced about and what "Eizene Kop" now required him to say. He said he was not a *Tsaddik* and that nobody should think he was. And he added that he was a sinful man, like everybody else, if not still more sinful.

His words had an unexpected effect.

"Do you hear how humble he is?!" cried some.

"Did you ever see such humility?!" others shouted in amazement.

If the Chassidim had gone to Lublin in their hundreds before this, they now went in their thousands.

Iron Head's disappointment was great indeed.

"Now you must show the people that you are not modest and humble as they think you are. That'll put a stop to it. You must tell them at the top of your voice that you are a saint!"

"Never!" answered the saint of Lublin. I shall never say that I *am* a saint. I refuse to *lie*. . . ."

A short while after this the saint of Lublin told one of his disciples:

"You had better go and see how the chief Rabbi is getting on."

The very same day the disciple left to visit Iron Head. It cannot be denied that he felt no small surprise that his saintly teacher should show such concern about his enemy's welfare and send somebody out on such an errand. The disciple came to Iron Head before afternoon prayer.

After prayer two men brought their case before the chief Rabbi. The Rabbi and his two assessors, all three of whom were real experts in Talmudic law, heard out the two contending parties, after which they sent them out of the court room to take counsel together. The chief Rabbi, whose word was decisive, inclined towards the plaintiff's side. However it had been clear from the outset to the Seer's disciple that it was the defendant who

183

was in the right. He could not understand how anybody could hold the opposite opinion. Especially a Talmudist like Iron Head. He, a mere disciple, knew the very place in the commentary to the Talmud which could show up the incorrectness of the chief Rabbi's opinion.

True, Iron Head was an opponent of his beloved teacher but for all that the disciple from Lublin had no desire to put a learned man to shame. So he took the relevant tractate of the Talmud from the Rabbi's library. Then he pretended to be deeply engrossed in the volume and not to take any notice of the dispute. The judges were just about to pronounce judgment when the disciple went up to Iron Head and asked him to explain a passage in the commentary which he could not understand. The Rabbi rebuked him, telling him that he had no time to explain it just then. But the disciple would not give up and pushed the open volume under Iron Head's nose. Willy-nilly Reb Azriel glanced at the book—and understood. The case was settled in accordance with law and justice.

The holy Seer welcomed his disciple back with great joy and said:

"You have done something that is very pleasing to God. Know that those three men, the plaintiff, the defendant and Iron Head, their judge, have been on this earth *ninety-nine times*. In each lifetime the two men have brought the same case and each time this Rabbi has been their judge. But he has always made a mistake and sentenced them unjustly. Again and again all three of them have had to be born until their case was settled in accordance with the Law. Now this has happened. Thanks to you they have been redeemed from *gilgul*,[1] from going round and round for ever."

Some say that Iron Head did come to believe in the saint of Lublin before his death and found salvation. Others, on the other hand, maintain that he remained obdurate. As it is written in the Talmud: "Not even on the threshold of Hell do sinners repent of their sins."

[1] 'Gilgul', the transmigration of souls.

One of the disciples was reproached by the saint of Lublin with not pronouncing the prayers properly; the saint said he "swallowed" them.

"I swallow them because they're sweeter than honey," said the cunning fellow by way of excuse.

"Do you think I don't find the taste of the words just as sweet as you do? Yet I don't swallow them."

"You can't! For your praying—is *fire!*" replied the disciple.

One of the inhabitants of the holy community at Lublin was a great sinner. He wasted no time in committing any jolly old sin he could and was never happier than when he fell into temptation and could give way to it. He was never sorry on account of his evil deeds, and his vices were a source of pleasure to him.

You would certainly never have shaken hands with a man like that, nor would you have spoken to him. In fact you would have given him a wide berth.

Not so the saint of Lublin. There was nobody he enjoyed talking to so much as this rake. Whenever he came to visit him, he always gave him a more joyous welcome than he would have given to the greatest saint.

The Chassidim were greatly upset by this.

"He's a rare fellow and deserves our admiration. I don't know anybody else who is so gay the whole time as he is," the holy Seer would instruct his disciples. "Know then," he continued, "that when the Tempter entices a man to sin, he is not so concerned that the poor fellow should actually sin as that he should feel that familiar depression, that nagging of the conscience and melancholy of the soul which follows in the wake of sin. That is what the Tempter aims at. For sadness is the greatest evil in the world. It is an evil against which we must keep on warning ourselves. But this sinner never grieves for his sins in the least, and never ceases to be joyous and contented."

It was maintained by eyewitnesses that they had seen the saint of Lublin walking with a deceased person. But for the most part it was only the *souls* of the dead who would fly to him. They used to fly to the window of his room and hand him their *kvitlach* and gifts through it. They would beg him, at least now they were dead, to grant them "correction".

The correction which saints dispense to the *souls of the dead*— we say of sinners, even during their lifetime, that they are "dead" —is a special, magical operation, the mystical intervention of the *third*, spiritual hand of the cabbalist into the entrails of a sick soul; intervention by which their organs, made crooked through vice, are straightened out. We call this correction *tikun*.

All his life the saint of Lublin was engaged in a struggle with the powers of Evil. It was his saintly custom to prolong the peace of the Sabbath as long as possible, for even devils are obliged to hallow the holy Sabbath. As long as the Sabbath lasts they may not torment the souls of the deceased in hell. The souls have a day off.

As the holy Sabbath draws to a close we sit down in the evening twilight to the third, mystic, Sabbath banquet. As soon as the stars come out, we get up from the table for evening prayer during which we bid farewell to the Queen Sabbath. At that moment the souls of the damned return to their torments.

The holy Seer used to sit at the third meal with the Chassidim of Lublin till late into the Sunday morn. So long as they did not rise from table, the devils in hell could not restart their iniquitous activity.

Once, when the saint of Lublin had prolonged the Sabbath an unusually long time and was sitting at table with the Chassidim after midnight, the devil gave them no mean shock. To show that duty called, and that he had to get down to work again, he rapped on the holy Seer's window. . . .

The saint of Lublin forecast that the Chassidim would not keep the day of his death like the anniversaries of other saints' deaths. He said that on the day of his death we should neither light lamps of remembrance nor drink brandy.

Let us hear how his prophecy was fulfilled.

Lublin is a large town, a very large town. It is not a quiet and peaceful place like the villages where the other saints live. There is noise and bustle all day long. Only at night is it a little quieter, but only for us ordinary people, of course. Saints cannot allow themselves any rest. "The learned have no peace, either in this world or the next,"—says the Talmud. And the Lublin houses! How unlike our villagers' cottages! Two storeys they have, even three! It was in one of these tall houses that the holy Seer lived—right up in the attic, too. A small vestibule led straight into the saint's room. The room had no other exit. You could see the courtyard from the window of the room. We have already had occasion to mention that window. We know that the souls of the dead used to fly to it and ask the saint of Lublin for correction. You had better not go to the window and look down into the court, if you are unused to living in a town. It is immensely high, and if you are tired, overwrought or over-worked, the big drop attracts you like the soft voice of a beautiful woman. More than anything else you would like to jump headlong into the abyss and find blissful and eternal oblivion in the cold embrace of nothingness. You know such moments.

For fifteen years the saint of Lublin lived in that room, and never once did he look down into the street from the window.

However, the saint of Lublin had determined to break the power of Satan and bring the Messiah to the earth. In the magical preparations he made to this end he had to be watched night and day by some of the most devoted of his people. He himself ordained it so.

On the fateful night—the night of the festival of the Joy of the Law—it was the turn of his wife, Beyle, to stand guard over him, and Beyle never let him out of her sight in any case. The hours of the watch passed and everything was perfectly in order. Nothing unusual happened. But all of a sudden, his wife imagined she heard somebody sobbing in the hall. Yes, without doubt, there was a child crying there. Beyle wanted to go and see whose child it was, but then she immediately remembered that she had not to leave her husband alone a single instant. What was she to do? The child cried and cried. What mother could hold back?! Then she thought to herself: I shan't be forsaking my husband. Supposing I just open the door a little bit to see whose child it is sobbing out there?

The woman went and opened the door, without asking her husband.—That very moment the crying ceased.

Beyle peered into the vestibule, standing in the doorway and not leaving the room. Where was the child?—Nowhere to be seen. Was it an hallucination?

In the meantime something terrible, something indescribable happened. When Beyle turned round and looked in the room, she stood rooted to the spot. Her husband was not there. He had disappeared without leaving a trace.

It was nearly midnight when Reb Leizer of Chmelnik passed by the house. In the darkness he heard the sound of quiet groaning. Somebody was lying on the ground.—It was the saint of Lublin, his limbs horribly crushed. They carried him away and laid him on a bed. He was still whispering the midnight prayer. But he did not disclose his secret to anyone.

He suffered for a further nine months before he breathed his last. It was Tishebov, the ninth day of the month of Ab—the day that Titus destroyed our Temple and so many ills befell us.

From time immemorial Tishebov has been a day of the most profound grief for the whole of Israel. We bewail the loss of the holy city of Jerusalem, we fast, we do not eat and we do not drink. In the evening we sit in the half darkness. Only a dim light burns in the synagogue. So the saint of Lublin had been right in his prophecy. He is the only saint on whose anniversary the Chassidim light no lamp of remembrance and drink no brandy.

> "The ways of Zion do mourn,
> All her gates are desolate,
> And the daughters of Zion are afflicted.
> She weepeth sore in the night, and her tears are on her cheeks.
> Her adversaries are the chief, her enemies prosper,

For the Lord hath afflicted her with bitterness!
He was unto me as a bear lying in wait, and as a lion in
*   secret places. . . ."*

Thus do we lament on that one night, year after year, with a prophecy of Jeremiah made three thousand years ago.

It is fitting to recall three circumstances which show how great the power of Satan is. The window was so high as to be level with a person's head, and nobody could jump out of it. That this in fact did not happen was clear from the panes placed side by side in the window—none was moved from its place. But the strangest circumstance of all was that the saint of Lublin was found fifty paces from the house. A man cannot jump as far as that. The Evil One had carried him there.

The saint of Lublin has left us three books: "Dyvre Emet", "Zichron Zot" and "Zot Zichron" (Words of Truth, Remembrance is This, This is Remembrance). Few human hands have written such sublime works.

The saint of Lublin never pronounced the name of God in conversation. Instead of God he said *Kroyn*, which means: Crown. But when he said *Kroyn*, all the heavens shook. We would not know this of course if we had not been told of it by one of his foremost disciples, Reb Chayyim Halbershtam of Sanz (Nový Sandec), the holy Dyvre Chayyim ("The Words of Life"), as we call him after his book.

This holy Dyvre Chayyim was an unusual saint. He would not allow a single heller to stay in his house through the night. Whatever he received from the Chassidim during the day, he gave out to the poor by the evening, like the holy Rebe Reb Shmelke and the holy Baal-Shem. The holy Dyvre Chayyim died on the 25th day of the month of Nisan.[1]

---

[1] Recently a lawyer, Dr. B., died in the Ruthenian town of S. As he was born shortly after the death of the holy Reb Chayyim of Sanz, his pious father gave him the name of Chayyim. Dr. Chayyim B., who was a university graduate and a very well educated man, was not of course outstanding in piety and had no

One day a poor girl came to him and asked him for a contribution towards her trousseau.

Hardly had the words been spoken when the holy Dyvre Chayyim gave her almost everything he had—enough to make it quite unnecessary for her to go begging anywhere else.

"Father, what are you doing?!" cried his own daughter. "I've been going about with my boots all torn for a whole month now, and you won't even give me the money to have them repaired."

"Quiet!" the holy Dyvre Chayyim shouted her down, "this bride here is the daughter of a learned man!"

"But Rabbi," exclaimed those present, "your own daughter is also the daughter of a learned man!"

"She's also the daughter of a learned man?" the modest saint repeated, somewhat sceptically. . . .

"Ah well, in that case it's my duty to support her, to be sure. . . ."

Thus saying, he took out the remaining few coins he had and gave them to his daughter. She too should have her shoes repaired, if people said she was the daughter of a learned man. . . .

The holy Dyvre Chayyim achieved no small fame by his struggle against the Sadagor Chassidim. But more about that on another occasion.

The holy Dyvre Chayyim was taught to love music and singing by the holy Reb Naftali of Ropshitz. As a result the town of Sanz in those days was a paradise for musicians and singers. Day and night there was a growling and a buzzing, a humming and a roaring, as in a beehive or at a weir. How those musicians studied and practised for Reb Chayyim! But when they came to perform together! I wouldn't like you to think they all

feeling whatsoever for mysticism. Nevertheless there is a certain mystery connected with this man's life. Dr. Chayyim B. was a healthy man and lived to a ripe old age. *Throughout his life,* from earliest childhood, he always fell ill on a certain day in the year: the 25th day of *the month of Nisan,* the anniversary of the death of the holy Reb Chayyim of Sanz (whose name he bore, having been born immediately after his death). In the end, Dr. B. also died on the 25th of the month of Nisan.

played or sang the same note. Far from it!—The double bass would in all probability be playing something entirely different from the violins, and while the voices of the younger children were twittering like larks, the voices of the older lads would break in like thrushes or nightingales. In short it was some kind of polyphony, or whatever it's called. But it was all in perfect tune and very refined.

It is a pity I have forgotten the name of Reb Chayyim's bandmaster. Look it up in the musical records! You are sure to find it, but should you be unable to, you can think up your own name for him. For never since the days of our King David was there a musician like the holy Reb Chayyim's bandmaster at Sanz. Every week he devised some new song and forthwith started rehearsing it with his singers. Well, it is no wonder that every prince in Christendom envied the holy Dyvre Chayyim his band, and not even the holy Reb Yisroel of Rizhen had better musicians at his famous court at Sadagor than were these lads of ours at Sanz.

There was one condition, however, that the holy Dyvre Chayyim insisted on: his singers and musicians were not allowed to play or sing from music. They all had to learn everything by heart. Why, they were not even allowed to understand musical notation!—"For the song which a person plays from music is a mere paper song. It does not come from that mysterious chamber of God high up in the heavens, from which all true music wells forth." Such was the teaching of the holy Dyvre Chayyim—may the Light of his merits protect us!

In addition to this earthly music of ours there is another kind of song, namely, the familiar chanting which helps to inspire us when we meditate on the holy Talmud. You call it monotonous? You could never manage it, I'll be bound. Not on your life! What a ceaseless rise and fall of sound! Long drawn out, of course, and invariably in a minor key. When we have climbed up to the top—the top of knowledge—we make it a tiny bit more gay, with a kind of victorious trill, then we start slowly down again, to the valley of some new problem in our study of the Talmud. Here we soften down our voices to a somewhat meditative, lugubrious pitch, then the song goes slowly up again and then down again, dragging on and on *ad lib*.

If this seems monotonous to your ear, then I really do not know what to say. But to the holy Dyvre Chayyim it was never monotonous. The holy Dyvre Chayyim would much more enjoy listening to his diligent disciples chanting away in this way than to all the songs sung by his beloved musicians and singers.

One winter evening he was hobbling home from the House of Prayer. He used to walk home alone as he did not have far to go. On this particular occasion, however, being absorbed in thought, he lost his way. All of a sudden he found himself in a small, dark alley where he presumably had never been in his life before. He must have been guided there by the gracious Lord Himself, for as he was walking along he suddenly heard some diligent disciple learning the word of God in one of the cottages. The holy Dyvre Chayyim stopped and listened. It was such a pure, innocent voice. No angel could have had a lovelier one. It drew him like a magnet. He went to the very door of the cottage and pressed his holy ear up against it so as not to lose even a single trill. He listened and listened. I couldn't tell you precisely which interesting piece the disciple was learning at that particular moment: whether it was the one about the two men who found a piece of cloth and how each of them insisted to the judge that he was the one who had actually found it, or whether it was the story of the drop of milk that dripped into the pot of meat, or maybe the one about the sons of Rabban Gamliel returning home from their carousing in the morning and asking their father if there was still time to say their evening prayers; or how King Solomon had the prince of spirits put into fetters so that he might help him in building the Temple at Jerusalem. There are many, many things we can learn about in the Talmud. But actually it is not what the disciple learns that matters. The main thing is *how* he learns! Does he learn in a genuine way and with all his heart, thereby serving his gracious Creator? It is possible to observe this from the manner in which he intones. The holy Dyvre Chayyim stayed on and on, listening to the exquisite singing. He was so absorbed in it that he took no notice of any-body else. The passers-by likewise took no notice of this shape pressed up against the door in the darkness. Nor of course *would* they keep an eye out for such a sight, for who knows if there might not be some sinful couple there, locked in each other's arms, and what devout eyes would look upon such things? So the holy Dyvre Chayyim listened on undisturbed, standing with his ear to the cottage door.

Meanwhile at home they were getting worried. What was keeping the saint so long? Did he not usually come straight home from the House of Prayer?!

It was already morning when they found him. There he was, nestling up against the door of a humble cottage—still listening, for the disciple was still practising. However, when they tried to drag the saint from the door, they found that it could not be done—his holy beard was frozen to the door handle, and they had to bring hot water to set him free.

"Believe me," said the holy Dyvre Chayyim by way of excuse, "if on this night they had opened the gate of paradise before me and told me to enter—I should not have obeyed. I would have preferred to stay here and listen."—The holy Dyvre Chayyim—what a character!

The disciple's name was Jacob Yitzhak, and he came from Ziditchov.

We Chassidim never say the Ani Maamin—the Jewish creed drawn up by the holy Maimonides in thirteen Articles of Faith. This is not because we do not believe. God forbid! We believe as fervently as the rest of them, if not more so. None the less we do not say the creed, even though it is to be found in every prayer book. God alone knows why we do not say it. The holy Dyvre Chayyim did however endeavour to recite it once. He began: "*Ani maamin beemuno shleimo*, I believe with firm faith. . . ." But he broke off immediately, saying to himself:

"Chayyim, you're a liar! If you really believed in the one God, could you sin, Chayyim? Even if only for a moment? Even if only in thought? . . . If you *really* believed?!"—

193

A moment later he began a second time: "I believe with firm faith. . . ."

Again he broke off:

"Chayyim, you're lying again!"

This went on for some time. Finally he gave it up. Since then he has never tried to recite the holy Maimonides' thirteen Articles of Faith.

FROM THE WISDOM OF THE SEER

I would rather have a rascal who admits he is a rascal than a saint who is conscious of his sainthood. A rascal who admits to the truth lives out his days in the Truth. And the Truth is God. In other words, even a criminal lives in God. On the other hand a person who thinks himself to be a perfect saint lives in a lie, and God abhors a lie. The truth is that nobody is perfect in this world.

All matter is permeated by the spirit. The spirits which are incarnate in food pass into us when we eat and digest food, and become joined with our spirit. Through prayer, study and good deeds we raise these spirits to higher degrees of perfection. But if a man misuses the strength he has gained by eating and drinking, he commits a sin and offends his Creator, both by his movements and by his thoughts. Not only does he not raise up the spirits that have entered into him, but he causes them to be forced into sin so that they too sink with him.

A person subject to nervous disorders should concentrate his thoughts on this passage in the Talmud: "Akavya, son of Mahalel, said, Reflect upon three things, and thou wilt not come within the power of sin: Know whence thou camest, whither thou art going; and before whom thou wilt in future have to give account and reckoning. Whence thou camest: from a fetid drop; whither thou art going: to a place of dust, worms and maggots; and before whom thou wilt in future have to give account and reckoning: before the Supreme King of kings, the Holy One, blessed be He." If you think on these three truths, you will recover your health. For all the substances that go to make up the world are delicately dispersed in the human body. Moreover all means of healing are contained in the body of each person; but this is unknown to the doctors. Pride coarsens the human spirit, and a coarse spirit cannot properly sift and appropriately blend the delicate substances, necessary for health, which are contained in the body. It is therefore essential that a person should achieve true humility and modesty. In this way his spirit is refined and he acquires the ability to make correct use of the healing substances of his body, according to his need, and he will be healthy. We achieve complete humility only when we realize the three truths shown to us in the Talmud: the meanness of Man's origin, the pitiful end to which we must come, and the responsibility we have before the face of Eternity, against which we so grievously err.

"God creates the universe and He also destroys it,"—says the Talmud. This means that God not only creates the universe but also, in His mercy, grants life to the wicked, even though they destroy His work by their sins. The passage in the Talmud therefore means: God creates the universe and those who destroy it.

Why does the holy book "Zohar" call penance "Mother"?— Because the human soul after repentance is as purified as the pure soul of a new-born child immediately after it leaves its mother's womb. (Rebe Reb Ber of Mezeritz also taught that a man is stirred to thoughts of repentance by the image of his mother's face. See also page 219 in this book.)

The verse in the psalm which reads, "Moses and Aaron are amongst His servants," means that if people sincerely serve God He will incarnate the spirit of Moses and Aaron in them.

Once again I have forgotten something immensely important! The holy Dyvre Chayyim of Sanz, the Seer's disciple, was the incarnation of the Hebrew poet, Avigdor Karo, whose bones rest in the old Jewish cemetery in Prague.

Therefore you who wish to live, enter with me into another Gate, for there you shall read:

—how wine fermented at the beginning of the world, or how blood is very holy—How the Holy Old Man performed a deed and why everybody in heaven took heed of Pinchas' word— And what the end of the story was—How the son of a rich man sinned very grievously, until he fell out of bed—How the holy Reb Pinchas succeeded in deceiving the heavenly court and saved a consumptive—How deeply modest he was, how he honoured his son and loved his enemies—Whereupon there follows why a proud person is incarnated in a bee, and how the holy Reb Pinchas liked quoting Gentile sayings—How he never spoke an untruth, yes, and how he recommended business men to do the same—How his song is itself God—How the birds would fly down and listen to his singing—How his son was an expert craftsman, and about his grandsons and the tortures they went through.

The Ninth Gate

Most secret brain of Greatness and Wisdom;
fifty gates of Light. (They were revealed to him.)
Even as noontide sun can have no added radiance,
so a king extolled is not thereby the higher raised.
For all praise
changes in his countenance
to quiet and silence.

Our teacher and our master

THE HOLY REB PINCHAS OF KORITZ

may the Light of his merits protect us exceeding clearly!

THE NINTH GATE

In the future world we shall not drink any young wine at all. In the future world the wine will be extremely old and valuable. "Wine that has fermented in its grapes since the beginning of the world,"—this the Talmud promises to all just people.

The blood that flowed in the veins of the holy Reb Pinchas of Koritz was both as precious and as old as the wondrous wine of the world to come.

One day Pinchas fell seriously ill. This was during the lifetime of the holy Baal-Shem and he was still very young.

Apparently the only way Pinchas could be saved was by bleeding. The holy Baal-Shem warned the surgeon:

"Make sure you cut him in the right place, and see that the lad doesn't lose a single drop of blood more than he need to enable him to recover. If you are not quite sure about it, then give it up altogether! I would rather place my hand on his, and have my own arm cut, than allow a single drop of his blood to be wasted. That boy's blood is immensely dear to me. It is a wondrous fluid, which was created at the very beginning of the world."—That was what the holy Baal-Shem said. May the Light of his merits protect us!

For many years the holy Reb Pinchas lived unnoticed and unrecognized in a little town and served God in secret. He lived in direst poverty with wife and children.

This was in the time of the Holy Grandpa of Shpole.

Holy Grandpa is the name we give to Reb Leib of Shpole on account of his having taught his entire illiterate community how to read the prayers, like a grandfather teaching his grandchildren.

The Holy Grandpa of Shpole had a Chassid who was a very unhappy man in spite of the fact that he was endowed with

worldly wealth far in excess of the normal share. He was unhappy because he had no children, and he who has no children
is accursed of God, as the Talmud says. The Chassid's name was
Reb Zanvl, if I am not mistaken.

In vain did the good Zanvl beseech the Holy Grandpa to entreat the Most High to grant him a son—so that he might have
somebody to pray for the salvation of his soul after God had in
due course called him to Himself.

Somehow the Holy Old Man always succeeded in putting
him off. The years passed, and Reb Zanvl remained without an
heir.

Once the Old Man advised him to treat the Chassidim to
brandy and then get them to wish him a son over their glasses.
This might help perhaps.—But all to no avail.

So it went on until one day he came upon the Holy Old Man
as he was deep in meditation.

"Now's a good time!" Zanvl thought to himself. "At this
moment the saint's spirit is without doubt soaring aloft in the
higher worlds. Who knows if it is not even now at the very
throne of God!" For the face of the Holy Grandpa was shining
like the face of an angel of the Lord.

The good Zanvl was determined to take advantage of this
hour of grace and impel the Holy Grandpa to take a decisive
step while his spirit was in the realms above.

But all his appeals were quite in vain. It seemed that the Old
Man did not even hear. Then suddenly, as though awakened
from a dream, he turned to Zanvl and said:

"I promise you—that you will never have a son! . . . There
are nobler things than keeping your line going. . . . Why have
you disturbed me?!"

Hearing these words, Zanvl sighed and wept. He sighed—out
of regret that he had disturbed the saint in his meditations. He
wept—because he was not to have a son.

Then he bid farewell to the Holy Grandpa and journeyed
forth into the world, to implore other *Tsaddikim* to intercede
with God on his behalf.

He was not sparing with gifts, but nowhere could he obtain

help. Where was the *Tsaddik* who could prevail against the word of the Holy Grandpa of Shpole?!

So Zanvl wandered through the world, from saint to saint, from town to town, until he came to the little township where the holy Reb Pinchas served God in secret.

Zanvl entered the House of Study there, and before he had so much as turned round in it, he was fascinated by the sight of an emaciated young man who was seated in a corner poring over an enormous book. He was evidently so engrossed in his study that he was quite oblivious of what was going on around him. His slender body and head moved forwards and backwards over the open book in a continuous rhythm. One, two, one, two, up, down, up, down.

He was learning out loud, of course. But the melody which accompanied his repetition of the words did not resemble the chant we use when reading from the Talmud. It sounded exactly like a prayer and at moments his spirit seemed to writhe in convulsions, as though he were confessing to the most grievous sins, so plaintive and doleful was the melody. A moment later, however, and it had changed into a joyous paean of praise to the Lord, as when we sing the Psalms of David at the great festivals. At other moments it sounded as innocent and sweet as when children at school learn the Song of Solomon.

Zanvl had seen many saints in his day, but he had never heard anyone studying like this before. No, never! All at once he realized what the entire town had not suspected in so many years: this emaciated young man was an exceptional saint, a saint with scarcely an equal in this sinful world.

He did not want to interrupt. He had had enough experience of that! From people in the House of Study he had learnt who the young man was. They told him it was "a fellow by the name of Pinchas".

Zanvl sought out Pinchas's home. Here too was such poverty as he had never seen in his life. Moreover it was the very eve of the Passover!

Reb Zanvl therefore wasted no time in purchasing everything that was necessary—unleavened bread and wine, eggs and bitter herbs, fish and meat, new clothes for Reb Pinchas, his wife and children, and even essential pieces of furniture.

Naturally he did not forget the thirty-six candles either. Thirty-six—the number of tractates in the Talmud and the number of hours that Adam beheld the mystic light of the Beginning of the World before God hid it from sinners for the world to come. Thirty-six—the number of times the word "light" occurs in the Five Books of Moses and the number of the *Tsaddikim* in each generation. Thirty-six is also the number of candles they use in faraway Tibet.

Indeed he bought two sets of thirty-six wax candles for the two evenings of the festival, for this time he had a strong feeling that he would most surely receive assistance.

He caused everything to be brought to Pinchas's home on the eve of the festival, partly to surprise him and partly so that the gifts could not be refused.

In short, when Reb Pinchas returned from the House of Prayer on the eve of the festival, he was unable to recognize his own home. He saw the hand of God in all that had been wrought, and his joy at such clear evidence of Grace knew no bounds. It goes without saying that the kind person responsible had to become his guest and share the family devotions, the *seder*.

Never was there a more beautiful *seder*!

Never had the ancient "Four Questions"—"How does this night differ from all other nights. . . ."—sounded so sweet as when, on this occasion, they fell from the darling little lips of Pinchas's youngest child.

It was the true piety of family happiness. They blessed the Lord, they spoke of Redemption and Salvation, they ate the unleavened bread, tasted the bitter herbs and emptied the first two cups of the festival wine. The thirty-six candles shone in Pinchas's holy eyes and the good Zanvl revealed his great wish.

"I swear to you," cried Reb Pinchas, "I swear that you shall have a son within a year from now!"

Zanvl could not believe his ears, the blood raced in his veins for utter happiness. He quivered with bliss.

While Zanvl quivered with bliss, the heavens quivered with consternation. The oath of a saint is a fiery sword. Pinchas's words thrust their way through the seven heavens to the very throne of God.

Would it also cleave and unloose that which had long since been so firmly secured by the Holy Grandpa of Shpole?!

Thus it was that they determined in heaven: If it be found that Reb Pinchas has never uttered an empty oath in his life, then he, and not the Old Man of Shpole, shall be heard. Then they looked up the records that are kept in heaven of every person's deeds, and found that Reb Pinchas not only had never yet uttered an oath, but even that he had never yet spoken a single empty word in his life. . . .

The saint of Ruzhen, who told this story, used to add: "You see, we should always pay heed to the wishes of the holy *Tsaddi-kim*, however unfortunate they may seem to us at first sight. Perhaps it would have been better if that Chassid had not been granted an heir, as the Holy Grandpa of Shpole ordained, for that shameful informer, Samson, who caused Reb Pinchas's grandsons to undergo such fearful torture fifty years later, was the son of the son who was born to the Chassid in answer to Reb Pinchas's prayers."

We shall hear more about that later. In the meantime I shall tell you another wonderful story about the holy Reb Pinchas.

At the end of every year, the holy Reb Pinchas used to send out two disciples to go round and collect contributions from the rich. He would draw up a list and enter opposite each name the sum of money which that person had to contribute. From the godless, of course, he took nothing.

One day he crossed out the name of a certain wealthy person and wrote down his son's name instead. Sure enough, when the disciples came to the rich man's home, they heard the tragic news. The devout and worthy man had died. Every year after this the required amount was paid by the son.

One year, however, the holy Reb Pinchas took his pen and crossed out the name of the rich man's son also.

The disciples supposed that the young man must have died, as the father had died years before when the holy Reb Pinchas crossed his name off the list. When they came to the town, however, the news they heard was even sadder than death. The man had not died, but had gone to the bad. He had started wearing the type of clothes worn by Christians, eating forbidden foods and publicly contravening the commandments of God and the sacred customs of our forefathers. Each year the things the disciples heard about him got worse and worse.

Then one day the holy Reb Pinchas took up his pen and again wrote the name of the rich man's son on the list.

Upon their arrival at the town the disciples heard that the man had mended his ways. He had given up his sinful life and started doing good deeds. No one knew the reason for his sudden conversion.

The disciples made their way to his home with all speed. He gave them a joyous welcome, instantly paid the sum of money and bestowed further generous gifts upon them. They were unable to refrain from asking him why he had suddenly changed over to leading a good life, and they told him how Reb Pinchas had crossed out his name from the list of the godly and how he had recently put it back on the list again.

"Listen, then," said the penitent. "Sit down and I'll tell you all about it.

"One day, less than a year ago, I dozed off after lunch and had a strange dream. I dreamt that I was on a journey. I travelled on and on. Suddenly I felt very hungry. So I made my way to the nearest town, went into an inn and ordered lunch. They brought me roast pork. It didn't worry me that this was forbidden food. I was just about to put the first mouthful into my mouth when a man came up to me and said: 'I've come to bring you to court. A legal action has been brought against you.' I told him I wasn't conscious of having done anything wrong, but that if anybody had a claim to make against me, he should simply present me with the proper evidence in support of his claim and I would immediately pay him without taking the matter to court. 'Not at all,' said the stranger, 'your case is required to come up before a court of law. You have been summoned to appear and the court undoubtedly has its reasons for this.' The stranger's appearance was so dignified, his voice so grave, that I got up from the table willy-nilly and followed him, without taking a single mouthful. We entered the court building. In the entrance hall a servant came up to us and asked me my name. When I told him he frowned and said: 'Yes, you have been summoned. But for the time being the court has no time to take your case. Go back and wait!' I returned to the inn and sat down to my meal. But once again the stranger came up to me and asked me to go to the court with him.

"I answered him crossly. Did he not know that the court was busy with another case, and besides, was I not ready to pay up everything, as I had said I would? I told him to leave me alone and let me continue my meal in peace and quiet. But the man insisted on having his way, and I had no option but to do as he said, being overwhelmed for the second time by his dignified bearing. Everything happened exactly as before. Again the servant came out and told me that the court had no time to take my case for the moment and that I should therefore go back and wait. I went back to the inn thoroughly angry, sat down at the table and prepared to eat. By this time I was ravenously hungry. For the third time the stranger came up to me and told me to follow him. I did not wish to and refused with all my strength. But once again my resistance was broken down by the man's mysterious gravity.

"This time the servant threw the court doors wide open in front of me and called out: 'Enter! You will now be judged.'

"I entered a magnificent room in the middle of which stood a large table. Around the table sat dignified old men with long, white beards; these were the judges. Then the man who had accompanied me stepped before the judges and recounted all the sins I had ever committed. Black sins there were, so that my hair stood up on end in horror; others, both lesser and greater, had grown pale, being sins which I imagined that I had long since forgotten. But the prosecutor described them in such detail that I remembered them all. I stood as though frozen with fear.

I wanted to run away but could not. My legs were like wood. Drops of mortal sweat broke out on my brow. It seemed that the reckoning would never come to an end. My sins heaped up before me like hideous heaps of dead rats and other unclean animals—like scorpions and snakes. At last the prosecutor stopped speaking. The ensuing silence was like the grave. All I heard was my own heart beats, coming, it seemed, from infinitely far away. Those were horrible moments indeed. They weighed upon me like leaden rocks and melted away into the endless nebulae of eternity.

"Finally one of the old men broke the silence:

" 'What punishment shall we mete out to him?'

" 'What punishment shall we mete out to him?' repeated the others in ghastly unison. Again there was silence.

" 'It will take a lot of time to pass judgment on him,' they said after a while. 'In the meanwhile let him stay here until we have properly discussed everything.'

"I realized that it was all only a dream. But something told me that my sleep was to last for all eternity and that I should never wake from it. I began to wring my hands, to weep, and implore my judges. To win their pity I protested that I was still young, that I still had a chance of mending my ways.

" 'That's true,' said one of the old men. 'The man can still mend his ways. We must give him a chance to do this and send him back to life.'

"I looked up. Who could be pleading for a person as unworthy as I was? I looked at his face and lo!—it was our holy Reb Pinchas. 'Since he assisted me once I am indebted to him and I ask that he be released.'

" 'That is not in accordance with law and justice," returned the other judges, 'but since it is none other than Reb Pinchas of Koritz who intercedes for him—let it be! . . .'

"At that moment I fell out of bed.

"That was the day when my new life began. But I am unable to rid my mind of that dream. Whenever I remember it, I tremble like an aspen leaf." . . . Such was the experience which the rich man's son related to the disciples from Koritz.

It was indeed an unusual dream. It had shaken the conscience of a thoroughly hardened sinner. We can see from this that the holy Reb Pinchas used to sit in the heavenly court while he was still alive. Other saints do not become members of the court until after death.

Doubt in matters of Faith can cause a person great difficulty. One of the Chassidim was greatly troubled in this way: how could God possibly know all the thoughts of every single person?

If only the foolish fellow had confided in an older colleague, he might have obtained proper instruction on this point. Did not our famous philosophers write at length on this subject centuries ago? This fellow however was ashamed of all his doubts, and that of course was a great mistake. How fortunate for the salvation of his soul that he was inspired to have the idea of making a pilgrimage to Koritz! What a happy chance that he had mercy on himself and obeyed the inspiration!

The holy Reb Pinchas happened to be looking out of the window at that very moment. Seeing the Chassid approaching, he called out to him when he was still some way off: "Why shouldn't God know—when even I know!" Thus it was that the Chassid came to be saved.

One day a man came to Koritz grievously ill with consumption—may our merciful God protect us from all evil! Some saint or other had prayed for his recovery, and the poor fellow had even been to the doctors—but it was all to no avail, his illness had got worse and worse the whole time. It was plain that heaven had passed judgment on him. But when the holy Reb Pinchas prayed for him, he was cured, he became "as healthy as a Gentile".

"Don't think they like me better in heaven than the other saints who prayed for him. And don't think that my prayers are more valued in heaven than the prayers of anybody else!" the modest Reb Pinchas told the Chassidim by way of apology. "It's simply that I set about it in a better way than the others. That's all.

"When I ascended to heaven during prayer, I found that the

gate of life was shut in front of this man. I knocked on the gate and implored them to open it, but all to no avail; the gate remained closed. So I went to the provisions gate. This one I found wide open. Here I asked for as much food for him as I could carry. They gave me plenty, enough to last for the longest human life. What had happened was that the celestial provisions office had made inquiries at the life authorization office and had been told that the applicant's fate was already sealed. They had then said to themselves: 'Why shouldn't we give the poor fellow some food since he won't be able to finish it in any case?' If a man's fate is sealed, he has to leave everything to other people and go. So after they had given me what I asked for the man," continued the holy Reb Pinchas, "I returned to the gate of life. As soon as they saw me coming, they instantly closed the gate. 'Give him life!' I shouted.—'Give him life? Most certainly not,' came the answer. So I went to the window and started waving the food permit which had been given to me at the provisions gate. 'So you want me to twist the sacred truth of the Talmud, do you?!' I cried. 'Is it not written in the Talmud: "To whom doth God give nourishment?—Only to him that shall live." If he has been granted food, then you are bound to give him life as well, as it has been ordained, otherwise you will be making a lie of the eternal truths of the Talmud.' What could they do against my objection? Nothing! Willy-nilly they were forced to do as I wished. So you see, I didn't do the least miracle when I made the patient better. I only asserted for his sake the truth of an old-established law, as our holy savants have expressed it in the Talmud."

Modesty and humility were the holy Reb Pinchas's greatest virtues. He was always pleased to hear anybody slandering and humiliating him. But if people paid him tribute, he was very troubled. He used to say that honours caused him greater pain than blows with a knife. In this profound humility he would speak as respectfully with his own son as a servant speaks with his master. He used to teach that we should all love one another. And if anybody hurt or insulted us, we should love that person even more than before. One day he read in a book that we should love all God's creatures—not only Jews, but all peoples, even if they do us harm and humiliate us. After this he could never stop praising this book on account of these words. There was a man where he lived who was absolutely illiterate and the simplest of the simple. This man was Hershel, the water carrier. The fellow was not even married, although he was well past forty. What an untutored, coarse chap he was! Nevertheless the holy Reb Pinchas held him in exceptionally high regard. Once he said to his wife: "Whenever I see Hershel, I tremble all over with respect for the man. What a rare *saint* he is! When he brings a person water, even if that person is the most ordinary citizen there could be, he positively melts in abasement before him. What must he feel when confronted by a person of consequence?! I'm sure that at such moments he is really conscious of all his human wretchedness and baseness. How deeply he must be loved by God for his humility! What a pity it will probably never be granted to me to achieve such perfection as his!"

The holy ARI teaches us that when a conceited person dies his soul is incarnated in a buzzing bee. We know that this punishment is a truly appropriate and just one, and that the life of a bee counterbalances the damage done by human conceit. For the bee is a creature that never thinks of itself. All its thoughts, feelings and acts are exclusively devoted to the general happiness of the entire hive. But the holy Reb Pinchas interpreted this law of *gilgul* (transmigration of souls) in his own way—one might say, almost phonetically. He said: "Your conceited person is continually saying: I am . . . —in Yiddish: *ech bin.* . . . For instance: I am a writer—*ech bin a mechabr.* I am a singer—*ech bin a zingr.* I am a savant—*ech bin a talmud-chochem.* By speaking like this he incarnates himself in a bee. For in Yiddish, we also use the word *bin* for a bee—exactly the same word as in 'I am'—'*ech bin*'."

The holy Reb Pinchas was not very fond of cleverness. He used to say: "There's only one thing I fear in the world: that I might become more clever than devout."

He liked using Ukrainian sayings. Among his Chassidim was one by the name of Yankel. Yankel was not a learned man but he was endowed with great physical strength and skill. There was probably nobody whom the holy Reb Pinchas was so fond of as this man. He used to say that he was a person who belonged to the world of Perfection. As proof of this he would add, in Ukrainian, that he was *"at home both in palaces and cottages"*, in other words, that he belonged both among the exalted and the simple.

Another Ukrainian saying the holy Reb Pinchas liked to use was: "Without God cross no threshold." Without the strength which God continuously transmits to us we cannot take the least step or make the least move, we cannot even think of doing anything.

He had a great love of truth. He used to say that if it had been granted to him to know something of the mysteries of the Lord, this was due solely to the fact that he had never spoken any untruth throughout his life. He believed that the best guide to success in any profession was: never tell a lie, however small. A man should prefer to give up the ghost rather than to breathe a single untruthful word. If people looked upon a lie as a sin no less serious than incest, the whole world would have been saved long ago.

Some songs, when we sing them, link us with God. But there are other songs—the holy Reb Pinchas said—which are themselves God. But ever since David the King no one had sung these songs, until now, when he, the holy Reb Pinchas, began singing them. May the light of his merits protect us!

The holy Reb Pinchas wanted to die in the Holy Land. "For to a man who dies in the land of Israel," says the Talmud, "it is as though he breathes his last in the arms of his mother. So Reb Pinchas set out. But he did not get far. The Holy Land came to meet him—in Russia. He died on the tenth day of the month of Elul in the year 5551 (1791), at the town of Shpitevke, where he lies buried.

The Chassidim mourned his loss deeply. None grieved more than his son Moyshele. I must tell you something about

Pinchas's Moyshele for he was in very truth a *silken* young man. Not only was he very learned and devout but he was also a skilled calligrapher and draughtsman. He was adept at various crafts and at making beautiful objects. His dear father, therefore, thought very highly of him throughout his life. And as for his lovely voice! When Moyshele sang, the birds would fly down to him from all directions, from distances of up to forty miles, to learn some of his songs.

Moyshele did not become a Rabbi. He set up a printing works at Slavuta. This was a most successful undertaking and brought him great merit. He printed three editions of the entire Talmud and also some cabbalistic writings, the letters for which he made with his own hand. Those of us who possess some of the works printed at Slavuta in our libraries are very proud of them and treat them as precious relics. There is of course yet another reason for this which we shall hear about directly, as I promised you a long time ago.

Two of Moyshele's sons helped their father in his business. The elder son was called Shmuel Abe and the younger Pinchas, after his famous grandfather. They were known as Rabinovitch. One morning a man was found hung in the House of Prayer at Slavuta. He was an employee of the printing works, Leizer by name, a drunkard of ill repute. It is not known whether it was a crowd of Chassidim who killed him and then hung him, in a fit of fury at his incorrigible drunkenness, as was whispered by some evil tongues at the time, or whether he hanged himself under the influence of the depression which follows upon the return to sobriety, as the Chassidim maintained. A personal enemy of the Rabinovitch family, by the name of Samson, went so far in his blind hatred of Moyshele and his sons as to denounce them to the Czar, averring that the Rabinovitch family had arrogated to themselves royal power over the Jews and even sentenced people to death. Leizer, they said, had been condemned to death in this way.

This shameless and totally unfounded accusation aroused indescribable indignation among all Jews throughout Russia. Even the most inveterate opponents of Chassidism, who on

other occasions did not shrink from turning informer if by doing
so they could harm their Chassidic kinsmen, were seized with
loathing and shame. No Jew could believe that the Chassidim
would actually kill drunkards. It is true—they would say—that
there are many scoundrels, criminals and debauched persons
among us Jews, no less than among other peoples. Indeed we
are all their innocent victims. But even granting all our mistakes
and vices nobody denies that we are truly a chosen people;
brutal murderers are almost unknown among the Jews. For
thousands of years the Jewish murderer has been an even rarer
phenomenon than the illiterate Jew. Only one out of the fifteen
million Jews in the world commits a murder in five or ten
years, and then usually only under the most exceptional circumstances. "My son, you may hear of a Jew being a swindler and
taking other people's money," Jewish mothers have told their
children, "you may even hear of them bearing false witness or
perjuring themselves. It would not be abnormal to hear accusa-
tions of this nature. There are a number of rogues among us. If
the Emperor's ministers are wont to steal, so are his Jews. But
never believe it if you hear of a Jew shedding blood. That is sure
to be a false accusation. Jews do not kill!"—The possibility of a
Jew shedding blood is indeed very slight. It hardly ever happens.
There have been no bestial murderers, fratricides and parricides
among us for centuries. In this we are different from every other
confession, and from every other people, from one end of the
world to the other. Nevertheless the fact that the idea could even
arise that Jews might have been responsible for the death of a
drunkard is in itself striking evidence of the disgust felt by Jews
for drunkenness. Naturally the Chassidim enjoy having a drink
together. But always in moderation. This their opponents are well
aware of. To assert that the wise and foreseeing Moyshele would
have sentenced Leizer to death was of course an almost ludicrous
assertion. It would be contrary to Talmudic jurisprudence.

In spite of this the Emperor gave orders that a strict investiga-
tion was to be held, and entrusted the responsibility for this to
Vasilchikov the Governor. Vasilchikov went into the matter
very thoroughly but with the best will in the world was unable

to find the accused even remotely guilty. Old Moyshele was immediately cleared of the charge. But just as it seemed that his two sons were about to be released from custody, these two inexperienced young men did something very foolhardy which was to have fatal consequences for them. To make sure that they would be released as soon as possible from their cruel prison they offered Governor Vasilchikov *one thousand five hundred* rubles in gold—something which was quite normal with the Russians in those days. But Vasilchikov brought a charge against them. The sum of money was far below his dignity, and his hatred of the Jews was greater than his craving for money. Both young men were convicted—for offering bribes, of course. A fearful sentence was imposed on them: *one thousand five hundred* strokes of the knout. In spite of all the appeals and intercession that was made on their behalf, the sentence was carried out to the full. They were driven naked through "streets" of Cossacks who beat them mercilessly. Not one stroke was remitted. Only one concession was allowed to them. Being Rabbi's sons they were permitted to keep their little caps—their *yarmelkas*—on their heads, since it is a sin for us to walk about with our heads uncovered. The story goes that one of them lost his cap as he was being beaten. He only noticed this after it was over and, not wishing to commit the sin of walking about uncovered for any length of time, he returned voluntarily for his *yarmelka* and had to endure further blows from the Cossack's knouts.

Under the terms of the sentence the two offenders were to be exiled to Siberia after the strokes with the knout had been administered. This part of the sentence, however, could not be carried out. The two Jews lay on the ground in a pool of blood. The flesh hung in shreds from their bodies and they no longer resembled human beings created in the image of God. The *muzhiks*, who had watched the spectacle from beginning to end, took pity on the victims. They killed two young rams and wrapped the tortured Jews in their skins while they were still hot and bleeding. No one had ever survived such terrible treatment with the knout. But the grandsons of the holy Reb Pinchas of Koritz stayed alive and recovered.

Later they were moved to Moscow. When the wife of the younger of the two, Pinchas, came to visit her husband and saw his face so fearfully ravaged by the suffering he had undergone, she died of heart failure on the spot.

It is said—although it is doubtful if it is true—that all this was God's way of punishing the two young Rabinovitch lads for a sin they had once committed in *offending a man of learning*. Apparently they had maintained that Akive Eger, the famous Talmudist, head Rabbi at Kalish, had accepted bribes in some court case, whereupon Reb Akive Eger had declared: "With all my heart I can forgive them for insulting me. But they can never be forgiven for the offence they have thereby committed against the Law of God whose representative I am."

The printing press at Slavuta fell on evil days. The father of the two lads, Reb Moyshele, son of the holy Reb Pinchas, whose early years had been so full of promise, wandered disconsolately through the world with a beggar's stick and died in extreme poverty. "I was young and have grown old, but I have never seen the just man forsaken and his children's children begging for their bread."—Thus it is written in the Holy Scriptures, and what is written is the highest truth. But the judgements of God are inscrutable.

FROM THE WISDOM OF REB PINCHAS OF KORITZ
(From his book: "Midrash Pinchas"—The Searching of Pinchas.)

All pleasures come to us from paradise, even good jokes.

Joy is on a higher plane than grief. Even with the new-born child, tears come first and smiles only later. Joy constitutes a higher stage, for it springs from the higher worlds, from the Glory of God. Thus it is that joy washes away all sin.

If a man falls into vice, it should not cause him to fret overmuch. He must hope that God will set him right and purify him. For it is only in the matter of deciding in favour of good or evil that we have freedom of will; the carrying out of our intentions and everything else is exclusively in the hands of God. But if a man sincerely chooses to do good, God will certainly help him to perform it.

If a person is beset by worries, his wisest course is to go to sleep. In sleep his soul merges with the Infinite in which all care dissolves into nothing.

Each thing sleeps in its own way. Vegetation and water also sleep. There are times when the angels of the Lord sleep, too, in their own way, and even the Law of God is wont to sleep.

Dreams are the refuse of the brain. Nonetheless they always reflect the personal qualities of the person who dreams them.

If a person moves amongst ignorant people, he stifles his spirit in the same way as if he were to dwell in a temple of idolaters.

Camels copulate back to back. This is the reason why the camel is the stupidest of beasts. With other kinds of animal the male usually faces the female, and only the female turns her back. There is therefore some wisdom in these animals. But people usually copulate face to face. This is the reason why they are so wise.

The Holy Scriptures are the link between the material world and the higher worlds. Solomon's Song of Songs is the link between the higher worlds and the Infinite. That is why no one can fully understand it.

Every human word contains elements of the world of the spirit, of the world of the angels, and of all creatures that exist. This is true of even the simplest everyday word, except that in such words these elements are at a lower level than is the case with words that are pleasing to God.

Some people have had to be born only in order that they should perform but one specific good deed in the course of their entire lives, and maybe even only one specific movement on one particular occasion.

Some souls, when they wish to become incarnate even for a short while in the brain of a person, will begin by reducing him to tears. And all the souls and all the worlds will help to make tears form in that person's eyes, for tears purify the brain.

A man should look upon himself as a complete idiot. In this

way he will renew his spiritual capabilities. And because a man has several souls within him, all of them renew their strength at the same time as he does.

The spirit of Moses pervades all generations and all souls.

In length there is neither breadth, nor right, nor left. For this reason it will not be possible in the future, long, eternal world to acquire either merit or blame, nor the rewards or punishments connected with these.

It used to be a custom with the Turks that when a Governor was deprived of his power, all his servants and slaves were paraded before him anew. At this ceremony, however, they all had to be as silent as if they were actually dumb. People who during their lifetime have not fulfilled the commandments of God as they should have done, will be treated in paradise in the same way as the deposed Turkish dignitaries. Each good deed we do turns into an angel. But if a deed is not absolutely perfect, that deed produces an imperfect angel. A dumb one, for instance. It will be a severe disgrace for a person, if when he comes to sit in paradise, he has dumb angels to wait upon him. Or if one of his angels has a hand missing, another a leg missing. These imperfections in his angels can only be put right by the self-sacrifice of the person concerned. But this is something you cannot understand. It is too profound a thought.

A man's good thoughts are his guardian angels. If we speak well of any one, even if that person be dead, our words clothe him with the garment of Wisdom.—Thus saying Reb Pinchas started singing the praises of the holy Rebe Reb Schmelke of Mikulov, saying that he was an outstanding saint the like of whom was not to be found in his generation throughout the world.—

God has made Himself incarnate in the food and drink which we use on the Sabbath and in our sleep on the Sabbath. This is in the nature of a *contraction* of the Infinite before the creation of the world.

Even as the world has its centre and this centre is Palestine, so does Wisdom have its centre and this centre is the Law of God. The other sciences are the enveloping cover of the Law; hence

216

if any one knows any of the sciences, this does not mean that he is capable of understanding our Law. On the other hand, a man who understands the Law will have no difficulty in understanding any other science. In a similar way the Law of God has its inner part and its outer part. The inner part consists of the sacred mysteries of the Book of Zohar and the writings of the holy ARI. It is for this reason that they were revealed in Palestine, which is the centre of the world, in the same way as they are the inner part of the law which is the centre of all wisdom.

All living things make up a unified whole which has the characteristics of the human figure. Israel is the brain of this whole, which accounts for our fondness for professions requiring a great deal of thinking. Other nations have the functions of hands in this living whole, and therefore they are above all such skilful craftsmen and artists. The animals, on the other hand, are merely the legs in this whole. Their characteristic activity is in their legs, and in consequence the lower types, such as insects and mice, are almost incapable of walking slowly, but can only run and jump. Thus it is with creation as a whole, and man as an individual. When a child begins to walk he does not do so like an adult; he either runs or stands still. He is therefore primarily *legs*. Subsequently, as he grows up, he becomes basically *hands*. And so, at a certain age, he spends the whole time playing. Thus my son, although he does very well at his lessons, likes most of all to do the work of a craftsman because he is still a boy. In old age a man is primarily *brain* and, in the last resort, finds his satisfaction not in talking but in silence and thought. Youth is innately hot-blooded and eager to fight, whereas in old age a man is more restrained. God, too, first revealed Himself—in the flight from Egypt—as a warrior, whereas subsequently, during the reign of Solomon, a great Peace held sway. (The word Peace, in Hebrew, is "Shalom"—Solomon is one of the attributes of God.) In the reign of Jeroboam, of course, dissension broke out again, for Jeroboam was a return to a lower level.—Now you have seen an interesting thing: you have seen how I began with the divine Being as the principle of all that lives and I end with the sinful Jeroboam. It is the same with the "Book of the Tree of Life" by the holy ARI which begins with the Being above this world and ends with the Gate of the Powers of Evil.

All happenings can be classified either as *outward-shining* light or as *reflected* light. For instance, if we lend somebody money we perform a deed that is outward-shining. The payment of a debt, on the other hand, is in the nature of reflected light. What a father gives to his children while they are young is outward-shining light. On the other hand, what the children pay back to their father in old age is reflected light. Outward-shining light constitutes the principle of Grace and Love, reflected light only the principle of mere law. The saying that one father will support ten children but ten children will not support one father is therefore quite correct. For the principle of Love is more powerful than the principle of Law.

A man should eat as little as possible, for his fate is determined by his manner of eating. It is not true that the more a man eats the longer he lives. Some animals eat a great deal and live only a short while. On the other hand other animals live a very long time even though they eat very little.

Everybody has a special light burning for him in the higher world, totally different from the light of every other person. When two friends meet in this world, their lights up above unite for a moment, and out of the union of the two lights an angel is born. However the angel is only given sufficient strength to live one year. If the two friends meet again within the year they give the angel a further lease of life. But if they do not see each other for a whole year the angel wastes away and dies for lack of light. The Talmud bids us, when we see a friend whom we have not seen for a whole year, to bless God for "raising the dead". This is a strange commandment indeed, since neither of us have died. Whom then has God raised from the dead? Surely none other than the languishing angel whose lease of life is renewed each time we meet.

218

Finally something for Freud and Darwin:

If a man has *sinful thoughts*, let him recall his mother's face and he will be delivered from them. If he is tempted by megalomania, let him imagine his father's face.

Among all creatures there are some types that are transitional. There are those that are transitional between plant and animal, and there are plants that are transitional between grasses and trees. *Monkeys are transitional between animals and man.*

How a pilgrim accompanies you on the way to Kotsk and what strange things happen there. On the journey there you learn that Moyshe Leib of Sassov was a merry child—Something about the sort of business man he was and what happened to a drunken *muzhik*—Why the Holy Jew understood the animals' language, or his wondrous discovery of the world, and the story of the frozen Seraph—Why Simche Binem travelled to the sea and became associated with the theatre there—How he played cards and saved a soul—Next it is related how Eisik, the son of Yekl, journeyed to Prague and how he returned home to build a House of God—How a *muzhik* studied the scriptures—Upon which there follows what Reb Meir of Dzikev related about Mendele of Tomashov, or how he made him out to be more handsome than he was—Where Reb Mendele kept his foot and how difficult it was to do so—How he prayed while still a small boy and how God sent angels to him—How Reb Mendele of Kotsk went to Prague and prayed for three mystic favours at the cemetery there—How he made Rabbi Loev a teacher—About a lazy fellow and his grave sin, and how things went with a saint in a fur coat—What a holy thing silence is and what scoundrels we Chassidim of Belz are—What happened to the good Mendele at Lvov and how strangely it all turned out—How the wise Rim stood in front of the heavenly gate, or what a mighty thing eating is—How we went to meet the Messiah with brandy and why God had to punish us so severely—How we would welcome our Saviour, our Prince and King, and so on and so on, and how it is all contained in our Cabbala—In which we finish our journey to the honour of God and to our own praise.

Therefore all ye who wish to live, enter with me into this Gate, for there ye shall read all these things.

The City of Wisdom

"*Rabbi José, the son of Kisma,*[1] *said, I was once walking by the way, when a man met me and greeted me, and I returned his greeting. He said to me, Rabbi, from what place art thou? I said to him, I come from a great city of sages and scribes. He said to me, If thou art willing to dwell with us in our place, I will give thee a thousand thousand golden dinars and precious stones and pearls. I said to him, Wert thou to give me all the silver and gold and precious stones and pearls in the world, I would not dwell anywhere but in the town of*

KOTSK

which is the home of knowledge."

As it is written by the hand of the prophet Haggai: The silver is mine, and the gold is mine, saith the Lord of hosts.

[1] Talmud, Aboth.

THE CITY OF WISDOM

On our pilgrimage from Belz to Koritz we have tasted enough of the honey of simplicity and faith to make us thoroughly sated with it. Let us now try a little of the pepperiness of Kotsk! It is a long journey of course—several miles towards the rising of the sun before we reach the crystal clear river which is called Veprsh.[1] But the time will soon pass. If you will tell me one of those lovely stories about the saint of Berdychev or the holy Ber, I will tell you as many as seventy-seven stories, if need be, from Kotsk. So we shall not be bored, thank God.

The empire of the people of Kotsk is indeed an inhospitable, poverty-stricken, dreary region, as you will soon learn. But there is a sea of Jews there—Talmudists, traders, labourers and craftsmen. You will find that the butchers, coachmen and black-smiths all wear handsome side-whiskers. You will meet very few Gentiles; it appears they are in a disappearing minority. You will find it strangely amusing, when we go through the towns, to see Gentiles and not Jews as the outcasts. There are so few of them there, these wretched Gentiles. There is great misery and still greater dirt. It goes without saying that the Jews likewise do not live in any too great prosperity in these confines. The majority of them are beggars—yes, beggars they are, the poorest of the poor. Just wait, we shall soon be meeting long processions of them—carrying sticks in their hands and bundles on their backs as they journey in droves from town to town, village to village, like the locusts in Egypt. They are none too gentle-hearted, these beggars, it must be admitted. They have their pride. Be very careful not to offend or provoke them. Even if we are dirty and clothed in rags, we are still all equal, we sons of Israel. We are all descendants of Abraham, Isaac and Jacob, all of royal blood, and we take care of our dignity. Indeed,

[1] 'Veprsh' means 'pig'. Translator's note.

of all things, this is the most important for us. But if things are bad, we can be content with a single match acquired by dint of hard begging. Match after match, and by evening, with the help of the Most High, we shall have a whole boxful. And that is a commodity worth having! We can exchange it for money in the town and then we can buy a good hunk of bread. But as a rule it is not as grim as all that. On the contrary, taken as a whole, life is gay on this earth. Not a day passes without some festivity or other, a circumcision, or a banquet, and none of these can take place without us beggars. We must be there. Have we not then reason enough to be proud of our condition as beggars? You, uninvited guests, are not required by anybody. You are no good for anything.

Yes, taken as a whole, life is gay on this earth. Everybody must acknowledge that. So let us not frown and grumble at the world, and we shall be content. But for God's sake let us not be like that *bad guest* on the earth, whom we read about in the Talmud—that bad, ill-mannered guest who is not happy with anything, not even when our good Host gives him everything he could possibly want. Let us rather be that "good guest" who can be content with little, and who with a sweet smile on his lips will thank his heavenly Host for everything He sets before him, even if it be only a dry slice of bread and a gulp of water. Only by being contented with everything, by accepting everything as it is, do we show forth our exalted origin, that good upbringing and gentleness of soul such as belongs to and becomes those who are truly noble. So let us be genuinely modest! That is my advice. And there is one more piece of advice I would give you on the road to Kotsk: Put on the breastplate of flexibility and arm yourself with the shield of patience! Another thing—please do not think that you already speak perfect Yiddish! Why?—Well, because when you get to Kotsk you will have to relearn Yiddish, all over again from the beginning, just as though the language they speak there were entirely strange and unknown to you. Why the breastplate of flexibility and the shield of patience?—You will soon see.

The Chassidic people are on the whole a kind and friendly

people. We of Belz are not too good in this respect, it must be admitted. But the Chassidim at Borislav, Stretena, Tchortkev, or even Karlin and Kossov—they have no equal under the sun in kindliness, gentleness, friendliness and courtesy.

But the Kotskers?—By heaven, they are really coarse!

It is as if their souls never even went to Mount Sinai on that early morning when God enjoined us to keep the rules of courtesy and decency before He gave us His holy Law. It is as if they have never learnt the "Derech Eretz", that part of the Talmud which deals exclusively with the subject of polite behaviour.

"Sholem aleychem" is a greeting of peace and quiet, but at Kotsk they say it in such a terrible way you think they are cursing you. If you ask for bread and salt, they will throw them in front of you, almost as if you were a dog. And if you once complain that there is bran in the bread, or that it is mouldy, or that a dried herring is not actually a herring but a piece of shoe leather which you cannot get your teeth into, or if you make a fuss about there being nails, among other things, in the mash, yes, nails, if you please! then you can be quite sure that you will complain only once and make a fuss only once. You will never try to do so a second time. In the same way you do better never to ask anybody the way to the House of Study if you chance to lose your way in the *town* boulevards! It will fare ill with you. And when finally you are standing in a corner of the *Bes Hamidrash* and pouring forth your heart's affliction in quiet prayer to God, you can be sure that some clumsy lout will suddenly bump into you and the next thing you will know is that you are at the other corner of the House of God. And you will not be allowed so much as to open your mouth.

Nevertheless, in the middle of all this, do not imagine that you must be among a gang of toughs from Sodom rather than among Chassidim. In case you do not know, it was the Sodomites who smeared an innocent girl with honey, and left her at the mercy of the bees, merely because she had given a little water to a beggar and sinned thereby against the unnatural laws of Sodom, which forbid one to do good and command one to

225

do evil and harm, as the Talmud tells us. Far from it! The worthy citizens of Tomashov, Kotsk, Pzhysha, Alexandra and Gera are in no way like those Sodomite scoundrels. They are Jews like ourselves, *chaste, full of sympathy and given to works of mercy*, like ourselves. But they have a strange philosophy of life, a most original one. They say that being treated with courtesy and kindness makes people conceited, and that kindliness and friendliness are therefore only imaginary virtues whose value is highly questionable. Their effect on a person is morally injurious, encouraging pride and arrogance—the worst of all the vices. It is therefore in the interest of the eternal beatitude of our neighbours that we should treat them as roughly as possible and that we should not be too kind and polite with them. On the contrary, the more coarse a person is *"the more he is worthy of praise."*

Against this logic no objection is possible, not even from the point of view of the delicate ethics of the *chabadniks* of Lubavitch,[1] not to mention us *chnyoks* of Belz. However there are thousands of other things they do which can justly arouse general indignation. It is enough to recall how they will crumble their unleavened bread into coffee or soup at festivals—not even the "last" and worst of other Chassidim would think of doing such a thing—or how they will eat the precious Baal-Shem dumplings made of beaten unleavened bread (*matzot*) on the very first evening of the festival—whereas the rest of us Chassidim would not think of touching them till the eighth and last day of the festival. The Chassidim at Belz were quite justified in coining a well-known phrase to describe the Kotskers: *"They think of their dumplings and not of the holy conversation of freedom and Salvation. . . ."*

It is said that on one occasion the Kotskers decided not to put on their phylacteries for three days on end. Apparently they wanted to see what influence this might have on world events. I do not know how the experiment turned out or what

[1] Schneur Zalman of Lady (whose son settled at Lubavitch) founded a trend in Chassidism known as Chabad from the three Hebrew words: Chochmah, Binah, Daat (wisdom, intelligence, knowledge). Translator's note.

results it had. But I doubt, I very much doubt, if it is even possible to tempt God in such a blasphemous way. But who knows? Evil tongues even assert that the Chassidim at Kotsk ate the flesh of geese which had been forcibly fed on fir-cones or maize. But that is probably only unfounded calumny. They were indeed a wonderful set of Chassidim!

In order that we should have some idea as to who's who in that Kotsk crowd, we ought to take a brisk look at the genealogy of the Kotsker saints. We have observed earlier that our holy Rebe Reb Shmelke of Mikulov had a disciple by the name of Reb Moyshe Yide Leib of Sassov. Well, one of the disciples of the holy Reb Moyshe Leib of Sassov was *the Holy Jew*. The Holy Jew—who also of course went to visit the holy Seer of Lublin and the holy Preacher of Koznitz—had a disciple by the name of Reb Binem, Reb Simche Binem of Pzhysha. One of the latter's disciples was Reb Mendele of Tomashov, who subsequently became Rabbi at Kotsk. Finally Reb Mendele had a disciple named Itchey Meyer, also known as the wise Rim, who became the famous Rabbi of Gera. That is enough for the time being.

I have already told you something about the holy Rebe Reb Shmelke. Now I shall tell you something about his disciple, the holy Reb Moyshe Yide Leib of Sassov, in order that the Light of his merits may protect us. You will remember it was he who sailed across the Danube with the holy Rebe Reb Shmelke in a kneading-trough. Moyshe Leib was a gay lad. A gay lad likes to have gay companions. Whenever he had time off from his lessons he would be having fun and running around with his playmates. His father did not like to see this, but he said nothing. However it was a more serious matter when the young Moyshe Leib announced one day that he was much attracted by what the Chassidim were preaching at that time throughout Poland about a new way to God. It was still more serious when all of a sudden his son gathered his belongings together and left home—not to go to a high school of Talmudic learning, a *yeshive* at Vilna or Lvov, which his father would have been quite pleased about in point of fact, but—and this is what was so

227

terrible—to Mikulov. Yes, to Mikulov, to the holy Rebe Reb Shmelke. Meanwhile, at home, his father cursed and swore. At first he determined that he would never again acknowledge his son. What disgrace he had brought upon him! The son of an honest Talmudist, now a vulgar Chassid! But then he said to himself: "He is my child after all. When he comes back I'll punish him. I'll teach him!" Thus saying he went out and purchased a cane. The next day he threw the cane away. Why? Because he bought another one, a more springy one. He went on like this day after day, all through the years when his son was learning to serve God at Mikulov. The slender green willow switches, whose leaves we beat off in the House of Prayer at the festival of Hoshana Rabba, are not so dear to us as was the sight of a new cane every day to Moyshe Leib's father. "You just wait, you're for it!" the words were balm to his soul. But in the end the father did nothing at all, for when his son finally returned he was no longer just Moyshe Leib! He was the holy *Reb* Moyshe Leib, and he no longer belonged only to his father, he belonged to us all, to the whole of Israel.

But it is not only to Israel that the holy Reb Moyshe Leib belongs; he belongs to the entire world. One night, the holy Reb Moyshe Leib was sitting at home studying the Talmud, serving God. When a saint serves God the whole world looks at him and all creation listens to him in silent devotion. But Reb Moyshe Leib was suddenly disturbed. Somebody was rapping at the window—rapping so hard as nearly to break the glass. It was sure to be a Gentile. No Jew would bang like that. The holy Reb Moyshe Leib looked out of the window and, sure enough, it was a Gentile, and drunk into the bargain. A drunken *muzhik*! You know what they are capable of. The drunk asked for a bed for the night. Shocked at hearing such a request for hospitality, Reb Moyshe Leib was on the point of giving vent to his indignation that a drunken Gentile should have had the effrontery to disturb him, Moyshe Leib, in the service of God, when he suddenly recollected himself and held back his just anger. What did he do? He went to the door and let the man in, then he remade his own bed for the drunken *muzhik* to sleep in. For the holy

Reb Moyshe Leib spake thus to his heart: "If God Himself serves a drunkard like this, looking after him and giving him the world He has created for the satisfaction of his mean desires— then you, Moyshe Leib of Sassov, the humblest servant of your Lord, shall not act differently towards him."

Of course he could not be angry with *them*, the unfortunate Gentiles—unfortunate because they had never tasted the sweetness of keeping the commandments of God, or the joys of studying the holy Talmud, which will delight our souls even after death. He could not be angry with *them*. Do we not pray day after day that they may be enlightened? Why, even if we have once had occasion to drink at a well, we are forbidden ever afterwards to throw a stone into it and thereby reward it with ingratitude. Are we not bound to honour all persons who have ever taught us anything useful as though they were our actual teachers, and even as God Himself? Moreover it was no small thing that the Holy Reb Moyshe Leib had learnt from the Gentiles. Had they not taught him how we have to fulfil the greatest and most noble of all commandments—the commandment to "love thy neighbour as thyself", which the Talmud declares to be "the sum and foundation of the entire Law of God"? It had been a *muzhik* like this, a drunk like this, who had interrupted him in his devotions many years before and had shown him how we must love our neighbours.

It happened like this: One day, Reb Moyshe Leib was caught in a downpour which was so severe that he had to take shelter in an inn. In the inn two *muzhiks* were sitting at a table. Both were drunk—that goes without saying. All of a sudden one of them put his arms round the other's neck, as drunkards will, and cried: "Brother, how I love you!" At that moment the other had an accident. He pierced his finger with a knife which he was playing with on the table. The first man did not notice that his friend had hurt himself.

"How can you love me," exclaimed the injured *muzhik*, "how can you love me, if you don't even know that I've cut my finger so badly that it's bleeding?!"

When the holy Reb Moyshe Leib heard this, he thanked God

for having caused him to enter that inn. He said: "Lord of the Universe, now I know how we have to love our neighbours. We must love them so much that when anything hurts them we feel as though our own body was hurt."

From that day this was the guiding principle in the life of the holy Reb Moyshe Leib. Few could equal him in his love for his neighbour.

I want now to tell you a very nice story about this, and I trust that you will be good enough to give a little thought to it.

Well then!

Let us enjoy our lot here on earth in joy and gladness. Such is the teaching of the wisdom of the Talmud:

"Eat and drink, and make haste about it! For the world to which we shall have so soon to bid farewell is a like a wedding procession. It passes us by so quickly. So let each one hurry to seize what there is!"

This of course does not mean that we have only to think of ourselves. It does not mean that we have to eat and drink everything we have, to deny things to others, not to give anybody anything. It is our duty to give one tenth of our earnings to good purposes. This is enjoined on us by the Holy Scriptures. If you give more than it is your duty to give, you are worthy of praise. But your beneficence must not exceed one fifth of your income. That would not be beneficence but waste. Thus it is written in the Talmud.

The amount we can give to the poor is unfortunately considerably limited. But the good we can perform by *deeds* is unlimited.

"Here are things to which *no limit is set*, here are things on which we can enjoy interest while we are still in this world and whose everlasting capital is laid up in the world to come: tending the sick, burying the dead, comforting the sorrowful, healing the quarrels of those who are set at variance one with another, giving support to the joy of lovers, praying devoutly. *But the reading of a good book is above all these things.*"—Thus is it written almost word for word, in the holy Talmud.

Let us not suppose, then, that our best deeds are those that we buy for ourselves with money. There is something higher and nobler than this.

Therefore keep always in your heart the story I am going to tell you. Talk about it together and tell it to children. Write it at the entrance to your homes and on the gates of your cities!...

On the stroke of twelve, the holy Reb Moyshe Leib rose from his bed. After he had washed he praised God that He had given us His Law.

Then the holy Reb Moyshe Leib put on the clothes of a *muzhik* and went to chop wood. With a bundle of wood on his back he set out into the frost and the night.

He walked softly through the sleeping town, totally unaware that a watchful disciple was following in his footsteps at a distance.

Reb Moyshe Leib crossed the square, avoiding the Christian church but equally avoiding the synagogue. He headed for the outskirts of the town, the little alleys where the poorest people have their homes.

He walked on and on, without stopping, until he had left the town and was ploughing through snow drifts. Where was he making for?—In the distance could be seen the outlines of a cemetery.

Reb Moyshe Leib passed the tangle of poor houses, passed the place of death, and did not stop until he came to a remote cottage.

He put down his bundle and knocked at the window.

"Want any wood?" he asked in the Gentile language.

"Wood!—Of course I do! It's terribly cold here! But I can't buy any. I haven't got a farthing. I'm only a poor widow."

"I'll leave you my bundle and you can pay for it later. I'm in no hurry for the money. What's the point of my trudging about with this load on a frosty night like this!" said the *muzhik*-saint.

"No, no!" objected the widow. "It wouldn't be any use to me in any case. I'm a sick woman and my child has the fever. I can't move from his side. I can't light a fire."

231

"That doesn't matter, I'll light it myself," said the *muzhik* and, without waiting for an answer, he stepped inside.

The disciple drew close to the window and looked in: the saint was lighting the fire, and as he did so his holy lips were trembling and tears were running down his cheeks!—This, then, was how he prayed the midnight prayer! The first midnight prayer, Rachel's prayer, the prayer of the grieving mother:

"A voice was heard on high, lamentation and bitter weeping, Rachel weeping for her children and refusing to be comforted. Lo, the archangels mourn and the angels of peace sob bitterly."

The saint placed the chopped wood on the fire, piece after piece, and his lips trembled. But his tears had stopped and his eyes shone!—Now he would probably pray the second midnight prayer, the prayer of Leah, the mother of old, the mother exultant. Exultant over her sons.

"Weep not, Rachel, let thy tears no more flow, thy hopes shall be fulfilled, thy children shall return. . . ."

The fire crackled merrily in the hearth and the wretched room was filled with pleasant light and warmth. And the light and the warmth filled the heart of the poor mother and all the heavens.

Thus it was that the holy Reb Moyshe Leib of Sassov prayed the midnight prayer, and thus it was that he served God all the days of his life.

All the good Chassidim of Sassov followed his example. At one time there used to be many of them. Reb Moyshe Leib had his imitators not only in Poland itself but also beyond the country's borders.

Now there are only a few of them. *Sed omnia praeclara tam difficilia, quam rara sunt.* Yes, all sublime things are as difficult as they are rare.

Perhaps in their goodness they will forgive me for having applied to them the words of that accursed apostate, Baruch Benedict Spinoza.

The holy Reb Moyshe Leib was not in fact a Rabbi. He was a shopkeeper. A truly remarkable shopkeeper. There are not many like him. You could get anything you wanted in his shop at Sassov. It was like a sort of Maison du Louvre at Paris. Only somewhat smaller, of course. After all Sassov is not Paris. In fact Sassov is not even as big as our Belz. In other words, Reb Moyshe Leib was not a rich man. Why, he could not even afford a belt. You have not forgotten what a belt is, have you? It is that silken cord we put round our waist before we pray.—If you do not possess a belt, then at least you must tie a piece of ordinary string round your waist before you pray. But the holy Reb Moyshe Leib did not even have enough money to buy some string. So he tied a wisp of straw around his waist. He was so thin that it was quite sufficient for him. His shop was not open the whole day; there was no need for it to be. An hour or two was quite enough. When Reb Moyshe Leib had made enough money to buy himself bread for the day, he would close the shop and go to the House of Study. Moreover he never tried to prevail on his customers to buy at his shop. When anybody came he would begin by telling him where such goods as he sold could be found cheaper and better in Sassov. With these business methods, as I have said, he was of course never able to afford a belt. But if I have said that Reb Moyshe Leib was not wealthy, then I must hasten to correct myself. He was wealthy, excessively so in fact. Not even Reb Anshel Rothschild of Frankfurt was as wealthy as our Reb Moyshe Leib. For: "Who is wealthy?" —asks the Talmud. "He who is content with what he has."

The holy Reb Moyshe Leib had indeed reason to be contented. No Rothschild ever had a disciple such as he had. I shall now tell you something about this disciple. I have nothing further to say about the holy Reb Moyshe Leib in any case and he does not really belong in the region of Kotsk. This disciple of his was called Jacob Yitzhak. But we do not call him by that name. We call him the Holy Jew.

I think I have already told you that the holy Rebe Reb Shmelke of Mikulov was like the Comte de Lautréamont in that he never slept. Our Holy Jew was also like your *Lotrmond*, only

233

in a different way. The Holy Jew was never known to *laugh* throughout his life. Not even the least smile flickered over his holy countenance.

Why do we call him the Holy Jew?—

One morning, as he left home, he remarked: "The prophet Elijah will appear to me today." And so it came about, in this wise: The Holy Jew walked on and on through the town until he came to the market, where he stopped and looked around. But he saw nothing out of the ordinary. Then all at once he beheld a sight which caught his attention—an old peasant with a bundle and a stick. He stared and stared at the man, unable to tear his eyes away, until finally the good *muzhik* lost his temper (he did not lose his temper; but it looked as though he did) and said: "Why do you look at me like that, *Jew*!?"—It is because the *muzhik* called him "Jew" on that day that we too call him the Jew; the Holy Jew. That *muzhik* was Elijah in disguise.

It is a very truthful story. As sure as the sky is above me! But if it does not carry the same weight with you, then I will confide to you the real reason why we call him the Holy Jew. We call him the Holy Jew because the soul of the Old Testament Mordecai was incarnate in him, and the Book of Esther in the Bible calls Mordecai "the Jew"; "the Jew Mordecai". For this reason, too, Jacob Yitzhak, or the Holy Jew, was a perfect saint from the day of his birth. As a young lad he used to preach the law of God to the goats grazing in the meadow and led them on the road of peace and forbearance. On account of this he was the darling of the animals until the end of his life. Wherever he went they would welcome him with joy. No one else understood them so well. One spring day, for instance, he went out into the countryside with one of his disciples, named Perets. Perets heard all God's animals chatting merrily together and saw the saint's face becoming brighter and brighter. "If only I understood what they were talking about," sighed Perets to himself, "it's certainly most beautiful."

"You stupid fellow," said the Holy Jew, "it's only too easy! If people *knew what they talked about themselves*—they would understand the animals."

234

As a result of his marriage the Holy Jew came to live at Apta. At that time of course he was still called Jacob Yitzhak. No one had any idea as to who he really was, least of all his father-in-law, who had no understanding whatsoever for his son-in-law's piety and diligence. Perhaps it was quite impossible for him to understand. An ordinary baker himself, he wanted nothing more than that his son-in-law should also be a baker. But his son-in-law sat in the House of Study and cared nothing for any trade. He refused to submit to his father-in-law's will, and his father-in-law refused to feed him for nothing. Why did he need to eat at all if he did nothing? Studying the Talmud was not to be considered work and certainly would not keep anybody from hunger. In short, the Holy Jew might very likely have starved to death if it had not been for his young dryad. She was the only soul who understood him. Somehow she always succeeded in surreptitiously obtaining some food for him, without her father knowing. In one matter, however, father-in-law and son-in-law resembled one another. They were the only citizens of Apta who stayed up the whole night long, the father-in-law at home at his trade, the son-in-law in the House of Study at his books.

One winter's night a rich merchant drove to Apta. Thick snowdrifts lay across the road, and the sledge became more and more submerged. Finally the horses came to a halt and refused to budge any further. So the rich man ordered his coachman to unharness one of the horses and ride on to Apta for help while he waited in the carriage. Apta was still a long way off, a few hours' journey, but there was nothing else to be done. So the coachman mounted the horse and rode off. The frost was cruel.

At Apta everybody had long since gone to bed. The only light the coachman saw was in the House of Study where the Holy Jew was still studying. Entering the *Bes Hamidrash*, the coachman went straight to the stove. At this moment the Holy Jew raised his eyes and saw the unfortunate fellow all numb and shaking with the cold.

"What shall we do now?" asked the coachman, after he had somewhat recovered and had related the misfortune to the

THE CITY OF WISDOM

studious young man. "My master's freezing to death. And here
in the village everybody's asleep."

The Holy Jew thought for a moment, then he said:

"I'll come and give you a hand myself." He felt so sorry for
the ill-starred travellers.

The coachman glanced mistrustfully at the emaciated young
man. He would have needed somebody stronger. A team of
horses in fact. But what was the point of such musing? He could
be glad that he at least had this man to help him. But would the
horse be able to carry the pair of them? It looked as though it
was ready to give up the ghost at any moment.

"To horse, and away we go! There's not a moment to waste!"
the young fellow broke in on his thoughts just as if he had read
them.

This was no longer the humble disciple giving modest advice.
It sounded to the coachman like the voice of a general.

They leapt into the saddle and rode away. Rode?—No, they
flew. No sooner did the horse feel the new rider on his back
than it rushed off as though possessed. The coachman could
hardly hold the reins in his hands. He knew not whether he was
shivering from the cold or with fear. No, there was something
unusual about it all. A moment before his horse had been so
weary and half frozen that it had hardly been able to carry him,
now it was suddenly galloping faster than the wind, apparently
quite oblivious of its double load. The snow-laden trees and
hills flashed by in ghostly fashion in the dark night. Before the
coachman could recover from his astonishment, the wild ride
was over, and they had reached the sleigh, which by this time
was half covered in snow. "Let me sit in your place at the
front, or else I'll go at the back," said the Holy Jew. Then, as
though speaking to himself, he remarked: "It doesn't make
much difference either way."

The coachman made no objection. He knew his part by now.
But the master, who had been eyeing the young man, blurted out:

"The horses won't be able to pull us out of the snow by themselves! How do you think you'll get them moving? All three of
us had better try and push the sleigh out of the drift!"

236

Nor did he wish to entrust the young man with the leading rein, for at the very first glance he had seen that he was an ill-fed student, incapable of doing anything but pray and swot over the Talmud. There were thousands like him. Not one of them could control a horse.

"Don't waste your strength on the sleigh, please," said the young man to the trader, while the coachman harnessed the horses. "Just stay quietly in your place. That's it! There, that's better." And so saying, he mounted the back seat of the sleigh.

The coachman cracked the whip and in a trice the sleigh was out of the snow! It might have been feather-down, not snow. Already the horses were at the gallop and before you could have prayed the "Ashrei" they were at Apta. It was a ghastly experience. The coachman went through it twice and the trader once; for both it was nothing short of a miracle.

As soon as they arrived at the township, the young man got down from the sleigh and returned to the House of Study, as though nothing out of the ordinary had happened. The other two did not follow him. Trembling with fear even more than with the cold, they preferred to remain outside. Looking round the square they noticed that after all there was a light in another house. They went in. It was a bakery.

The baker—the Holy Jew's father-in-law—was busy at his baking. He had little time for talking just at that moment. But hearing the strange tale of the newcomers he could not contain his amazement.

"Whoever could it have been? Who could have rescued you in this way?"

"Indeed, that's what we'd like to know."—"Let's hope it wasn't some accursed magician making use of evil sorcery! God protect us!" At that moment it did not occur to the baker that the only person still up at that late hour was his son-in-law in the House of Study.

While the baker put his loaves into the oven, all three had plenty to talk about. Again and again they went over what had happened, and each time their amazement grew. All the bread had been put into the oven, and they were still unable to overcome their astonishment. Suddenly the door opened, and the Holy Jew stepped into the bakery.

"That's the man! That's the man!" whispered the two strangers, rising respectfully from their seats as the Holy Jew entered.

Seized with fear, the baker fainted on the spot.

That morning the people of Apta very nearly went without food, for all the bread would certainly have been burnt in the oven had not the Holy Jew—may his Light protect us!—immediately brought his father-in-law round from his state of unconsciousness.

"Forgive me, please, for all the wrongs I have ever done you!" the baker begged his son-in-law, at this late stage, with tears in his eyes.

"It's too late now," replied the Holy Jew in a grave voice.

In very truth it was too late. All too late did the father-in-law express sorrow for his evil deeds. His fate had long since been sealed. Not even the Holy Jew himself was able to change the judgement of Heaven. Shortly after this the father-in-law died. This was God's just punishment for all the offences he had committed against so learned a man as his son-in-law. From that day the sun of the fame of the Holy Jew, the miracle-worker, began to rise—a sun which never sets.

The Holy Jew treated his wife with the deepest respect and dignity all the days of his life. Indeed this was to be expected. He would certainly have honoured her even if she had not been such a pillar of strength to him in all his privation. We all honour our wives, as the holy Talmud counsels us: "Honour your wives and it shall be well with you!"

The punishment which befell the father-in-law for all the wrongs and insults he had heaped upon his learned son-in-law bears out the truth of other words in the Talmud: "Warm yourself at the fire of the learned, but take care not to burn yourself! For the mordacity of the learned is like the bite of the fox, and their pungency like the sting of the scorpion, and familiarity with them like a snake-bite. The least word of the learned is a glowing coal."

238

The Holy Jew was a learned man in very truth. Not even the most scholarly works of the ancient Talmudists could stand up to his keen intellect and critical spirit. We ordinary folk feel our heads spinning round when we take a look at the complicated reasoning to be found in such masterpieces as the "Urim Vetumin" by the famous Prague Talmudist and Cabbalist, the holy Rebe Reb Jonathan Eibenschütz. But the Holy Jew, when he had read the book, declared that he had found only three "slightly remarkable passages" in it. . . . That's all!

The Holy Jew was not only an exceedingly learned man, a great worker of miracles, and a model husband. He was also an expert at telling delightful anecdotes, and most instructive ones, as we shall see immediately from one of them.

One day a husband came to him to complain of his wife's stinginess. The Chassidim were totally unaffected by the wretched man's misfortune. Instead they made fun of him. You know what the gentlemen of Kotsk are like! The Holy Jew was the only one who did not laugh at him. After graciously listening to the unhappy husband's moaning, he started telling the following story in a quiet and almost timid voice.

Once upon a time—long, long ago, of course—there lived in an out-of-the-way village a devout man who had a very niggardly wife. She was so niggardly that she would not allow the house to be heated in the winter even when the frost was at its keenest. In consequence the pious man was unable to say his prayers in winter. As soon as he got up in the morning he left the house to go out on the village green. Even in the frost and wind he found it warmer there than in his home. When he returned home in the evening he had perforce to go straight to bed so as not to freeze.

When the fellow came to the end of his sorrowful pilgrimage on this earth and stood before the gate of Heaven, the celestial judges asked him about his prayers on winter days and winter nights.

"I couldn't pray. My wife wouldn't make a fire."

His wife wouldn't make a fire! Upon hearing these words the celestial judges at the gate of paradise stroked their chins. They stroked their chins and their minds went back to all the joys of married life—married life down there on earth, long years ago. His wife wouldn't make a fire! They stroked their chins and were on the very point of opening the gate of forgiveness, freedom and salvation.

The man's soul rejoiced.

But suddenly, out of the blue, a little Seraph appeared on the scene. A little urchin he was, and quite inexperienced! But all glow and fire, as Seraphim are.

"What?!" he shouted at the venerable judges."You're going to let a sinner like that into paradise? If a man's wife won't make a fire, can his spirit be allowed to forget his Creator and the Lord of the Universe? He ought to be ashamed of himself behaving like that! Even if the winter was like in Siberia. . . ."

Before he could utter another word the judges cut him short by throwing a copper sieve over him. It was the same type of sieve as that used by our teacher Moses in the wilderness to cover the eternal fire at the altar, so that no one should be burnt when the Tabernacle was moved. Before the Seraph realized what had happened, his flames were placed in fetters and he was given the shape of a human being of flesh and blood. In a trice he was popped into a human skin, and there he was, down on the earth, standing in front of the door of a widow in mourning. In heaven, as you should know, everything moves like clockwork.

Willy-nilly he knocked at the door. The widow, he found, was a decent, orderly woman, modest and not ungracious. In due course, when she came out of mourning, she became his wife. For some time everything went swimmingly. In this heaven of married life the Seraph had no yearnings for anything better. He forgot everything he had known up above and came to accept the fact that he was only an ordinary mortal. He decided that after all it was quite good to be a human being—but not of course if one had to live on one's own. But then came the winter . . . Oh Lord! . . .

"Wife, come and make up the fire, please!" he begged. Nothing happened. "The fire, my darling!" he pleaded. Again nothing happened. "Make a fire, make a fire!" he implored, entreated, scolded and swore. But his wife would not make a fire. What was the point? Every penny spent on a fire was a waste of money!

In such a keen frost you do not stick your head out of your warm lair, not even if you have been a fiery Seraph. Our Seraph did at least try it once, to say his prayers. But he straightway crept back again, half frozen. He—a fiery Seraph! There could be no thought of prayer when the weather was so frosty.

He was fortunate indeed that they soon felt sorry for him in Heaven and freed him from his sufferings in good time. Who knows what would have become of him? Ever since then our good Seraph has had nothing to say when anybody has come to the gate of heaven blaming his wife.—The Holy Jew narrated this story in a very quiet voice, looking round cautiously in all directions as he spoke. Very likely he himself was that frozen Seraph—in an earlier incarnation, that is. Or did he have other reasons for being so vigilant?

The Holy Jew was fond of drinking. On one occasion—he was still only a disciple at Lublin at the time—he declared: "I will sell all my happiness in the hereafter for a gulp of brandy!" But not one of the Chassidim wanted to pay so dearly for his happiness in the hereafter. . . .

Reb Binem of Pzhysha was the Holy Jew's most famous disciple. The Holy Jew esteemed him above all others. No one else could take the liberties that Reb Binem was allowed. The souls of many sinners used to come to the Holy Jew to ask him for correction (*tikun*), just as they used to come to the holy Seer of Lublin and other great saints. One day, the Holy Jew refused to administer correction to the soul of a most grievous sinner in spite of being earnestly entreated to do so. Then Reb Binem said to his teacher: "If you do not administer correction to this sinner's soul and have mercy upon him, you are no longer my teacher and I am no longer your disciple." The Holy Jew did not wish to lose his most beloved disciple and he was therefore obliged to administer correction to that sinful soul. Then he made this wisecrack about Reb Binem: "Der junger Mann is a *Spitzel* vun mein Harz."—a quip which can be understood in two ways. It means: "The young man is a part, the *sharp end*, of my heart," in other words, I am deeply fond of him; but it also means: "The young man is the sleuth, the policeman, of my heart," in other words, I walk in fear of him.

The holy Reb Urele of Strelisk described Reb Binem of Pzhysha as follows: "Reb Simche Binem was a great saint. He wished to show the world an entirely new way to God, but he died before his work was complete. As a result of this those who have succeeded him have taken a wrong course." Thus spoke the holy Reb Urele, Seraph of Strelisk, may his merits protect us!

Like the holy Reb Moyshe Yide Leib of Sassov, Reb Simche Binem was not a Rabbi by profession. It is due to this that the Kotsk saints are not Rabbis today. To the public they are merely traders, after the example of these precursors. Reb Simche Binem started as an apothecary, a real Magister Pharmaciae. He took his exams at Lvov, passing them without the least difficulty. Then he gave up the profession of an apothecary and became a timber merchant. What, a real merchant? Yes, a wholesale merchant, a real wholesale merchant. His business travels took him as far as Leipzig, and even to Danzig, or Gdansk. Danzig is a sea port, and it was natural that Reb Simche should have to go there. Let us not forget that the soul of Zebulun was incarnate in him, and Zebulun was one of the twelve sons of Jacob and was also a merchant. It is written of him in the Holy Scriptures: "Zebulun shall dwell at the haven of the sea. . . ." Reb Simche Binem used the same words about himself. So he had to become a merchant and had to travel as far as the sea coast, that is, to Danzig.

One day, Reb Simche Binem went to the theatre at Danzig, when he was on one of his business journeys. But he did not go to the theatre to see the sparkling comedy which was being played there at the time! Far from it. He went for a much more important reason—and he even made a personal appearance, as a singer. Not on the stage, but in the auditorium. He sat on the floor in the darkest corner and, ever so quietly, chanted the Psalms of David. He was not interested in what was going on on the stage. He would never for a moment have gone into a theatre at all, if he had not at the time been concerned about saving a stray soul. When subsequently he heard people bewailing the depravity of modern youth, and how easily young people give in to the wiles of the Tempter, and so on and so on, Reb Binem would cut them short with a melancholy sigh: "Be silent! You don't know the strength of the snares of the present-day world. It is written in the Talmud: 'Judge not thy fellow-man until thou art come into his place!' But you have never found yourselves in the position of the youth of today. You have never even been in a theatre. I have, and I will not condemn anyone."

To go to the theatre, needless to say, is a great sin, for the theatre pollutes the spirit. But it is a still worse vice to play cards, and Reb Simche Binem even played cards on one occasion, though only for the greater glory of God. Under such circumstances this is an act to be commended. As it is written in the Talmud itself: "To commit a sin for a good purpose is better than to perform a meritorious deed for material motives." It is also written in the Talmud that "he who saves even one single soul in Israel does as much as if he were to save the entire world and all creation". Reb Simche Binem played cards for the sole purpose of saving one such straying soul.

It happened on this wise. On one of his business trips Reb Simche Binem met up with a young man in whom was incarnated a very saintly soul. Reb Simche Binem recognized this at once. But unfortunately the young man was a fearful gambler. So one day, in order to save him from the snares of the Devil, Reb Simche Binem consented to play cards with him and the company he sat at table with. He had not the least idea how to play and he was totally unfamiliar with the cards. He merely threw them on the table as they happened to come to hand. Surprisingly enough, he won game after game. Was it so ordained by God, or was it perhaps that the Devil was out to ensnare Reb Simche Binem himself, and lure him into his cunning wiles, so that he too should fall a victim to gambling? Who knows? Reb Simche Binem of course knew neither when nor how he won, nor wherein in fact victory lay. But when he saw the other players leaving money on the table and looking at it in bewilderment, he divined that he must have been the winner and that the money belonged to him. And so it came about that Reb Simche Binem piled heap after heap into the capacious pockets of his caftan.

From that moment the young man began to hold him in deep respect. It can only be, he thought, that Reb Simche Binem is conversant with various cabbalistic mysteries which make him win. In short, the young man literally worshipped Reb Simche Binem for the mysteries which he supposed he possessed. He followed him about everywhere in the hope that Reb Simche might one day reveal these mysteries to him. One day Reb Simche Binem went for a walk out of the town. The young man went with him. Silently they traversed fields and meadows. The young man had a presentiment that Reb Simche Binem intended to surprise him that very day. "I'm sure he's going to tell me his secrets," he told himself delightedly.

Dusk fell, and the stars came out in the sky. Finally Reb Simche Binem interrupted his silence. Raising his eyes to the stars, he exclaimed, in the words of the prophet Isaiah: "Lift up thine eyes to the hills and know who hath created them." His voice sounded superhuman. Something mysterious could be discerned in it, something that the young man had never known until that moment: the heart of a saint. For the first time in his life the young man was aware that there were other, nobler and more beautiful things in this world than gambling. He saw the light and was saved. He never touched cards again in his life and became a true Chassid. As it is written in the Talmud: "Some people win eternity through one hour of their lives."

"There are two things which are always able to convert a person and bring him to a state of ecstasy," declared a wise man on that day at the other end of the world: "The sight of the starry sky and one's own conscience."—The name of that wise man was Kant. Reb Simche used to say: "I can convert any sinner, except liars and swindlers."

The Holy Jew died in the year 5575 (1815) and Reb Simche Binem took his place. If the Holy Jew acquired incalculable merit through correcting the souls of numerous sinners who had departed this life, as he had been taught to do by the holy Seer of Lublin, Reb Simche Binem acquired still more merit thereby.

Disciples who visited Reb Binem in his room used frequently to hear somebody weeping and moaning outside at the window. Once they summoned up sufficient courage to run to the window and look. When they saw no one there, they were seized with fear. But Reb Simche Binem was not scared in the least. The moaning came from the unhappy souls of the dead who had come to plead with Reb Simche Binem, hoping that now they were dead he would administer them correction.

One day Reb Heynech of Alexandra came to visit him. "The souls of such great people come to me," Reb Simche Binem confided to him, "that I do not dare even to look at them, so noble and holy they are. Yet in spite of this they are unable to help themselves in that world and are obliged to ask me for correction, even though I am not worthy to be the heel of their boots. Only in this material world can help be given to them."

When Reb Heynech visited him a second time, Reb Simche Binem asked him if he had read a book by a certain author. The author was long since dead.

"Yes," replied Reb Heynech, "I have read it. But I must say that I have read better books."

But he quickly corrected himself, and started lauding the book to the skies. Why?—Well, because Reb Simche Binem trod on his foot under the table. He stamped on it good and hard, in the way only the people at Kotsk are capable of. Why did he tread on his foot? Good Lord! That is quite obvious! Because when the author's soul heard them talking about the book in Pzhysha, he flew there as fast as he could to hear if they were giving it all the praise it deserved.

Even when Reb Heynech of Alexandra came to visit him a

third time, Reb Simche Binem still expressed his heartfelt thanks to him in the name of the wretched author, assuring him that he had done the dead writer a great service through his eulogy of him—up there in that better world, at least. . . .

These are terrible things. Let us rather not speak much about them. But do not think that they took place only with those saints at Kotsk! Things were not different with us at Belz, in fact they were a good deal more curious. One day, for instance, our holy Reb Sholem was visited at Belz by the young grandson of the holy Reb Urele of Strelisk, Reb Urele of Podolsk—peace be to him! It was the Feast of the Day of Atonement. In the evening the two men were joined by Shiyel, Reb Sholem's son, in the study of the Talmud. They soon left off however and went to lie down, because they could not see to read owing to the flickering of the lamp. No sooner had they lain down, however, than Urele of Podolsk suddenly noticed that the table, at which they had been studying a moment before, was moving about as though it were alive. The table stood up on its hind legs, then on its front legs, and in this fashion jumped about the room, like a young kid before it is slaughtered. As it is written by the hand of King David:

"Wherefore do the mountains jump like young lambs and the hills like young bullocks?"

When Urele saw the table carrying on like this he was seized by a severe fit of trembling.

"That's nothing," said Shiyel, calming him down, "it's only some unhappy soul asking us for correction. If you're going to be afraid of such things you won't have to sleep in our house. You'd better go somewhere else!" So saying he took his companion off to some friends of his. It was some time however before Urele overcame his fit of trembling. I too tremble all over whenever I remember this terrible happening. As it is written elsewhere by the hand of King David:

"Let the earth tremble before the Lord,
Before the God of Jacob, AMEN!"

"If somebody tells you: I have looked but I did not find—do not believe him! If he tells you: I did not look but I have found —do not believe him either! But if somebody tells you: I have looked and found—believe him; that man speaks the truth." Thus it is written in the holy Talmud. Reb Simche Binem demonstrated the truth of these words with a beautiful story. It resembles your *Peer Gynt*.

Long, long ago—Reb Simche Binem related—there lived at Cracow a devout scholar, Reb Eisik Yekls by name. Reb Eisik Yekls lived in direst poverty and was totally unable to better his lot. "Only a miracle can help me," he used to say. One night he heard a mysterious voice in his dream: "Eisik! Eisik! An infinitely precious treasure is destined to be yours. Go to the city of the Kings of the Czech Lands, which is called Prague. When you are there, look under the Stone Bridge which arches over the River Vltava!" Eisik Yekls was not a superstitious person. He was familiar with the Talmud and had learnt from it that what a person thought about for days on end he would also dream about at night. But his dream returned a second night and then a third. So Reb Eisik knew that his dream was no ordinary dream and that the voice he had heard was inspired by the Angel of Dreams. He therefore took his stick and set out on his journey.

In those days the road from Cracow to Prague was a bad and dangerous one. But it was worse still if a man's conscience was burdened by the thought that he was leaving his dear ones in hunger and misery and going after a dream.

But when after his long and arduous pilgrimage he stood on a hill, covered with green trees, and saw in front of him a glorious castle on a high mountain and under the castle a town spread out on both banks of a wide river, and when he glimpsed a mighty bridge, built throughout of stone, Eisik's heart thumped with joy. He felt that he had reached his goal and that what he saw was Prague; "*Prag hamaatyro, Ir ve-Em be-Yisroel*, Prague, Crown of the World, City and Mother in Israel". It was a city in all respects like that with which the Angel of Dreams had fired his imagination. And Eisik recognized the river as the

River Vltava and the stone bridge as that which arched over the treasure of pearls and silver. Indeed he was not mistaken. There were no other bridges over the Vltava in those days.

But the bridge was guarded by soldiers. Eisik Yekls stepped back a little, but after a short while he returned to the bridge and started looking underneath it, seeking a place where he could search for his treasure unnoticed.

The gendarmes caught sight of him. He was seized and led before the commander. When questioned Reb Eisik Yekls held nothing back and informed the guard commander of the secret of his dream. He was not asked his name nor where he came from.

"You fool," exclaimed the officer with a sneer when he heard Eisik's explanation. "I was really unaware that there are such madmen as you among the Jews, who would go wandering off after dreams. If I were to believe in dreams, I should have to go all the way to *Cracow*. I had a dream that there is some wonderful treasure there hidden near the fireplace in a room occupied by a Jew. The name of this Jew was declared to me in my dream. In fact I remember it very well! His name was . . . *Eisik Yekls.* . . . Do you think I'd want to drag my weary body all the way to Cracow to go scratching for treasure near the fireplace of some confounded Jew?! Dreams are lies and deception. Only old women believe in them!"

When the gendarmes released him Reb Eisik gave thanks to the Lord. The matter was settled in a blast of mocking laughter. Eisik returned home without delay and found the treasure near his fireplace.

To this day the synagogue which he subsequently founded at Cracow bears his name. Everybody knows the "Reb Eisik Yekls-Shil (Schule)" at Cracow. The caretaker there will tell you its story.

But Reb Simche Binem, who used to relate the story to every novice who came to study with him, would always add:

"So you see, my boy, there is something of inestimable value which you will always be seeking as in a dream, and which you will probably never find in the whole wide world. Very

likely you will not even find it here with me, and yet there is
one place where you could find it." . . .

It is written in the Talmud that a person who limps or appears
crippled when in fact he is neither lame nor crippled, will be
punished for this godless shamming. He will finish up by being
genuinely lame or crippled. From this Reb Simche Binem de-
duced that it would be exactly the same with a person who
pretended to be a saint even if he was not: he would finish up by
becoming a genuine saint. As a sort of punishment. . . .

Reb Simche Binem illustrated the truth of this with a story
that has a very original ending.

A nobleman saw a *muzhik* lying dead-drunk on the road. The
nobleman was a great wag. "You wait, you old boozer, I'll get
you properly mixed up!" He gave orders for the drunken
muzhik to be placed on a cart and taken to his castle. There the
man was undressed and put to bed. His *muzhik's* clothes were
taken away and replaced by those of a priest. When the man
came to, he was at a loss to understand where he was. Finding no
other clothes to hand, he dressed up in the priest's robes. No
sooner had he left the room than the lord's servant, making a
deep obeisance before him, asked the worthy father what he
could do for him. The *muzhik* was taken aback: "Am I really
a priest," he thought to himself, "and did I only dream I was a
muzhik? Or am I really only a *muzhik* and simply having a
dream that I'm a priest?"

So the *muzhik* told the servant to bring him the Holy Scriptures. If I am really only an ordinary *muzhik*, he told himself. I
shall not be able to read and I shall not know what is written in
the book. In this way I shall make sure whether I am a priest or
a *muzhik*.

The servant brought the book and the *muzhik* scanned its
pages intently. He saw all manner of letters but understood nothing of what they meant. He was just about to admit that he
was not a priest but only a simple *muzhik*—why, he was not
even able to read, and any true priest could do that!—when it
occurred to him: Supposing the other priests also understand

249

nothing of what they see in their books but just pretend to study them so learnedly so as not to have to do any work, and be honoured and revered by everybody, and have a good time?

So the *muzhik* did not close the book. Instead he closed his mouth, which he had already opened to make his admission. He started poring over the book, and in this way became a real priest.

Thus it is with many a "saint". Day and night they sit over their studies, delving into cabbalistic books and not understanding the least thing. They tell themselves: "The others do not understand it either!"

They sit and sit; at least they do no harm. In short they end up by becoming real saints.—That was what Reb Simche Binem of Pzhysha used to tell his disciples.

He departed this life for eternity on the twelfth day of the month of Elul in the year 5587 (1827).

The Holy Jew and Reb Simche Binem of Pzhysha had a disciple by the name of Reb Mendele of Tomashov. As a young man, Reb Mendele also went to visit the Seer of Lublin and the saint of Koznitz. Subsequently he became a Rabbi at Kotsk. He shook the Chassidic world to its very foundations.

"God set aside but one single drop of His infinite Wisdom, and with this drop created the entire world. Nor did He use the whole of this drop, but only one half of it. For the other half was poured into the heart of Reb Mendele of Tomashov."—So spake Reb Meir of Djikov of our Reb Mendele.

Speaking of himself, Reb Mendele said: "With one foot I stand in heaven, but with the other I stand in the deepest abyss of hell. Do not think that that is easy!"

He declared: "If I so wanted, I could make Chassidim of all people. But it would not be desirable."

The souls of the dead used to flock to Kotsk in regiments. The poor things would queue up in front of Reb Mendele's house and await their turn to be corrected by his magical power. The power of his soul was indeed immense. From earliest childhood he had thought of nothing else but God!

By the time he was three years old he had ceased to ask anything of his parents. He called on God, and God alone, all the time: "God, give me a piece of bread! God, give me some water! God, I want that, God, I want this!" Nor would he give up his shouting until God in truth took pity on him and dispatched him a guardian angel in the form of his father or mother, using them to bring him what he had asked for.

Reb Mendele of Tomashov had another teacher beside those that have been mentioned already. A most unusual teacher. You would never guess that this teacher was none other than the Great Prague Rabbi Loev. This came about as a result of Reb Mendele of Tomashov making a journey to Prague, where he prayed for three favours at the grave of Rabbi Loev. No one knows what favours he asked for, but ever since that time the Great Rabbi Loev of Prague was Mendele's teacher. Anyone who is familiar with the writings of the Great Rabbi Loev has only to consider the sayings of Reb Mendele and he will immediately recognize that this is so. In fact it is thanks to him that the works of this writer from our Old Prague are to this day studied more diligently in the far-off Kotsk region than anywhere else in the world. Reb Mendele used to say that a true Chassid should have two teachers—one alive and one dead.

Reb Mendele was not a man of many words. We ordinary people are in the habit of asking one another: "Fin vant zent ir? —Viazoy haist ir?" (Where do you come from? What's your name?) Reb Mendele merely said:

"Fin?" (Whence?)

"Viazoy?" (Name?)

Everybody had to understand. . . .

One day a man was saying the prayer of the Eighteen Benedictions in the House of Prayer. This prayer is always prayed quietly, with the eyes closed, and the hands folded on the breast. The supplicant may stand motionless or he may throw his body about, but the prayer must always be in a whisper and must not have anything added to it! This man however was saying it out loud and kept on calling on God: "Father, Father—oh Father,

Father!" One of the disciples wanted to rebuke the simpleton and tell him to keep quiet. But Reb Mendele prevented him from doing so, saying: "Let him be! He'll go on saying it so often—until it's really true."

The difference between a lazy person and a deliberate person was defined by Reb Mendele as follows: "In their outward behaviour the two are very similar to each other. It is always a considerable time before either of them does anything, but for quite different reasons. The deliberate person takes a long time about each decision because he first of all considers what is the right thing to do, whereas the lazy person is so lazy that he does not even trouble to consider."

Reb Mendele described one famous scholar as a "Rabbi in a fur coat". What did he mean?—Well, it's like this: "People fight the cold either by heating their rooms or by protecting themselves by means of a fur coat. Those who heat their rooms give warmth to others as well as themselves. On the other hand, a person who merely protects himself against the cold, warms his own body, but does nothing to stop other people from freezing. It is the same with a saint who, while capable of warming the whole world with the light of his soul and the warmth of his heart, nevertheless wraps himself in silence, as in a fur coat, and keeps all his warmth exclusively for himself."

However silence is at the same time a very holy thing. "Silence is a fence behind which spreads out the field of wisdom," says the Talmud. There is another interesting thing about silence which we learn from the Talmud: it can help us to lengthen our life on this earth. We know from the Talmud that, every now and again, death makes a mistake and takes away somebody whose hour has not yet struck and who ought by right and justice to live many more years upon this earth. When this happens, the angel of death proceeds to make very intelligent use of the years which the unfortunate deceased has been deprived of—he adds them to the life of another person. It was in this way—as the Talmud tells us through the actual mouth of such a person—that a particular *scholar* was allowed to live longer. When, in the course of his learned disputes with his colleagues, this man would sometimes have very effective arguments to hand, arguments which could stun any adversary, he would instead curb his mouth and say nothing—*he would keep silence.* Such is the great worth of silence. It prolongs life. Look it up in the Talmud, you will find it there. . . . And the holy ARI—may the Light of his merits protect us!—teaches that a man who can keep silent for forty days on end shall surely obtain the gift of a holy spirit. Moreover it is common knowledge that the holy Reb Nachman of Brazlav used to prescribe for his penitents a day of silence instead of fasting. Now that you know what a beautiful thing silence is, I shall tell you a nice story about our Reb Mendele.

It happened when Mendele was still a disciple of the Holy Jew. One day he met Reb Leizer, the grandson of the holy Preacher of Koznitz. The two young saints sat down side by side on a bench. They then sent all the Chassidim out of the room and remained seated in silence. They sat for an hour in silence, they sat for two hours in silence. Every now and again the Chassidim would look inquisitively into the room. Each time Reb Leizer drove them away with a powerful gesture of his right hand. For three whole hours the two saints sat in silence. Finally Reb Leizer opened the door and called out to the impatient Chassidim: "All right. You can come in now. We've finished all we had to say. . . ."

Mendele did not break his silence. He got up, and walked all the way to Pzhysha, without saying a word. When he arrived, the Holy Jew greeted him unusually cheerfully. He told him a number of delightful stories and, at the end of each one, looked inquisitively at him to see what he would say. Mendele said nothing. He remained as silent as a statue. Finally the master asked him straight out: "Mendele, wherever did you learn to hold your tongue so well?" Mendele half opened his mouth, and was about to reply, when he immediately thought better of it and—*kept silent.*

Reb Mendele used to put the verse in Ecclesiastes: "He that increaseth knowledge increaseth sorrow" into the imperative tense. It thus acquired a different sense in the Hebrew, and in translation would appear as follows: "Let a man continually increase his knowledge, even if he increases sorrow for himself thereby!"

On one occasion Reb Mendele asked his disciples the question: "Where is God?"

"Where is God?—Any child knows that! God is everywhere."

Reb Mendele shook his erudite head. His disciples were nonplussed.

"God," he said, "is where He is allowed to be."

In our hearts, if we do not shut Him out.

Reb Mendele did not observe the prescribed times of prayer. If he had merely said the morning prayer at noon, as we do at Belz, this could still, although with some difficulty, be justified according to the Shulchan Aruch. After all, Heaven is quite accustomed to the Empire of the Chassidim being a little late in sending out their morning prayers. But just imagine, Reb Mendele—and it goes without saying that all the people of Kotsk followed his example—often did not say his "morning" prayers until the evening! Our prayers, you will remember, must be said not only with our souls, hearts and mouths, but with our entire bodies, with every single limb. That is self-evident. As you know, when we pray we stagger about in all directions, shaking ourselves and waving our arms. King David —peace be to him!—says in his Psalms: "*All my limbs* tell of thee, o Lord!" This, Reb Mendele maintained, was the reason why we should pray as late as possible. Our limbs, he said, do not all wake up at the same time, and when we get up in the morning some organs of the body go on sleeping. We walk about, talk, eat and work, and these sluggards are still dozing within us. They do not wake up till the afternoon, maybe, or even not till the evening, when we are going to bed again. If then we really want to pray with *all* our limbs and *all* our organs we must be patient and wait till the evening. Naturally the people of Kotsk were in agreement with this teaching of their saint. But you can just imagine what the other Chassidim, beyond the confines of the kingdom of Kotsk, had to say about this flouting of our ancient regulations regarding the times fixed for prayer!

One day, first thing in the morning, Reb Mendele remembered that prayers were to be said early that day, in the morning half-light, as it ought to be. He was all ready to walk to the House of Prayer. But at the door he suddenly turned back because an interesting solution to a *toysfes* had just occurred to him and he had to take a quick look at it so as not to be obliged to think about it during prayers. That would have disturbed his devotions. I take it you know what *toysfes* are? The little annotations in the Talmud, which are all the more incomprehensible and difficult, the shorter they are. Proper crossword puzzles. The commentaries that have been written on these mediaeval glosses in the Talmud! In short, Reb Mendele left the door open, went back into the room, took out the relevant volume of the Talmud, opened it at the particular page and looked at his gloss. Fortunately it was quite a short one and he was sure to have it done in a jiffy. You probably know the one it was. I expect you remember reading it over and over again and finding something odd about it. It is only two and a half short lines. Reb Mendele gazed at this tiny gloss, which lost itself in the vast volume like a drop in the wide ocean. He put his foot on the chair, and using his leg as a good firm upright placed the open volume on his knee. Under his arm he had his bag containing his prayer mantle, or *talis*, and his phylacteries, or *tfilin*. After all he was going straight off to the synagogue for morning prayers. Especially early, in fact, that day. But just for the time being he did not go. He stood bending over his knee, and on his knee rested a volume of the Talmud. He stood there, without a movement, like a statue, staring with compressed lips at two and a half lines. He stood and stood. Naturally nobody dared to disturb him. Finally he straightened himself out. "At last I have it!" he exclaimed exultantly. He looked round the room. It was twilight, as in the moment when he had taken out

the book—except that it was already the twilight of evening. . . .
Luckily it was summer-time, and the day was long enough for
a man to take in two and a half lines of the holy Talmud. If it
had happened in winter, when the day is short, the people of
Kotsk might very likely not have said their morning prayers at
all that day. A moment later three stars came out in the sky and
it was time for *evening* prayers. They had only just had time to
say their "morning" prayers a moment before. In great haste, of
course.

You will certainly have noticed that in speaking of the saints
of Kotsk I have not been using the title "holy" for a long time,
although a man like Reb Simche Binem certainly deserved it.
Please do not think that this omission on my part is due to irre-
verence or lack of respect. On the contrary, I assure you that my
esteem for the people of Kotsk is not a whit less than for other
just and righteous persons. Indeed of late I have felt particular
esteem for them. But nobody who has ever tasted the *mash* we
eat at *Belz* could ever call the Kotsk saints holy.

I had almost forgotten to tell you how it came about that Reb
Mendele of Kotsk shook the entire Chassidic Empire to its very
foundations. If I had not already promised this, God is my witness, I would rather not speak of it. But there is nothing for it,
it is our duty to keep a promise once it has been given. Otherwise you would be able to pronounce a curse over me: "By God
who sent the flood on the unbelievers, etc. . . ." I am therefore
compelled, willy-nilly, to give you a faithful account of everything. Somehow my pen seems not to want to write either, to be
sure. But I shall tell you everything, thoroughly conscientiously,
and you will not have to ask anybody else about any of the
details. (Though it would be best if you never even mentioned
it.) I will not conceal anything from you, nor will I make any
embellishments; at the same time I will not exaggerate, nor will
I slander or ridicule anybody. I shall speak as an impartial
spectator and eye-witness, as an *eyd reiye (ed raaja)*, or reporter,
as you say.

But first, please, you must ponder well the words of the Talmud: "If you have seen a learned man commit a sin by day, do not suspect that he will sin at night as well! Maybe he will have done penance in the meantime."—Not "maybe". Certainly he will have done penance, we add. Naturally I do not want to maintain that these words are directly applicable to what I am going to tell you and that perhaps "he" really did *commit a sin*. But you shall judge for yourselves.

It happened in this wise.

Reb Mendele of Kotsk suffered with terrible headaches. I do not know if neurasthenia already existed at Kotsk in those days, but it must have been something of that sort. In short, Reb Mendele went off to Lvov to ask the honoured specialists there about it and to hear their advice as doctors. Naturally he did not travel alone but was accompanied by his entire staff. At Lvov the travellers stayed at a big hotel. They supposed themselves to be in perfect safety, although they could hardly have been ignorant of the fact that, from the moment they arrived at Lvov, their every step would be carefully observed by hundreds of unseen eyes. Chassidim belonging to other, hostile camps—foremost among which, of course, were our Chassidim at Belz—watched at every corner in the hope of catching the fellows from Kotsk committing some indiscretion which they could subsequently utilize for their *tsad*, or "side". And these chaps of ours from Belz were pastmasters at the art, make no mistake about it, real *same gekovete briyes*.

The King of Lvov, or chief Rabbi, at the time was Yeshiyes Jacob (Yeshuot Yaakov), as he was called after his famous work "The Help of Jacob". His real name was Reb Yakev Meshilem Ornstein. He was a strict Talmudist, a world famous scholar. His word was his bond; there can be no doubt at all of his absolute impartiality.

On the very first Saturday that the visitors from Kotsk spent at Lvov, a grievous report was brought to the office of the chief Rabbi. Some men—it is said they were Chassidim from Belz—who "by sheer chance" happened to be walking, at night, through the street where the Kotsk fellows were staying, had stated under oath, and with complete unanimity, that they had seen Mendele of Kotsk with their own eyes—they did not call him "Reb" Mendele of course—on the night of the Sabbath—*smoking* a pipe at his window, not even wearing his cap, his *yarmelka*, on his head!—I ask you, take good note of that fact: *he wore no cap* on his head!

Smoking on the holy Sabbath—as you must be aware—is a mortal sin, and such wilful profanation of the Sabbath, when committed in public as in this case, means that the sinner is automatically excluded from the entire Jewish religious community. In any case, therefore, the consequences are serious to a degree. We would not marry the daughter of such a man, we would not drink the wine he had touched, and so on.

The men from Kotsk swore on oath that this had been an error on the part of these "witnesses"—an optical illusion of some sort. They maintained that the man they had seen smoking had not been their Reb Mendele, and was not a Jew at all, but a bearded Gentile, who had happened to be staying at the room next to that occupied by Reb Mendele on that fateful night. A Gentile, needless to say, was allowed to smoke on the Sabbath. Or were those damned *chnyoks* from Belz out to stop even Gentiles smoking on the Sabbath?

The Chassidim from Belz laughed until their sides shook. Above all of course they were amused by the objection put forward, with the best of intentions, by the men from Kotsk to the effect that the witnesses' statement was in itself proof that the Sabbath smoker could not have been their Reb Mendele, nor in fact any Jew. It was obvious, said the Kotskers, that these were lying, perjured witnesses. . . . Why, they even had the effrontery to maintain that the smoker was not wearing a cap! This very fact was a proof that the smoker had not been a Jew at all. Every Jew wears his *yarmelka* cap at home, so the smoker without a cap must have been a Gentile. But the Kotsk fellows forgot that a person who profanes the holy Sabbath ceases thereby to be a Jew, and becomes merely a jew. He is no longer a Yehudy but only a *yahudy*, in other words almost a Gentile, worse than a Gentile in fact. A sinner like that, who does not observe the sanctity of the Sabbath, will certainly not be ashamed to walk about without a *yarmelka*.

In vain did the visitors from Kotsk implore the chief Rabbi of Lvov, in vain did they threaten him, in vain did they pronounce that if he accepted, as valid currency, the testimony of such villains as these Chassidim from Belz, then all the judgments he had given in the past and all he would give in the future would one and all be invalid.—All their entreaties and threats were of no avail. Reb Mendele of Kotsk, the supreme head of so many thousands and thousands, was brought to account.

Nobody in the world can tell you exactly what happened at the Rabbi's office in Lvov. Not even our Chassidim at Belz will speak of it. But this much perhaps I can tell you: the words that were pronounced there on that day were not altogether unlike a *curse.* . . .

There was an almighty rumpus as a result of this. Open warfare broke out between the Chassidim of Kotsk and the rest of the Chassidim, especially of course those at Belz. It is true there were many neutrals too, but even these tended to lean towards the Belz side. Everywhere people whispered the old Jewish saying: "A men esst nisht ka knobl—stinkt men nisht." "He who eats no garlic does not stink." Or as you would say: "There's no smoke without fire." What storms there were in the Chassidic world of the time! Only he who is familiar with our Chassidic temperament can have any idea how violent they were. The broad Polish land shook with the thunder of the hoofs of the Chassidic armies.

As I have already said, the opponents of the Kotskers were not recruited solely from the ranks of the *chnyoks* of Belz. Why, even the *chabadniks* of Lubavitch now had an excellent opportunity of paying back the people of Kotsk for all the wrongs they had inflicted on them over a number of years. Were they not always being reproached by the Kotskers, quite unjustly of course, that they, the people of Lubavitch, were only interested in metaphysics and that they paid no heed whatsoever to the laws which must govern a man's actions in this temporal life? The Kotskers formulated this reproach in their famous "delicate" way. They told the Lubavitchers: "Your Rabbi preaches the Law of Heaven. Our Rabbi preaches the Law—of the *Navel*...."

After his return from Lvov, Reb Mendele shut himself up from the entire world in the back part of his immense house, never once going out from there for the rest of his life. Totally alone, he sat for twenty long years in the empty rooms of his palace. Only a few select persons were allowed to visit him in his "most holy sanctuary", and even they could see him only very rarely. Grey spiders and huge tame rats, which ran around in packs at the saint's feet, were his only companions. Through the windows, by day and by night, columns of smoke ascended from his pipe to the gloomy Kotsk sky, like the smoke of burnt offerings. For twenty long years the prisoner of Kotsk lived on in this way. On the twenty-second day of the month of Shevat in the year 5620 (1860)—on the very Thursday when the verse from the Torah: "And it was said unto Moses: Go up to the Lord!" is read out in the synagogue every year—Reb Mendele departed this world, reconciled to his people and bewailed by hundreds of thousands of his faithful followers, at the blessed age of seventy-two years, the same number as the sum total of the numerical values of the consonants in the Hebrew word *chessed*, mercy, mercy of God.

It is said that Reb Mendele was good friends with a doctor who was very "enlightened" (the term "enlightened", meaning "educated in a European way", is an insult!). It would appear that by means of lying talk this "enlightened" doctor succeeded in arousing Reb Mendele's interest in other matters besides the Law of God and the mysteries of the Cabbala. But I do not think that this silly tale is true. I have also heard—though I do not like to repeat it of course—that Reb Mendele's daughters-in-law did not cut their hair, that they were not ashamed to shake hands with strange men and that they even went about with low-necked dresses. But what is the point of repeating old and unpleasant tittle-tattle and gossip? These, too, are sure to be only *same babske maisses*, old wives' tales.

The storms over Kotsk have long since passed over and died down. Only occasionally is there a flash of lightning or a clap of thunder in this or that place. Certainly these storms have not done the least harm to the people of Kotsk. Quite the contrary. They have cleared the air, and ever since then the ranks of the Kotskers have been noticeably increased and strengthened, and their teaching and knowledge has become more profound. The same thing of course has happened with us at Belz. We have all been tested and toughened in the struggle.

Needless to say, the Kotskers have long since given up some of their peculiarities. A great deal of the credit for this belongs to that most famous disciple of Mendele, Reb Itche Meyer, or Rim, as he is called for short, after the initials of his title and name.

Rim was a Talmudist whose like has not been known for centuries. He is the author of "Chidushei Rim". His complicated Talmudic problems and his learned solutions are so acute, subtle and involved that they have become proverbial. Whenever we want to describe something as being deliberately confused, we say it is like a "Rimian *kashye*", a "Rimian problem". Rim was Rabbi at Geru—"Gora Kalwariye" the Christians call it. It is not far from Warsaw, about five miles perhaps. There are some 3,000 people living there, and almost all the men wear side-whiskers and all of them work as tanners. The smell from the tanning is somewhat oppressive.

Rim was a truly devout saint. On one occasion he laid his head on the table after eating and stayed like that for about half an hour. He appeared to be asleep, but this was no ordinary sleep, for all of a sudden he raised his head and cried out: "Now I know that food is indeed a great and noble thing!"

"I have just been in heaven before the gate of paradise," he said. "While I was there, the soul of a saint who had just died arrived at the gate. Throughout his life this man had fasted, prayed and studied the Law of God. The gate was duly opened in accordance with his deserts. He entered paradise and was received into the bosom of the fathers. Once again the gate was closed. Next came the soul of a completely ordinary person, riding on a golden cart drawn by two pairs of white horses.

This time the gate of paradise was opened wide, and all the saints and angels of the Lord came out to welcome the new arrival. The heavenly musicians played the most beautiful wedding march that earthly ear has ever heard. "Who is this great saint?" I asked in amazement. "Why was the first, who was indeed a real saint, not received with the same pomp as this ordinary person?"

"It is true that the second one is no saint and not in any way equal to the first in the service of God," came the heavenly answer. "Nevertheless he was a decent, law-abiding, dutiful person and in addition to this he won great merit for himself in another way. Not only did he give hospitality to the poor in his home on the holy Sabbath and at festivals, as anybody does who has the wherewithal, but he also gave them to eat and drink on weekdays and grudged them nothing. The first one, on the other hand, merely prayed, studied and fasted all the time, but never gave anyone to eat. That is the reason why we have not welcomed him with as much pomp as the second."—

"Now at least I know that food is a great and noble thing," repeated Rim.

Once he taught his disciples this: "It is not good to be wise. A person who is too wise tends to become a sophist, which leads ultimately to disbelief. It is not good to be good. A person who is too good is soft and effeminate. Such a person has no tendency to disbelief but can easily become licentious. It is also not good to be devout. A man who is too devout tends neither towards disbelief nor licentiousness, but he thinks that he alone serves God as he should and that other people are no good at all, and therefore he hates everybody. In the end he turns out to be harmful to everybody, a real evil-doer."

His disciples were astonished beyond words at this.—"But, our teacher," they asked, "what then should a man be if he does not do well to be either wise or good, or even devout?" "What should a man be?" Rim answered them. "Well, wise, good and devout, all at the same time."—Then these three virtues mutually neutralize their undesirable by-products.

On one occasion Rim told this delightful story:

"In the time of the holy Rebe Reb Melech of Lizensk there lived a Rabbi in a little township. This Rabbi was a great saint but no one knew of this. Nor of course was he even aware of his sanctity himself. The caretaker, who was also his servant, noticed that two old men came to the Rabbi every morning. They were strangely dressed, and appeared to be exceptionally noble and dignified. As soon as they left, a third man would appear. He also was strangely dressed, but more simply, and he was far from being so noble and dignified. He would ask the Rabbi something and be off again at once. This was repeated in precisely the same manner, day after day, for years on end. The Rabbi was always perfectly calm when they came, as though nothing out of the ordinary was happening. In vain did the servant rack his brains throughout the long years as to who the three men might be. Finally, he plucked up enough courage one day to ask the Rabbi, his master, who they were. The Rabbi-saint was so modest that up to that time he had believed everybody to be as holy as himself and supposed that the three mysterious men appeared to each person in the same way. He was therefore greatly surprised at the servant's question. "Can it be that you don't know them?" he asked. "The two men are the Old Testament prophets, Elijah and Elisha, and the third man is their servant Gehazi. He is condemned for all time to go in search of his former masters, but never to find them. He is thus unable to apologize to them for not having performed his duties as faithfully as he should have done during his lifetime."

The servant was profoundly shocked and ran into the street to tell the people of the miracle he had witnessed every day. Everyone was dumbfounded. Up to that time they had not known what a saint they had in the Rabbi, a saint to whom the ancient prophets of the Old Testament appeared. Now however the Rabbi too had at last learnt that the three men did not visit other people but only himself.

The next day a new surprise awaited the Rabbi's servant. The prophets did not appear. Nor did Gehazi, his model colleague. "Why did they not come today?" the servant asked the Rabbi.

"Now that I know they do not come to other people, I have asked them to leave off making their visits to me, for I cannot understand why they should respect me more than other people," answered the Rabbi-saint. So great was his modesty.

Great is the suffering that we children of Israel have had to bear among all nations for so many centuries. Our heavenly Father punishes us grievously indeed. Not a single little shortcoming does He overlook. He beats us with forty stripes for every little sin. Why should He be so strict with us in particular? Are not all people His children, has He not created us all equally, as it is written? And yet He is so kind to them, and so hard to us! The answer to this question is obvious: "Because the child that is the most severely punished by his father—that child shall surely one day bring forth some great thing." Something along these lines was said by King Solomon.

But how is it possible that in spite of all these sufferings we have never yet perished, and shall never perish, until the coming of the Messiah? By what mysterious means have we kept ourselves in vigour and strength, what wondrous medicine have we used to heal ourselves, throughout the ages, from all our wounds?

Only the wise Rim was able to explain this to us. He said:

"In the time when the Jews were driven from Spain there lived a saint who bore the name of the prophet Samuel. This saint considered that our people's suffering had already reached its peak, that the times could never be worse than they were then, and that therefore the coming of the Messiah was at hand, in accordance with the old prophecies. So he commanded all who had not gone astray, but had remained faithful to the faith of their fathers, to come out to meet the Messiah in joy and good cheer. Everyone was told to take a bottle of brandy in his hand and, as soon as he saw the Messiah, to drink to his health and call out: 'Behold, Son of David, what we moistened our throats with, and how we fortified our hearts, during our most bitter Exile! With a draught of brandy. That gave us strength, so that we did not despair or perish.'

"That saint Samuel erred. The measure of suffering did not reach its climax in the expulsion from Spain, and the Son of David did not come. But I tell you," the wise Rim concluded his story, "that when the Messiah really comes, the Chassidim will take a *little Rabbi* under their arm and shall go with him to meet the Saviour, calling out joyously: 'Behold, Son of David, behold, who it was who comforted us with their words in our most bitter exile! Behold who strengthened us by their example and gave us courage and preserved us until Thy time was come!'"

"When Moses led us out of Egypt," said the wise Rim, "God performed great miracles. Before the eyes of the nations He broke the ancient laws which He had given to nature at the beginning of the world. Today, too, miracles take place, but only veiledly and secretly, not openly. They take place in such a way that people think the laws of nature remain unaffected. Why the difference?—God led us out of Egypt in order that He might give us, on Sinai, His common Law, His revealed Law. At that time He did not disclose His mysteries to us. In other words, the revealed miracles, which preceded the laws of Sinai on the way out of Egypt, were a preparation for the Law that was likewise revealed. But nowadays God performs for us secret miracles, hidden by a veil, the veil of the natural order of the world. For this time these *secret* miracles are a preparation for the *secret* Law, for the mysteries of God, which hitherto have been hidden from the understanding of all creation, the mysteries which will be revealed to us when the Messiah really comes."—Thus spake the wise Rim.

As it is written by the hand of the prophet Isaiah:

"FOR OUT OF ZION SHALL GO FORTH THE LAW, AND THE WORD

THE CITY OF WISDOM

OF THE LORD FROM JERUSALEM: AND HE SHALL JUDGE AMONG THE NATIONS, AND SHALL REBUKE MANY PEOPLE: AND THEY SHALL BEAT THEIR SWORDS INTO PLOWSHARES, AND THEIR SPEARS INTO PRUNING-HOOKS: NATION SHALL NOT LIFT UP SWORD AGAINST NATION, NEITHER SHALL THEY LEARN WAR ANY MORE:"

MAY THIS HAPPEN SOON, IN THE DAYS OF OUR LIFETIME,
AND HERE ENDETH THIS PILGRIMAGE TO THE
EMPIRE OF THE CHASSIDIM:
AMEN.